Jan Wloka

Tool-supported Refactoring of Aspect-oriented Programs

Jan Wloka

Tool-supported Refactoring
of Aspect-oriented Programs

Why Aspect-oriented Programming Prevents
Developers from Using Their Favorite
Refactoring Tools, and How These Tools Can Be
Made Aspect-aware

VDM Verlag Dr. Müller

Imprint

Bibliographic information by the German National Library: The German National Library lists this publication at the German National Bibliography; detailed bibliographic information is available on the Internet at http://dnb.d-nb.de.

Cover image: www.purestockx.com

Publisher:
VDM Verlag Dr. Müller Aktiengesellschaft & Co. KG, Dudweiler Landstr. 125 a, 66123 Saarbrücken, Germany,
Phone +49 681 9100-698, Fax +49 681 9100-988,
Email: info@vdm-verlag.de

Produced in USA and UK by:
Lightning Source Inc., La Vergne, Tennessee, USA
Lightning Source UK Ltd., Milton Keynes, UK
BookSurge LLC, 5341 Dorchester Road, Suite 16, North Charleston, SC 29418, USA

ISBN: 978-3-8364-8999-7

Abstract

Aspect-oriented programming offers a new modularization concept for improving the modularity of crosscutting concerns. This concept is mainly realized by an advanced mechanism for *composing program behavior*, called pointcut and advice.

Software evolution of aspect-oriented systems, and particularly software refactoring, has been considered as problematic, because even local changes in the source code can result in unpredictable effects on the behavior of an aspect-oriented program.
In a first part of this thesis, we classify general attributes of existing approaches for composing program behavior in AOP and illustrate how each attribute is responsible for the evolution-related problems in the context of refactoring. We conclude that pointcuts specify properties of program representations to capture a certain program behavior, and identify the missing connection between a specification of such a property and the targeted behavior as primary reason for the evolution problems.

To overcome these problems, we integrate ideas drawn from the study of automated software refactoring, static change impact analysis, and qualitative program analysis into an impact analysis approach for verifying the validity of pointcuts in aspect-oriented programs.
We propose a model for pointcuts that represents every specification of a property of a program representation explicitly by an individual element. Based on this pointcut model a change impact analysis for pointcuts can detect change effects on every specified property, assess how precise a matching element of a program representation is specified, and derive invalidated specifications. The change impact analysis is integrated into a refactoring approach that makes applied changes explicit and uses the impact assessment for an automated computation of pointcut updates.

We also present a prototype refactoring tool, called SOOTHSAYER, that implements our refactoring approach. The tool assists the developer in estimating effects on existing aspects, in detecting invalidated pointcuts, and in defining pointcut adjustments. An experimental evaluation of our approach using the tool has validated our expectations.

Acknowledgments

I would like to expression my gratitude to the people who helped me to make this dissertation a reality. First and foremost, I wish to thank my adviser, Stefan Jähnichen, who gave me the opportunity to work in an inspiring environment with the freedom to experience many different aspects of software engineering. I also want to thank the second reviewer, Robert Hirschfeld, for his very detailed and good critique on my writing, and his encouraging words in the final stage of this thesis.

Many thanks also to all the colleagues who have helped me during my work on this thesis. I am grateful to have had the opportunity to work with such outstanding people. In particular, I would like to thank Stephan Herrmann for inspiring me with his work on Object Teams and for kindly sharing with me his knowledge about many aspects of programming language design.

I would also like to thank my students, Jochen Hänsel, Jaroslav Svacina, and Sascha Kolewa, who contributed to this research with the work on their diploma theses and also often with lively discussions about this topic.

I especially would like to thank my friends for their support in various aspects of my life during the work on this thesis. Special thanks go to Thomas Dudziak, Rodger Burmeister, and Christian Storl for the sometimes thought-provoking but always inspiring discussions, and in particular for the tough job of prove-reading this thesis.

I am also very grateful to all people that supported and hosted me during my travels abroad. In particular, I thank Alessandro Garcia for making my visit in Lancaster possible. The time I got to spend with you was truly unforgettable. Thanks also to Claudio Sant'Anna (best Brazilian guitar player on planet), Luca Sabatucci, Vander Alves and the rest of the Brazilian connection.

Very special thanks go to my family. I thank my parents and my sister for their unending love and support, and for the wonderful environment I grew up in. I have had a magnificent time with you and I cannot express how happy it makes me to be part of our family.

Most importantly, I thank Dana, my love, my best friend, and now also my wife. This work would not have been possible without her love, admirable patience, and encouragement through the long writing process. There is nothing that could make me happier.

Contents

List of Figures

Chapter 1

Introduction

Aspect-oriented programming (AOP) has been proposed as an enhanced programming model for improving the modularity of software systems. In particular, it targets functionalities that are often implemented by several different parts of a software system, so called *crosscutting concerns* [53]. For example, in object-oriented programs functionalities like authorization, authentication, persistence, and transaction management, are often implemented by multiple parts of the program. AOP aims to improve the modularity of such crosscutting concerns and can result in simpler code that is easier to maintain and has a greater potential for reuse [52].

To this end, AOP introduces two advanced mechanisms for composing the structure of different implementation modules and for adapting the behavior of the program at runtime. While AOP as a modularization concept has shown several benefits [30, 57, 34], its composition mechanisms still cause serious problems when aspect-oriented programs are evolved [56, 65, 86, 94]. Any change in the source of an aspect-oriented program can result in unpredictable effects on the program behavior. This is particularly a problem when a developer, unaware of existing aspects, alters the parts of a program on which aspect-oriented compositions rely on.

Software refactoring is a well established technique for improving the design of software systems in a behavior-preserving way. In object-oriented programs, various refactorings support developers in changing the structure of a program in a controlled way. Tool-supported refactoring is less error-prone, reduces the required effort and accelerates individual refactorings steps. It is one of the key factors for successful software engineering in changing environments.

All software systems need to be changed throughout their entire life, including aspect-oriented ones. Hence, the success of AOP depends on how much the improved modularity supports the continuous evolution of a software system. AOP will only be adopted for industrial application development if resulting programs can be evolved with an effort at least similar to object-oriented programs. Tool-supported refactoring is one major means for keeping software systems evolvable and thus also needs to be provided for aspect-oriented programs.

This thesis presents the results of a systematic analysis of aspect-oriented composition mechanisms and a classification of their effects on refactoring tools, in order to expose the actual reasons for the evolution issues with AOP. This analysis has revealed a refactoring-compliant subset of aspect-oriented composition mechanisms for which a reliable refactoring support can be developed. In this thesis we elaborate the realization of such a refactoring tool for AOP as well as the reasons for which only specific language mechanisms can be properly supported.

1.1 The Problem of Refactoring Aspect-oriented Programs

Most software systems will have to change again and again, and that as long as they are alive. A system may change during its development, e.g., through addition of new functionalities, or during maintenance (even after its delivery), e.g., through changed or new requirements. This continuous adaptation is not always about changing the system's behavior, but also about improving its internal structure. Developers rename types and methods to give them a more reasonable name, extract some code into a new method to make it more reusable, or replace duplicated code with calls to a method. Meir M. Lehman identified this need for "continuing change" in his so-called first law of software evolution: Software "systems must be continually adapted else they become progressively less satisfactory" [62].

There is always pressure to change the system, and it is mostly an external pressure, originating from the customers (requirements, bug-fix, feature enhancement etc.) or the competition. This need to change a software system leads to a big problem. The changes are applied as fast as possible, as their are applied under the ever-present time and cost pressure. As a result, the system's structure gets not only more and more distant from the originally planned design, but becomes increasingly complex with every change, which in turn makes changing the system more difficult. Therefore, software developers need to be supported in keeping a software system evolvable.

1.1.1 Tool-supported Refactoring

Software refactoring is one of the most successful techniques dealing with how to change software systems in a controlled way. Refactoring means changing a system's structure in such a (disciplined) way, that the observable[1] behavior of the system is not changed yet its internal structure is improved [28]. In short, refactoring is intended to keep a software evolvable and should be an essential activity in software engineering, according to Lehman's second law "increasing complexity: as a program is evolved its complexity increases unless work is done to maintain or reduce it" [61].

Performing refactoring steps manually, however, is costly and error prone, so tools are the preferred means to achieve a design improvement in a fast and reliable way. Tool support for refactoring is offered as an integral part of many modern integrated development environments, such as Eclipse [21] and IDEA [44]. A typical refactoring tool assists

---

[1]Observable behavior most often denotes the functionality that is implemented by the refactored part of the system, i.e., the impact of refactoring on other aspects, such as runtime performance, are mostly unconsidered.

the developer in refactoring code rather than attempting to detect better designs and refactor the code automatically. It helps the developer to detect whether changes would alter the program behavior, identify a certain modification as reason for the altered behavior, and automate the particular refactoring steps.

Tool-supported refactoring significantly reduces the effort for achieving design improvements and allows developers to perform refactoring on a more regular basis. More frequently refactored software systems are generally considered to be easier to understand, maintain, and evolve [28].

Most refactoring tools have a straightforward implementation. The developer decides which refactoring to perform and selects the refactoring target (the part of the program to be improved). Then the tool (statically) analyzes the source code to determine if the refactoring's preconditions are satisfied. If the preconditions are not satisfied, the developer is notified and no action is taken, unless the developer still wants to perform the refactoring. If the preconditions are satisfied, the tool performs the refactoring in an automated way [75].

1.1.2 Aspect-oriented Programming

AOP introduces an advanced modularization concept to explicitly specify the composition of program behavior on top of existing concepts, such as object-oriented programming (OOP). Concrete AOP approaches usually provide a mechanism for intercepting the program execution at well-defined points, so called *joinpoints* [52], and to insert new behavior before or after, or to replace such a joinpoint. A joinpoint is, more technically spoken, an execution of a program element at runtime, such as executions of a method call, field access, or field assignment. The behavior that is inserted at a joinpoint is defined by a new implementation module, the so-called *aspect*.

An aspect can be seen as a class-like module that provides two additional features: pointcut and advice. The *advice* defines the interface for invoking the aspect behavior at a joinpoint and is bound to a *pointcut*, that specifies both the set of joinpoints and the information that is passed from the joinpoint's context to the advice's parameters. A pointcut uses query-like constructs that select joinpoints by specifying their properties. Every time the execution hits a selected joinpoint some runtime-support determines matching pointcuts and invokes the bound advices.

With this complex but powerful concept, aspects can explicitly define the adaptation of multiple implementation modules at a single place, even without modifying the source of any of these modules. This concept makes it possible to modularize crosscutting concerns and "achieve the usual benefits of improved modularity: simpler code that is easier to develop and maintain, and that has greater potential for reuse" [52].

Most AOP approaches realize the new modularization concept as extension to an existing object-oriented programming language. They provide certain syntactic means to support two composition mechanisms; one to adapt the structure of an implementation module, and another to select the joinpoints at which the program behavior is adapted.

In some cases, if an aspect inserts more than just a few additional statements at a joinpoint, additional structural support is required. To this end, aspects provide an advanced mechanism for composing the structure of implementation modules, the so-called **struc-tural composition**.

Current AOP languages provide various mechanisms for adapting the structure of implementation modules, ranging from the static introduction of single features [5] to the dynamic wrapping of an existing object with a role [69]. AspectJ-like programming languages provide a mechanism called inter-type declarations. It allows to introduce new members or new relationships, such as inheritance, to multiple classes. For example, an aspect can declare an implementation of a new interface to an existing class and add the methods needed to fulfill that interface [103]. Any introduction statically affects the program code, i.e., every instance of an adapted class holds the introduced members and relationships.

Other approaches, like OT/J [69] or CaesarJ [81], enhance the support for feature composition by using advanced inheritance concepts, such as multiple inheritance and mixin composition. These concepts are even more powerful. They can augment the structure of individual instances rather than apply the addition to all instances of a class.

Every approach to AOP provides a **behavioral composition** mechanism to insert a particular behavior at a joinpoint in the execution of a program. The mechanism uses information from the meta-level of the program, i.e., it refers to static and dynamic representations of the program (e.g., abstract syntax tree) and its execution (e.g., stack trace). To this end, AOP approaches provide a joinpoint model and a pointcut language. The *joinpoint model* defines the types of program elements whose executions are "observed" during runtime as well as which of these executions are generally available as joinpoints. In addition, it establishes the advanced program representations and defines the properties within these representation that can be used to select a particular set of joinpoints.

The *pointcut language* provides the means for specifying a selection of joinpoints. Various pointcut languages have been proposed, ranging from regular expressions [3, 52], over XML-based queries [24], to complete logic meta-programming approaches [50, 72]. Most languages differ in syntax, expressiveness and the supported joinpoint model, but they all provide query-like specifications of structural properties, i.e., they have reflective access to the program and its execution. The pointcut developer can specify structural properties of the program representations established by the joinpoint model to identify the desired set of joinpoints. Typical properties are code containment, inheritance relationships, and execution order.

1.1.3 Refactoring Aspect-oriented Programs

While manual refactoring seeks to preserve the observable program behavior [28], tool-supported refactoring informs the developer on the consequences of a particular change, but allows her to alter the behavior. The detection of change effects on the program behavior is achieved through precondition checks. These checks ensure that specific properties in the structure of a program are preserved by a refactoring. William Opdyke has discovered a set of syntactic and semantic program properties for object-oriented programs, which must not be violated if the program behavior should be preserved [70].

These properties are associated with inheritance, scoping, type compatibility, and semantic equivalence of references and operations, i.e., they are related to fundamental concepts of the programming language used to define the program behavior. A refactoring tool implements explicit precondition checks for these properties to detect behavioral changes.

Problem Statement:

> In aspect-oriented programs, the mechanisms for structural and behavioral composition can also be affected by a refactoring. Existing refactoring tools can neither determine whether a refactoring invalidates the composed behavior nor adjust affected references in aspects to restore the expected behavior.

The language constructs for *structural composition* refer to named elements in the targeted implementation module, and therefore have to be considered when the program is refactored. They use symbolic references to introduce new members or to declare new inheritance relationships, which can simply be adjusted during the refactoring. However, the adaptation of inheritance relationships requires additional and also more complex precondition checks. In addition, new or re-defined situations for dynamic binding have to be considered by aspect-oriented refactoring tools. Such dependencies require additional analyses of the inheritance relationships, but do not require a conceptually new approach to behavior preservation in refactoring.

The mechanisms for *behavioral composition* define invocations of a certain aspect behavior at selected joinpoints. Joinpoints have no (unique) identifier that can be referenced by a pointcut, they are selected via properties of meta-level program representations. Any change of a property that is specified by a pointcut, can alter the selection of joinpoints. Since a refactoring tool cannot always ascertain every joinpoint selected at runtime, it can only prevent pointcut-affecting changes by detecting change effects on the referenced program representations. Pointcuts can specify various properties of even *highly dynamic* program representations, such as stack trace or object heap. Every used dynamic program representation has to be statically approximated, because refactoring tools deal with the program's source code usually without access to runtime information. In addition, pointcuts can *specify a property incompletely*, which may intentionally capture additional joinpoints in future program versions. The use of dynamic program representations and incomplete specifications makes it even more difficult to determine whether a joinpoint is supposed to be selected by a particular pointcut.

Research Question:

> For which properties of (static and dynamic) program representations can a refactoring tool detect change effects on the composed program behavior and how do pointcuts have to specify these properties so that a valid update can be computed?

1.2 Our Approach

In this dissertation we propose an aspect-aware refactoring approach that is built on a change impact analysis. The approach consists of the construction of an intermediate pointcut representation, a change impact analysis for pointcuts, an heuristics-based update decision-making and a pointcut generator. The prototype refactoring tool SOOTH-SAYER implements the approach as an extension to the Eclipse Java IDE [21] and the AspectJ Development Tooling [1].

The *intermediate representation* for pointcuts describes every specified property explicitly and reflects the dependencies between different properties directly.

The *change impact analysis* computes static representations for every program representation used by a pointcut in the program and evaluates the specified properties within these static representations. The evaluation results before and after the refactoring are compared, and a pointcut impact representation of all pointcuts is produced.

A *set of heuristics* quantifies the change effects in terms of the pointcut (specification completeness, degree of dependency, and execution semantics), and with respect to the set of selected joinpoints (number of affected matches). Based on these impact measures and considering the responsible code change a pointcut update decision is inferred (Keep Pointcut, Update Pointcut, Cancel Refactoring).

The *pointcut generator* computes the updated pointcut. It tries to replace only affected parts of the pointcut, in the same way as they were specified before the refactoring. If the updated pointcut selects a set of joinpoints that differs from the original set, it excludes additional matches or includes missing matches by an explicit pointcut extension. The tool SOOTHSAYER supports an extended refactoring workflow that shows effects on existing pointcuts, proposes updates, and allows for a customized pointcut update if the proposal does not meet the developer's expectations.

The tool is applied to various aspect-oriented programs in order to evaluate the heuristics for classifying the change impact and the proposed update decision. In addition, specific and more complex pointcuts are constructed to expose and evaluate the limits of our approach.

Thesis Statement:

> A meta-model that explicitly represents the change effects on pointcuts, stating which part of the pointcut is affected by which program transformation, allows for minimal invasive adjustments, which keeps a pointcut recognizable even after multiple updates.

1.3 Contributions

The primary contributions of our research are:

- A *change impact analysis framework* for pointcuts of present AOP approaches, which computes the actually added and lost matches for every specified property of a joinpoint, and associates it with the responsible change. The analysis provides static approximations for dynamic program representations, and a pointcut matching algorithm which selects every element in the program code to which a pointcut refers to.

- A *change impact classification* distinguishes affected from invalidated pointcuts, using a set of qualitative heuristics to support the developer's decision making. The heuristics classify the effects on a pointcut (specification completeness, degree of dependency, and execution semantics), and in terms of the set of selected joinpoints (pointcut match impact).

- A *model for decomposing pointcuts* into elementary pointcut expressions is proposed, that makes matching elements of referenced program representations explicit, represents evaluation dependencies between pointcut expressions, and distinguishes between references to joinpoints (pointcut matches) and other references used for expressing a certain joinpoint property (pointcut anchors).

- A *prototype refactoring tool* automates the proposed aspect-aware refactoring process. It is realized as an extension to the Eclipse JDT refactoring support [22]. It appends three additional refactoring steps to the refactoring workflow: preview of impact on aspects, pointcut impact review and pointcut update. The tool implements the proposed impact analysis and pointcut update patterns as well as the impact visualization. It is the foundation for evaluating the change impact classification and pointcut update proposition strategy.

- A *heuristic-based pointcut update computation* proposes an update for every invalidated pointcut and labels the smallest affected pointcut part as to keep, to broaden (include lost matches), to narrow (exclude new matches), or to replace.

- *Pointcut update patterns* define, as general extension to existing refactorings, the least intrusive pointcut adjustment, the patterns to enclose a direct (or narrowed) replacement of an affected pointcut part, as well as the broadening or narrowing of the complete pointcut by explicit extensions.

- A *taxonomy for characteristics of joinpoint models and pointcut languages* in AOP. This taxonomy is a classification of general attributes of joinpoints, the means for identification, and the means for specification used in present AOP approaches considering their effects on software evolution.

- *Criteria for refactoring compliant AOP*. A particular subset of attributes of joinpoint models and pointcut languages has shown its suitability for the developed refactoring approach. AOP approaches following these criteria, can be considered as refactoring compliant with the conceptual framework of this thesis.

1.4 Thesis Outline

The remainder of this thesis is organized as follows:

Chapter 2 identifies the preservation of pointcuts as a conceptually new problem in software refactoring, and describes how refactoring can be made aspect-aware. We analyze the nature of the construct "pointcut", and present a general taxonomy for joinpoint models and pointcut languages in AOP. Furthermore, we illustrate this problem by examples, and discuss the effects of different attributes of joinpoint models and pointcut languages on software refactoring. In addition, we define the core vocabulary used throughout this dissertation, and present the key challenges in refactoring aspect-oriented programs.

Chapter 3 presents the state-of-the-art in aspect-oriented refactoring, evolution-specific tool-support and aspect-aware mechanisms at programming language level. We review the work of these three fields, and identify the lack of proper tool-support for detecting change effects on pointcuts and adjusting affected pointcuts as the major problem in the refactoring of aspect-oriented programs. We also discuss the key challenges in the development of such a refactoring support.

Chapter 4 gives an overview of our aspect-aware refactoring process and describes the additional process steps in detail. In particular, we illustrate how our tool supports the developer and present extensions to standard refactorings.

Chapter 5 describes our program analysis approach for detecting affected pointcuts and for classifying the change impact. We describe every analysis step in detail, and illustrate employed program representations, static approximations, and algorithms for constructing these representations. In addition, we present our approach for the static evaluation of selected joinpoints. Also, our heuristics for classifying the change impact are described and the results expected from their application are discussed.

Chapter 6 describes how our refactoring tool SOOTHSAYER computes update decisions and generates the adjusted pointcuts. We give an overview of the update determination process, present our update decision criteria, and explain how the impact measures are used to derive a particular decision. Furthermore, we describe the constraints for transformations that add, change, or remove matching element based on our impact measures. Also, we present our algorithm for computing the least intrusive update, and give illustrating examples.

Chapter 7 gives an overview of our aspect-aware refactoring tool SOOTHSAYER. We describe its architecture and its components implementing the impact analysis, static approximations, the pointcut handling and the impact visualization. In particular, we present important design decisions and explain how the developer is supported by the prototype.

Chapter 8 presents the evaluation of our approach using SOOTHSAYER. We describe the employed methodology, the expected results and three experiments considering independently developed aspect-oriented programs. We also present the detected effects, proposed update decisions as well as the updated pointcuts. The evaluation results are discussed and compared with our expectations.

Chapter 9 summarizes the primary results of our work and shows how they support the statement of the thesis. Moreover, we look forward to future work and relate it to known limitations of the current realization of our approach.

Chapter 2

Refactoring in the Presence of Aspects

In this chapter we identify the preservation of behavioral compositions in AOP as a conceptually new problem in software refactoring and describe how a refactoring can be made aspect-aware. We start our analysis of this problem by defining the key vocabulary used throughout this dissertation (2.2). In Section 2.3 we present an illustrating example to demonstrate how behavioral compositions can be interfered by standard (object-oriented) refactorings and depict different change effects on pointcuts in three refactoring scenarios.

In the main part of this chapter (2.4), we analyze the nature of the construct "pointcut" and present a general taxonomy for joinpoint models and pointcut languages in AOP as the result of a comparison of numerous approaches to AOP. Based on this taxonomy we discuss different characteristics of joinpoint models and pointcut languages and their effects on the realization of a reliable refactoring support. In Section 2.5 we present resulting challenges in preserving the behavioral compositions in aspect-oriented programs. We conclude that pointcuts are specification-like constructs that refer to (static and dynamic) program representations in order to specify the conditions under which the aspect behavior is invoked. Aspect-aware refactoring must detect change effects on these specifications and update invalidated ones rather than preserve the composed behavior of the aspect-oriented program.

2.1 Preservation of Structural Composition

Aspect-oriented modularization mechanisms enable various new refactoring opportunities [39, 78, 101], but also require a different approach for constraining the possibilities in which a program can be refactored safely [101, 102]. Structural and behavioral composition mechanisms refer to elements of the program and may be invalidated if these elements are changed.

The mechanisms for *structural composition* in AOP use symbolic references to declared program elements. An aspect can adapt the structure of every referenced element, e.g., add additional members to a class or object, or define new inheritance relations [43, 52]. However, an adaptation of containment or inheritance relationships does not only rely on the referenced program elements, it also assumes particular properties of the adapted structure, e.g., class members can only be added if they do not interfere with existing inheritance relationships (e.g., overriding), and new inheritance relationships can only be introduced if they do not conflict with existing members. Compilers for AOP languages are responsible to check these dependencies before the composition is performed.

Refactoring tools also have to be aware of such structural dependencies if undesired effects on structural compositions shall be prevented. A refactoring tool can be made aware of AOP-specific structural requirements by augmenting every refactoring with additional preconditions. Such preconditions perform two additional tasks: (i) check whether the refactoring can be safely performed in terms of defined structural compositions and (ii) reveal references within aspect modules to changed program elements. The particular computation effort for evaluating these preconditions depends on the adopted means for composition, e.g., generative, class-based inheritance or instance-based inheritance. The more the adopted mechanism interfere with existing program behavior, the more expensive are the required preconditions checks for every refactoring.

In the preparation of this thesis, we studied the interference of common refactorings for Java with structural composition mechanisms. As one result of this work, a refactoring tool for OT/J [69] was developed[1]. The tool is part of the Object Teams Development Tooling for Eclipse (OTDT) and is integrated with other tool support for OT/J. It provides OT/J-specific refactorings for renaming various program elements, and for moving and extracting methods.
The implementation of this tool has shown that extensions of existing Java refactorings are only limited in cases where the aspect-oriented language extension affects the semantics of existing Java constructs. The implementation effort for these refactorings was not exceptionally high, mostly because OT/J is a seamless extension of Java that provides nearly non-invasive composition mechanisms (i.e., instance-based inheritance) and new implementation modules with strict interfaces.
For additional details on the refactoring support for OT/J we refer the reader to the Object Teams website [69]. Additional information on the interference between refactoring and structural composition mechanisms are available in the corresponding diploma thesis [12].

The remainder of this dissertation focuses on change effects on the aspect-oriented concept for *behavioral composition* (pointcuts and advice), and a proper handling of pointcuts within a refactoring process. To this end, various approaches to AOP have been studied, concentrating on extensions to the programming language Java [5, 6, 69, 74, 81, 89, 91] and concepts for advanced pointcut languages [3, 24, 36, 50, 72, 99]. As one result, a general classification of behavioral composition mechanisms was developed, that categorizes the attributes of adopted joinpoint models and pointcut languages.

---

[1]Since OT/J does not provide a pointcut language, the refactoring support for OT/J is not integrated with SOOTHSAYER, the refactoring tool developed and evaluated in this thesis. However, SOOTH-SAYER was developed in a way that it can be integrated into the OTDT when a pointcut language is supported in a future version.

2.2 Core Terminology

Most of the vocabulary in this dissertation is borrowed from research about program analysis and compiler construction. The presentations of addressed problems and their causes, as well as the way in which corresponding solutions are described using the terms and definitions of these research areas. In the following, we present the basic terms and definitions that establish the key vocabulary in this dissertation.

2.2.1 Concerns in Software Systems

The term software *concern* is found in many publications about AOP, even though the term itself appears to be hard to define. Filman et al. define a concern as "a thing in an engineering process about which it cares" [27]. Another definition defines a concern as "an interest which pertains to the system's development, its operation or any other matters that are critical or otherwise important to one or more stakeholders" [98]. In this thesis we consider a concern as a concept, functionality or any kind of requirement, which is implemented by a software system.

A *crosscutting concern* is a concern whose implementation is scattered throughout the implementation of other concerns in a software system [27]. Especially concerns that cannot be modularized within a certain programming model are considered to be *crosscutting*, because the elements of their implementations are *scattered* and *tangled* within elements of other concerns.

The term *scattering* denotes the occurrence of elements that belong to the implementation of one concern in modules encapsulating other concerns, whereas *tangling* characterizes the occurrence of multiple concerns mixed together in one module. We use the term *crosscutting* to characterize scattered and/or tangled elements in the implementation of a concern.

2.2.2 AOP Language Terms

Most approaches to AOP introduce a new implementation *module*, i.e., a new abstraction in the adopted programming model. An *aspect* is an implementation module designed to implement a concern [27]. It can be bound to events in the execution of the program, so called *joinpoints*. The binding of joinpoints is completely specified inside the aspect and invisible to other modules of the program. At every joinpoint, an aspect can adapt the program behavior, by providing enhanced mechanisms for behavioral composition. To this end the aspect module holds additional features like advice and pointcut definition.

An *advice* is a method-like construct, in many AOP languages without a name, that can be invoked at a joinpoint. It can declare input parameters for accessing information that is available at a joinpoint. An advice contains a block of statements that are executed either before, or after the joinpoint, or replace it completely.

A *pointcut definition* binds an advice to a set of joinpoints through a specification of their properties. Every bound advice is invoked at any joinpoint that is selected by the pointcut. The term *pointcut* denotes a specification of joinpoint properties that is contained by a pointcut definition. A pointcut can be seen as a functional query that specifies properties and returns matching joinpoints. Most AOP approaches provide a separate language for specifying properties of joinpoints, a so-called *pointcut language*.

2.2.3 Joinpoints and Pointcuts

The term *joinpoint* denotes the central concept for describing the interaction of aspects with other implementation modules. Various definitions can be found in the literature, but it was originally coined by Kiczales et al., as a well-defined point in the execution of a program [52]. Filman et al. define a joinpoint as "a well-defined point in the structure or execution flow of a program where additional behavior can be attached" [27]. Another definition characterizes joinpoints as "points of interest in some modules in the software lifecycle through which two or more concerns may be composed" [98]. In this thesis, we need a more technically definition that defines a joinpoint in terms of the program representations that exhibit the program code or runtime conditions of its execution.

A program's source code can be represented by *static program representations*, such as an abstract syntax tree (AST). Its nodes represent the language constructs used in the source code to define its behavior, so called *program elements*. The runtime conditions of a program execution can be represented by *dynamic program representations*, like a stack trace or an object graph. These representations exhibit runtime conditions of a single program execution and are only available at runtime. In contrast to static program representations, they cannot be obtained directly from the program's code.

In AOP, static and dynamic program representations are used to reason about the program's meta-level, i.e., a pointcut specifies their properties to identify either elements in the program or in its execution. Since joinpoints are events at runtime and have no unique identifier, these properties are the only way to differentiate between different joinpoints. In terms of these program representations, we can define the term joinpoint in a technically more precise way:

> **Definition 2.1**: A *joinpoint* is an event in the execution of a program that occurs when a program element is executed. It has no unique identifier but it can be discriminated through properties of static and dynamic program representations that exhibit meta-level information of the program code or runtime conditions of its execution.

The program element defining the code region that the existence of a joinpoint depends on, is called *joinpoint shadow*. The shadow is defined as the static projection of a joinpoint onto the program code [64].

Joinpoints can be discriminated by several properties of various program representations, which we call *joinpoint properties* and define as follows:

Definition 2.2: A *joinpoint property* is the property of a program representation that represents the implementation of the program or runtime conditions of its execution.

Two different kinds of properties can be distinguished if the availability of a program representation is considered. A *static property* of a joinpoint addresses an element in the program code, whose executions represent joinpoints (i.e., the joinpoint shadow). Static properties can be used to identify all executions of a specific set of program elements as joinpoints. Individual executions can be distinguished from each other by their dynamic properties. A *dynamic property* of a joinpoint is represented by elements of a dynamic program representation. Dynamic properties denote the runtime conditions under which a particular joinpoint occurs and thus are related to a specific program behavior, rather than to its implementation.

At which joinpoints the execution of a program can be intercepted in general, is defined by the so-called *joinpoint model*. It can be seen as the common frame of reference defining what kinds of joinpoints are available and how they can be accessed and used [98].

The *pointcut languages*, as provided by most AOP approaches, enable a declarative specification of joinpoint properties. Nearly every AOP approach defines its own language, with its own syntax, expressiveness and semantics. Depending on the particular syntax, a pointcut can be defined as a combination of specifications for elementary properties. Such a specification addresses a single property of an element and is often called *predicate* or *pointcut designator* [98].

The term pointcut designator is defined in the literature as a description of a set of joinpoints [27]. This definition does not clearly differentiate between pointcut and designator. Moreover, pointcut designators as constructs in existing pointcut languages often address more than one joinpoint property. For these reasons, we introduce the term *pointcut expression* to denote a specification of a single property within a pointcut and define it as follows:

Definition 2.3: A *pointcut expression* is a specification $pce(p)$ that describes a single property p of a joinpoint. It can be evaluated for a particular program to select a set of elements that represent a joinpoint property within a certain program representation.

Pointcut expressions can refer to various elements of static or dynamic program representations, e.g., to express a particular property as a relationship to another element of the representation. These so-called *pointcut anchors* are elements of program representations that are referenced by a pointcut:

Definition 2.4: A *pointcut anchor* is an element of an arbitrary program representation, which is selected by a pointcut to express a joinpoint property. The set of selected pointcut anchors also includes joinpoint shadows, which are elements of a static program representation.

Using this terminology, a *pointcut* is just a more complex specification that aggregates pointcut expressions to describe several joinpoint properties. We can define a *pointcut definition* more precisely as a functional query that evaluates a set of pointcut expressions PCE for a particular program P to receive the elements of the program's static and dynamic representations that match the specified properties:

> **Definition 2.5**: A *pointcut definition* is a functional query $PCE \times P \longrightarrow E$ that evaluates all expressions of the set PCE for a particular program P and returns a set of elements E that exhibit the specified properties.

2.2.4 Refactoring and Program Transformation

Refactoring, or in particular **manual refactoring**, is defined as the process of changing a program's structure without altering its observable behavior [28]. The major problem within the context of refactoring tools is that behavior preservation is often difficult to prove and the analyses that must be performed to ensure it are difficult to compute [75]. In **automated refactoring**, a refactoring is defined as a program transformation that has particular preconditions which must be satisfied before the transformation can be safely performed [75]. Such a definition encompasses both behavior-preserving and non-behavior-preserving transformations. A typical example for a behavior-preserving transformation is the remove class refactoring. It only removes the class, if the class exists and if it is not referenced from other parts of the system. An example for a non-behavior-preserving transformation is the inline local variable refactoring. It replaces any occurrence of the variable by its initialization, which can alter the behavior if the initialization has side effects.

In this dissertation, we use the definition for refactoring of Donald Roberts (cf. [75], p.25):

> **Definition 2.6**: A *refactoring* is a pair $R = (pre, T)$ where *pre* is the precondition that the program must satisfy, and T is the program transformation.

The term **program transformation** was originally coined in the field of constructing interpreters, compilers and optimizers [2]. More recently, it is used as an approach for supporting various programming activities. Program transformations deal with elements of formalized program representations, such as abstract syntax trees (ASTs), call graphs (CGs), or control flow graphs (CFGs). Such a graph represents elements of the program as nodes and their relationships as directed edges. An AST, for example, represents the containment relationships of all program elements.

A program transformation modifies the program code by transforming the corresponding AST. It only performs changes for complete elements, i.e., a transformation cannot cause partial changes, incomplete edits with syntactic errors. We define a program transformation as follows:

> **Definition 2.7**: A *program transformation* is an operation $T(P, in) \longrightarrow P'$ that rewrites the AST of program P for a given input *in* into a new valid AST representing the changed program P'. The input *in* defines a set of input parameters, like change values and targeted program elements.

Since refactorings are program transformations, we call the program before the transformation *original program* (P) and the program after the transformation *refactored program* (P').

2.2.5 Aspect-oriented Composition

In general, the integration of multiple software artifacts into a coherent whole is called software *composition* [98]. AOP defines a more specialized integration of aspect modules with other implementation modules that is called *aspect weaving*. It is, e.g., defined by Filman et al. as "the process of composing core functionality modules with aspects, thereby yielding a working system" [27]. In most AOP approaches, this composition is asymmetric, i.e., only aspects can be composed with other implementation modules. We call these implementation modules the *base program*, in order to differentiate it from the program that is yielded by aspect weaving, the *composed program*.

Most AOP approaches provide two different composition mechanisms. A *structural composition* mechanism allows aspects to adapt the structure of one (or more) implementation module(s). Aspects can, e.g., introduce new members to a class or declare new inheritance relationships. The advice code of an aspect can use the augmented structures, e.g., for storing runtime values or invoking additional methods.

The *behavioral composition* enables an aspect to adapt the program behavior at a joinpoint. An aspect specifies a pointcut that binds an advice to this joinpoint and provides some code that is composed with the joinpoint's behavior.

Both mechanisms define the composition of multiple artifacts, but differ in several ways. The most important difference for software refactoring is in their concepts for referencing the artifacts to compose. All references to program elements have to be ascertained and adjusted, if the program behavior should be preserved. While mechanisms for structural composition use symbolic references to program elements, the behavioral composition, defined by pointcuts and advice, refers to (join)points in the program's execution. Moreover, joinpoints have no identifier that could be referenced but instead static and dynamic program representations are used to specify distinct properties for their selection. This significantly complicates the determination of referenced joinpoints, the preservation of their properties, and the adjustment of property specifications, if a refactoring has invalidated them by changing referenced elements.

2.3 An Illustrating Example

This section presents a small example program and three different refactoring scenarios. The program contains a few aspects whose behavior is affected by the refactorings. At first, the program behavior and its general design is briefly described, followed by a detailed description of each refactoring scenario and its effects on the aspect modules. Every refactoring scenario has a different effect on the pointcuts in the program, ranging from very obvious to almost undeterminable.

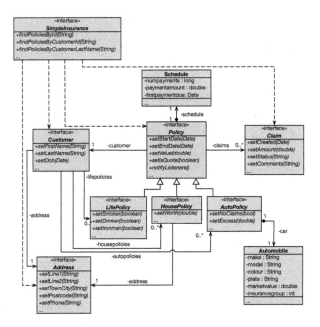

Figure 2.1: The domain model of the Simple Insurance Application.

2.3.1 A Simple Insurance Application

The example program is a scaled down version of an insurance application that keeps track of customers and policies of a fictitious insurance company. It is a slightly extended version of the *Simple Insurance Application* developed by Colyer et al. [16]. The basic use cases of the application cover standard customer management including the contracting of life, house, and car policies. For example, a new life policy can be created for a certain customer, considering her basic health attitudes and fitness. The application provides a rich-client user interface (UI), and a persistence layer that stores all entered data.

The program is an AspectJ application. Its basic architecture is represented through three logical tiers: presentation, business logic, and data. The business logic is implemented in pure Java, whereas the other tiers also contain aspects. Figure 2.1 shows the application's domain model, representing its basic abstractions. The figure represents only a selected subset of methods, the actual implementation contains for every attribute setter and getter methods. Each interface in the model is implemented by a class with a corresponding name, e.g., `LifePolicy` is implemented by `LifePolicyImpl` (not shown in the figure).

The implementation of the insurance application also consists of three aspects. Every aspect implements a certain behavior that is of minor interest here, but the pointcuts defined in each aspect exhibit different characteristics which arise interesting issues when the program is refactored.

The TrackFinders aspect uses the Java logging capability to log how many results are returned by a query method in SimpleInsurance. It defines a pointcut that enumerates three methods in SimpleInsurance that implement different possibilities to find a specific policy in the systems:

```
1 pointcut findPolicies(String criteria):
2  (execution(Set SimpleInsurance.findPoliciesById(String))
3   || execution(Set SimpleInsurance.findPoliciesByCustomerId(String))
4   || execution(Set SimpleInsurance.findPoliciesByCustomerLastName(String)))
5  && args(criteria);
```

The pointcut refers to each method by specifying its fully qualified signature and selects any execution of these methods at runtime.

The PolicyChangeNotification aspect implements a notification mechanism to observe updates of policies. The user interface is implemented as simple Model-View-Controller design. There is a small PolicyListener interface that clients can implement, and after registering themselves with a policy, they will receive a policyUpdated() notification whenever the policy is updated. The PolicyChangeNotification aspect defines a point-cut that is supposed to select every execution of a *setter* method defined in PolicyImpl class or its subtypes:

```
1 pointcut policyStateUpdate(PolicyImpl policy): execution(* set*(..)) && this(policy);
```

The pointcut identifies a *setter* method by the characters "set" at the beginning of a method's name and requires their containment by specifying the type of the object at which these methods are executed. At any execution of such a method it calls the method notifyListeners() at the underlying object.

The last aspect LifePolicyStatistics implements a handling of statistical data for contracted life policies. It uses a *cflow* pointcut that intercepts any creation of a LifePolicyImpl object when the Add-Button is pressed in the user interface:

```
1 pointcut policyContracted():
2  execution(LifePolicyImpl.new(Customer))
3   && cflow( execution(public void SelectionAdpater+.widgetSelected(SelectionEvent)) );
```

The pointcut selects the behavior "Add-Button pressed" by recognizing executions of methods with the signature widgetSelected(SelectionEvent) of SelectionAdpater types. A selection event in SWT[2] represents a mouse click on widgets in the UI, like buttons or menus. Any execution of the constructor named LifePolicyImpl(Customer)

---

[2]SWT is an abbreviation for the Standard Widget Toolkit [88], a library for building user interfaces used by the Eclipse Platform [21].

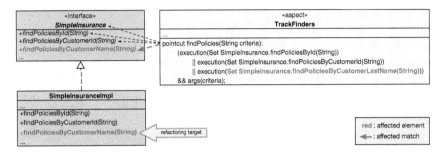

Figure 2.2: Effects of renaming method `findPoliciesByCustomerLastName(String)`.

within the control flow of such a method is selected as a joinpoint. Other instantiations of these objects are ignored.

2.3.2 Refactoring Scenarios

In this example, we rename two program elements using the Rename Method refactoring (cf. [28], p.273) and inline a local variable using the Inline Local Variable refactoring[3]. Each refactoring affects one of the pointcuts presented above. In the following sections, we describe every scenario and illustrate the issues that result from refactoring within the context of pointcuts.

2.3.2.1 Rename Method

The *Rename Method* refactoring changes the name of `findPoliciesByCustomerLast-Name(String)` in class `SimpleInsuranceImpl` to `findPoliciesByCustomerName`. It affects the pointcut `findPolicies(String)` in `TrackFinders` as shown by Figure 2.2. The refactoring renames a method that overrides other methods, thus every base method also must be renamed (cf. [28], p.273). The aspect's pointcut uses the signature of a base method to recognize the joinpoints at runtime. A change of this signature removes the identifier, so the pointcut cannot recognize any joinpoint that is anchored to this method after the refactoring.

The pointcut specifies three clearly separated sets of joinpoints, of which only one set (marked "red" in the figure) is affected by the refactoring. This set loses all matching anchors in the program, and thus all depended joinpoints. The renaming of the anchor made it impossible to identify the same joinpoints in the execution, because removed the used identifier.

An aspect-oriented version of the refactoring needs additionally to update the specification of properties that are used to identify a set of joinpoints. In this case, the rename

---

[3]The *Inline Local Variable* refactoring is an automated implementation of the *Inline Temp* refactoring (cf. [28], p.119), provided by the Eclipse Java IDE [22].

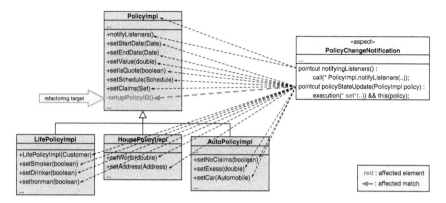

Figure 2.3: Effects of renaming method `createPolicyID()`.

refactoring changed a property of all matching anchors, so it is obvious that the specification can be adjusted in a similar way as for symbolic references. Such an update
would not only follow the developer's intention behind a pointcut, but also preserve the
program behavior.

2.3.2.2 Rename Method, again

In the second scenario, the *Rename Method* refactoring changes the name of method
`createPolicyID()` in class `PolicyImpl` to `setupPolicyID()`. The pointcut `policy-
StateUpdate(PolicyImpl)` of aspect `PolicyChangeNotification` selects all methods
whose names start with "set" in class `PolicyImpl`. Hence, the refactoring causes a
newly matching pointcut anchor for this pointcut. The Figure 2.3 shows the program
structure after the refactoring and indicates affected parts in "red". The affected part
of the pointcut incompletely specifies a method signature (name starts with `set`), but
defines the type at which the method has to be executed.
Even if such cases can easily be resolved by a human, no refactoring tool could infer
an updated proposal just from analyzing the program's source. At syntactic level it is
impossible to decide whether the additionally matching method `setupPolicyID()` is an
intended anchor.

An aspect-oriented refactoring tool can only recognize the additional match and warn
the developer of the poorly specified property. The information for deciding such cases is
not expressed in the program. If the program was developed using certain naming conventions, either the refactoring tool is made aware of adopted standards, or the developer
has to provide a decision by considering the behavior implemented by method.

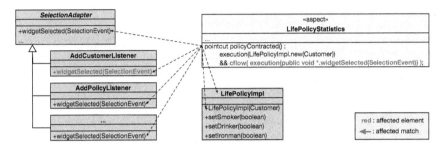

Figure 2.4: Effects of inlining the variable lp.

```
public void widgetSelected(SelectionEvent event) {
    if (lifePolicyButton.getSelection()) {
        LifePolicy lp = (LifePolicy)company.createPolicy(customer, PolicyType.LIFE);
        new LifePolicyEditor(
            myShell,
            SimpleInsuranceApp.getCompany(),
            lp,
            true);
        checkClaims(lp.getClaims());
    }
    else if (autoPolicyButton.getSelection()) {
        // ... create a car policy
    }
    else {
        // ... create a house policy
    }
}
```

```
public void widgetSelected(SelectionEvent event) {
    if (lifePolicyButton.getSelection()) {
        new LifePolicyEditor(
            myShell,
            SimpleInsuranceApp.getCompany(),
            (LifePolicy)company.createPolicy(customer, PolicyType.LIFE),
            true);
        checkClaims(((LifePolicy)company.createPolicy(customer, PolicyType.LIFE)).getClaims());
    }
    else if (autoPolicyButton.getSelection()) {
        // ... create a car policy
    }
    else {
        // ... create a house policy
    }
}
```

Figure 2.5: The Inline Local Variable refactoring performed on variable lp.

2.3.2.3 Inline Local Variable

The third refactoring is performed on the variable `lp` in method `widgetSelected-`
`(SelectionEvent)` of class `AddPolicyListener`. This refactoring replaces all variable
usages with its initialization and affects the pointcut `policyContracted()` of aspect
`LifePolicyStatistics`. The pointcut captures every instantiation of class `LifePolicy-`
`Impl`, if it occurs when a button in the UI was pressed. The aspect counts the number
of contracted policies and uses the *cflow* property to filter instantiations that occur in
other contexts.

The refactoring does not affect any referenced program element, as shown in Figure 2.4,
but it alters the control flow specified by the pointcut. Changes of dynamic properties,
such as the control flow, are especially difficult to recognize and an assessment of their
effects on selected joinpoints is nearly impossible without proper tool support.

In the example, the refactoring replaces two occurrences of variable `lp` with its initialization, shown in Figure 2.5. The variable's initialization, however, creates an object of
`LifePolicyImpl`. After the refactoring, the code creates two objects of the class, and
obviously causes a different program behavior. Object-oriented refactoring tools, like the
Eclipse JDT[22], do not check such kind of side effects, i.e., the developer may have not
noticed the alteration of the base program behavior. In addition, the refactoring leads
to additional invocations of the aspect's advice, which now would be invoked two times
if the corresponding button in the UI is pressed.

An aspect-oriented version of this refactoring can detect such situations and point a developer to the responsible program transformation, but the tool would not be able to
propose a resolution of such behavioral interferences. It can neither restore the original
behavior nor decide whether the intention behind the pointcut is invalidated. Nonetheless, an aspect-oriented refactoring tool could recognize the change effects and notify the
developer in case the refactoring alters the program behavior. With this information a
developer would be able to cancel the refactoring, if the changes are not intended.

2.3.3 Summary

Aspect-oriented programs need additional refactoring support as shown in the examples
above. Essentially, developers seek for tool support for three additional activities when
refactoring an aspect-oriented program.

First, a refactoring tool can filter the change effects on existing pointcuts and confront
the developer only with impacts on the program behavior. In particular, it could hide
changed pointcut anchors that are still referenced by the pointcut and only appear under
a different name or in a different part of the program. This is especially important for
pointcuts that tend to refer to a huge number of elements, such as the pointcut in the
second example. A developer then only needs to deal with really new or lost anchors.

Second, the tool could assess the change effects on the selected behavior in terms of the
specification. Affected pointcuts with very weak specifications, i.e., use of properties
that are unrelated to the selected behavior (set of joinpoints) or incompletely specified
properties, could be detected and expected issues reported to the developer.

Third, since pointcuts may intend alterations of their selected joinpoint sets, a refactoring tool for AOP should assist the developer in the decision, whether an affected pointcut has to be updated. In ordinary cases, like the first example, a refactoring tool should be able to propose an update decision and automatically generate the update for invalidated pointcuts.

Due to intended alterations of the composed program behavior, a refactoring tool for aspect-oriented programs cannot just restore the original program behavior. A new concept for behavior preservation in AOP is required, which enables the tool to differentiate accidental from intended behavioral changes.

2.4 Selection of Joinpoints

Various approaches for the selection of joinpoints were studied during the preparation of this thesis [3, 5, 24, 36, 50, 72, 74, 91, 99]. Most approaches differ in syntax, expressiveness and the provided joinpoint model, but they all select program elements by specifying properties of program representations.

These program representations implicitly define an interface either to the implementation or the execution of a program. A developer can select elements from a representation by specifying their properties (pointcut) and can bind an advice to it. An AOP-specfic runtime support would recognize every execution of a program element (joinpoint), that matches the specified properties, and would then invoke the bound advice code. The properties and program representations used by a pointcut define the **expected interface** for bound advice declarations.

Like "traditional" interfaces, these representations are *used* (even without any explicit declaration) as a facade to a possibly changing implementation of the program behavior. Hence, the developer expects that referenced representations and their specified properties remain unchanged during evolution of the program. The bound advice is called at all joinpoints matched by this interface. Hence, any refactoring that affects this interface should also adjust the pointcut that defines it.

Unlike "traditional" interfaces, these representations can be directly or indirectly *affected* by arbitrary changes in the program. Even changes of program elements that do not belong to the interface can affect referenced program representations. Furthermore, some advanced AOP approaches [3, 72, 99] also provide access to runtime representations, like stack trace, execution trace, or object heap. These dynamic program representations exhibit the runtime conditions of a program execution, which can be used by pointcuts to select a particular behavior at runtime. Such pointcuts would require a refactoring to adjust a specification of a certain program behavior, whenever it interferes with a dynamic property.

The general nature of this interface is defined by the joinpoint model and the pointcut language provided by a particular AOP approach. This section presents a **classification of general attributes** that characterizes the interface used by every studied AOP approach.

The interface consists of three separate parts, as shown in Figure 2.6. Each part deals

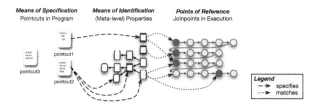

Figure 2.6: Constituent parts of the meta-level interface in aspect-oriented programs.

with a different type of information, with respect to the elements that can be referenced (***points of reference***), the properties that can be used for identifying these elements (***means of identification***) and the way in which the properties can be specified (***means of specification***). The classification presents general attributes of each part and characterizes the effects of each attribute on aspect-oriented refactoring.

2.4.1 Points of Reference

The joinpoint model of an AOP approach defines at which (join)points in the execution an aspect can be applied. It exposes executions of specific program elements, that can be intercepted to invoke the advice code. Three primary attributes of a joinpoint model mainly influence the way in which aspects can interact with other parts of the system: *visibility, granularity* and *symmetry*. In this section, these three attributes are described and resulting consequences on refactoring of aspect-oriented programs are discussed.

2.4.1.1 Visibility

The visibility of declaring elements in the program code, e.g., private, protected, or public, can be considered by the joinpoint model. Depending on the visibility of the declaration that is associated with a joinpoint shadow, two generally different types of joinpoint models can be distinguished: black-box and white-box.
A ***black-box model*** only allows pointcuts to refer to publicly exposed program elements, i.e., only exposed parts of the program's interface can also be used as joinpoints at runtime. Executions of other program elements are not intercepted by aspects.
A ***white-box model*** offers access to all parts of the program's interface, including elements declared as private.

Regardless of whether "private joinpoints" can be accessed by aspects, a refactoring tool needs a representation of the executed element in the program code. Otherwise, changes in the program's source cannot be mapped to a set of joinpoints. For white-box models, a refactoring tool requires a more fine-grained program representation to contain every program element that can be referenced by pointcuts. Thus, the computation can be more costly, which however is the only difference with respect to refactoring, as long as joinpoints are directly represented by their shadows in the program code.

2.4.1.2 Granularity

Similar to the visibility of declared elements in a program, only specific kinds of program elements can be allowed for a composition with aspects. In general, ***operation-level*** and ***statement-level*** access can be distinguished. The operation level considers every operation, i.e., constructor or method invocation, defined in the program as possible joinpoint. Statement-level approaches consider execution of much more program elements as joinpoints. They also provide access to every statement in the program. It is obvious that statement-level joinpoints are the more powerful approach, but at the price of several disadvantages.

Ossher and Tarr investigated the pros and cons of statement-level joinpoints and highlighted the unpredictability of change effects on statement-level weaving as major problem [71]. They state that statement-level changes are in particular difficult to predict, because they affect both the data- and control-flow properties of that code, which negates any guarantees that might have been made about the code. Furthermore, Ossher and Tarr point out that data- and control-flow analyses are inherently exponential, which makes it difficult even for tools to reveal all effects of statement-level changes. Although this problem is inherent to software engineering in general, the fact that aspects are oblivious to the code they are attached to, amplifies this problem.

Also, *Bergmans et al.* have discovered evolution problems arising from statement-level joinpoints. They emphasize strong dependencies to implementation details, which make aspects less reusable and more vulnerable to implementation changes [6].

So the question is, what additional problems may be caused by statement-level joinpoints that need to be taken into account if certain change effects shall be prevented by a refactoring tool.

First, existing refactoring tools only deal with effects of operation-level changes in detail. They mainly consider semantic equivalence of references and operations (cf. [70], Section 4.1.1), and provide just a few statement-level constraints, that basically allow a refactoring to simplify expressions, or to remove dead code. Less restrictive constraints would require, on the one hand, a more fine-grained definition of semantically equivalent statements, and, on the other hand, the usage of additional program representations to enable control- and data-flow analysis during the refactoring process.

Second, static control- and data-flow analysis is very expensive in terms of computation time and memory usage, and relies on conservatively approximated program representations. Hence, not all runtime effects caused by control- or data-flow changes can be represented by statically approximated program representations.

Third, statement-level changes are likely to affect the program behavior in more hidden ways than operation-level changes. A refactoring tool is required, on the one hand, to distinguish semantically equivalent but changed behavior from other behavior alterations at the statement level, and, on the other hand, to communicate the differences in those changes to the developer. For example, consider an error message during a refactoring that should present the reasons for a non-equivalently modified sequence of statements. How should the tool communicate all possible indirect and direct reasons in a comprehensible way, covering changes from a simple statement removal to arbitrary side effects. The requirement for statement-level equivalence constraints, stated above, would also soften the general requirement for behavior preservation in refactoring. It alters the general goal of refactoring and requires a more fine-grained model for supporting an automated decision making. Refactoring tools for present AOP approaches have to deal with effects on statement-level joinpoints, but in turn they require precise static representations of joinpoint properties and sufficiently complete specification, to provide checks for statement-level equivalence rules.

2.4.1.3 Symmetry

Most AOP approaches only consider joinpoints in the execution of the base program, the part of an aspect-oriented program that is adapted by aspects. A few approaches support *symmetric composition* [81, 91] that makes no distinction between aspects and other components of the system, and provides the same composition mechanisms for component-component, aspect-aspect, and class-class compositions [42].
In symmetric approaches, the execution of the aspect code itself provides joinpoints, in addition to the base program. Aspects can re-use the functionalities defined by other aspects, which make them more reusable [82, 100]. If such approaches are combined with white-box visibility and statement-level joinpoints, they provide the most powerful composition mechanisms in AOP. However, this power again comes with a price; huge additional effort needs to be exerted in order to detect interferences with known composition concepts, such as inheritance, and also between different aspect modules.

This causes three major issues with respect to refactoring tool-support: First, the program representations required for the analysis of change effects are getting even more complex. In particular, the inheritance relationships and control- and data-flows of already composed components have to be considered to reveal undesired interferences. Second, more research is required to identify *all* conflicting situations between different aspects and non-AOP components, such as discovered by Störzer and Krinke [86]. Third, the resulting constraints do not only affect new composition mechanisms, but inverse interferences have also to be taken into account, e.g., any definition of additional inheritance relationships would require a check for conflicts with AOP compositions.
In summary, all fully symmetric AOP approaches require more than an aspect-aware refactoring tool to support software evolution. We consider the specific issues arisen from fully-symmetric joinpoint models as out of the scope of this thesis.

2.4.2 Means of Identification

Joinpoints are executions of program elements and hence do not provide a unique identifier. Pointcuts specify properties of joinpoints to select individual executions of program elements for invoking bound advice declarations. During the execution of the program a particular execution of an element is recognized by these properties, in contrast to fully-qualified names that already identify the element in the program code. However, as a refactoring would adapt symbolic references to changed declaration elements, it also would be required to adapt specifications of joinpoint properties when a property is changed.

A symbolic reference refers to a declaration element in the code and is completely specified. Joinpoint properties, however, are usually exhibited by multiple elements, and also
more or less completely specified by pointcuts. A preservation of pointcuts that specify
these properties, therefore, differs in several ways from the handling of symbolic references in object-oriented refactoring. In this section, we discuss three characteristics of
joinpoint properties, *analyzability*, *dependency*, and *meaning*, that significantly influence
their handling in an aspect-oriented refactoring process.

2.4.2.1 Analyzability

With respect to the availability of the information represented by the program representations for refactoring, we can distinguish *statically available properties* of the program
implementation from *dynamic properties* of the program execution.
Static program representations can be directly built from the program code, whereas representations necessary for dynamic properties, like the stack trace, need a more advanced
processing when they have to be made statically available. They additionally depend
on input values available only during the program execution and therefore have to be
conservatively approximated. An approximated representation is a static structure representing all possible program executions, and may contain more executions of program
elements than actually occur at runtime, i.e., including false positives. An approximation can also be very expensive in terms of computation time and memory usage, and
for some dynamic representations it may be very imprecise. Some runtime information,
such as values of global variables, can hardly be approximated. In such cases, the corresponding static representation would contain all possible executions without runtime
values. Different specification of such dynamic properties cannot be differentiated.
Depending on whether a joinpoint's property is represented through a static or a dynamic representation, the properties are called either static or dynamic properties.

Static properties. A *static propery* is a property of a static program representation,
such as the abstract syntax tree (AST) or static type hierarchy. An AST, for example,
holds all elements of the program code and can be used to query the program's name
space and lexical representation. Its edges represent containment relationships between
different program elements. The type hierarchy represents static typing information,
holding all super- and subtype relationships. Static properties denote properties of program elements that are somehow associated with a joinpoint (e.g., joinpoint shadows).
They can denote the element's kind, name, source code location or inheritance relationships. For example, consider the following pointcut:

```
1 pointcut nameAdjustments() : execution(void Customer.setLastName(String));
```

The pointcut selects any execution of a method with the signature `setLastName(String)`
of class `Customer`. The pointcut specifies several properties of the method (joinpoint
shadow), to select it from the program's AST:

- element kind = Method Declaration

- name = "setLastName"

- return type = "void"

- parameter type = "String"

- within = type "Customer".

Static program representations are directly constructed from the program code, i.e., their elements have a non-ambiguous representation in the code. Source code changes can be mapped to these elements and change effects can be inferred directly. Because of this direct mapping, a refactoring tool can exactly detect the change effects on static properties of joinpoints. Furthermore, specifications of static properties directly match elements in the program. If a refactoring unintentionally affects a matching element, the specification can often be adjusted using the same change values.

Dynamic properties. The observation that any seemingly safe modification in the base program's representation can alter the behavior of aspect-oriented programs leaded to several enhancements to existing pointcut languages [3, 36, 72, 99]. Their common goal is to abstract from implementation details, so that specifications can describe a specific program behavior directly.

A *dynamic property* is a property of a dynamic program representation. Its elements represent executions of program elements and may denote a particular execution order, dynamic type, or a certain runtime value. Dynamic properties depend on the program execution, i.e., on the behavior that actually occurs during runtime. For example, consider the following pointcut:

```
1 pointcut bigDeals(PolicyImpl pol): set(double *.value)
2        && target(pol)
3        && if(pol.value >= 1000000);
```

The pointcut selects specific executions a any assignment to a field named `value` that is a member of an instance of class `PolicyImpl`. An execution of the field assignment is only intercepted if the field's current runtime value is bigger than 1000000. The pointcut specifies two properties that cannot be represented through a static program representation:

- executing object = instance of `PolicyImpl`;

- dynamic value of field `value` >= 1000000.

Some experiments have shown that pointcuts with dynamic properties are more robust with respect to structural changes [36, 72]. These experiments however did not consider the impact of behavioral changes and the inherently exponential effort for detecting change effects on dynamic properties.

Especially, the introduction of advanced dynamic program representations to the specification of joinpoints, allows for pointcuts that are not affected by simple structural changes such as rename and move. However, other refactorings, such as Inline Method

or Inline Temp (cf. [28], p.117, p.119), can also influence pointcuts with dynamic properties. The primary disadvantage that comes with the specification of dynamic properties
is the lack of suitable static representations. An approximation of these properties is expensive and often imprecise, and a reliable detection of change effects is even impossible
for various dynamic properties. In addition, affected specifications of dynamic properties
are difficult to adjust. Since a dynamic property denotes a particular behavior, its adjustment would require a refactoring tool to specify a different, but equivalent, behavior.
An automated generation of behavioral specifications is still a research problem in other
fields in software engineering (e.g., generative testing).

2.4.2.2 Dependency

If we consider the dependencies of a joinpoint property, we can make a further distinction: some of the properties inherently belong to the element representing the joinpoint
(or its shadow), e.g., its kind, name or dynamic value. These properties characterize an
intrinsic part of the element, that is completely independent from relationships to other
elements. We refer to those properties as *intrinsic properties*. The complementary
property is called *extrinsic property*, because it depends on the element's context.
A specification of an extrinsic property refers to other elements outside of the joinpoint
shadow and expresses the property as relationships between different elements of a program representation, e.g., within, contains, supertypes, subtypes, or cflow.
The *pointcut anchors* are used to express the context in which those elements that
represent the joinpoint are selected. A pointcut anchor is an element of an arbitrary
program representation that is selected by the pointcut in order to express an extrinsic
property. Since a pointcut anchor is used as a key for expressing a property's specification, its existence is essential to identify joinpoints that possess the specified property.
Pointcuts select anchors also through a specification of their properties. Therefore, the
existence of these *anchor properties* is the prerequisite under which a particular selection of joinpoints is defined. For example, consider the following pointcut:

```
1 pointcut nameChanges(): call(void Customer.setLastName(String))
2                         && within(Account);
```

The pointcut selects every call of a method `setLastName(String)` of a class `Customer`,
when the call is defined within a class named `Account`. The calls of method `setLast-`
`Name(String)` are the shadows of the selected joinpoints, which are identified by two
extrinsic properties: (i) is a call of a method and (ii) is contained in class `Account`. Both
properties refer to properties of other elements (pointcut anchors) that lead to a selection
of the joinpoints. Any modification of an anchor property would not just alter a property
of a selected joinpoint, but also would alter the context in which the joinpoint's property
can be recognized, and therefore the semantics of the property's specification. Such a
change does not necessarily affect any joinpoint shadow (method call), but any other
element the pointcut relies on.
Since joinpoints are executions of program elements and have no unique identifier, their
properties are the only means for their identification. Specified properties are the identifiers for joinpoints, similar to fully-qualified names for declaration elements. Their

specifications have to be preserved when a refactoring changes the underlying program representation. The preservation of a property specification, however, differs in several ways from the treatment of fully-qualified names in object-oriented refactoring. The number of joinpoints with a specific property at runtime is unknown, and therefore a preservation of every single joinpoint seems pointless, especially in the light of static approximation.

Symbolic references point to a single name within an object-oriented program; only inheritance relationships additionally influence the actually invoked element at runtime. Refactorings for object-oriented programs restrict the modification of existing inheritance relationships and update all symbolic references to fully-qualified names when a declaration element is changed. In aspect-oriented programs, the properties can belong to various program representations and can depend on properties of other elements. Hence, in addition to the program's name space and inheritance relationships, a refactoring for AOP also needs to deal with other program representations. For every employed program representation:

- Elements that exhibit a specified joinpoint property,

- Elements on which extrinsic properties additionally depend on,

- Specifications of properties of both kinds of elements, and

- Any specification of relationships between different elements in the representation,

have to be preserved, so the joinpoints can be recognized by the same properties at runtime.

2.4.2.3 Meaning

Joinpoints are selected by their properties which are represented by elements of program representations that can only approximate a particular program behavior. For this reason, one can distinguish between properties that are closer connected to this behavior and properties that have no behavioral meaning at all.

No behavioral meaning. The most obvious property with no execution related meaning is naming. A name of a program element can refer to anything the developer had in mind; simply unreachable for every refactoring tool. This is especially a problem, if simple, *unscoped names* are used to select elements from the program. Such names can match elements in any part of the system, including external libraries and any extension added in the future. This problem becomes even worse if names are partially specified. A specification of a *partial name* defines a specific string of characters, which may make sense in environments with strict naming conventions, but this conventions must be applied to any piece of code that can possibly interact with aspects, even binary and 3rd party libraries. Without an automated verification of applied naming conventions, a more concrete meaning for partial names cannot be ensured.

Behavioral meaning. A specification of name-based properties, however, is not in general meaningless, especially, if the names are bound to a particular context in which they have a concrete meaning. In object-oriented programming, the visibility of names is restricted, e.g., through the enclosing package, type, or block. A name can have a *scope* in which it represents a concrete behavioral meaning. AOP advances this concept of containment-based scopes and allows a pointcut to scope names also through other program representations. Basically, a pointcut can scope a specified name with a particular *containment*, *inheritance*, or *control flow* relationship. *Data flow* relationships are another possible means for scoping, but they are often hard to reason about, and the information is technically difficult to obtain. Each of these *scopes* can ensure that a specified name is only associated with the program elements that represent a particular program behavior, and thus it can supplement a name with a behavioral meaning.

A **containment-based scope** restricts potential occurrences of a name to a specific part in the program, which is not necessarily associated with a particular behavior. For example, package-level scoping is often too coarse-grained, it is more or less a general location for types that provide some implementation for the same functionality. However, a method-level scope directly specifies the statements among which the named element has to occur; it associates a particularly implemented behavior with the named element. For example, consider the following three pointcuts:

```
1 pointcut pc1(): call(void *.setLastName(String));
2 pointcut pc2(): call(void Customer.setLastName(String));
3 pointcut pc3(): call(void Customer.setLastName(String))
4                  && withincode(boolean CustomerEditor.applyChanges());
```

Each of them selects method calls specifying a method signature and some containment-based scope. The pointcut `pc1` does not scope the signature at all. All calls of any method with the specified signature, anywhere in the program will be selected by `pc1`. That makes it very difficult to assume a concrete behavior at executions of these elements.

The pointcut `pc2` restricts the declaring type, so the number of implementations that can be associated with the specified signature is limited. In fact, it selects all method calls of a single method that implements one particular behavior.

The pointcut `pc3` additionally restricts where the method's calls can occur in the program. It selects only those joinpoints of one particular method call that is associated with a concrete behavior implemented by the method `applyChanges()`.

A more execution related meaning can be achieved with **inheritance-based scopes**. In particular, a specification of overriding methods gives every method name in the selection a strong behavioral meaning. Newly matching methods override the named method and provide a different implementation to be executed at occurrences of the same behavior at runtime. Hence, an inheritance-based scope is an indicator for elements that are invoked at the same behavior in the execution of the program. For example, the following pointcut specifies all methods that implement a behavior that occurs if a "mouse click" selects a widget in the program's UI:

```
1 pointcut selectionObserved():
2     execution(void SelectionAdapter+.widgetSelected(SelectionEvent));
```

The pointcut selects all executions at runtime of every method that implements the abstract declaration of method `widgetSelected(SelectionEvent)`. Each of these methods is invoked if the same behavior occurs at runtime.

A *control flow-based scope* restricts the specified element names to a specific control flow. It associates occurrences of a named element with a particular behavior represented by a particular control flow. It can be seen as a temporal relationship that renders element names valid if the behavior represented by the control flow occurs. For example, consider the following pointcut:

```
1 pointcut policyContracted() :
2     execution(LifePolicyImpl.new(Customer))
3     && cflow( execution(public void SelectionAdpater+.widgetSelected(SelectionEvent)) );
```

The pointcut additionally filters executions of one particular constructor of class `Life-PolicyImpl`. It restricts the set of selected joinpoints not only by specific program elements, it also describes a particular program behavior that has to occur at runtime, before a constructor execution is considered as a selected joinpoint.

Reasoning about data flows, has not yet been achieved by existing AOP approaches, however single events in the data flow that create, exchange, or assign data still have a meaning related to a particular program behavior. An *object creation* can be observed and intercepted at several points in execution, e.g., at executions of *static initializers* when the object's class is initialized or at *dynamic intializers* and *constructors* when an object is created. Also, *data access* represents points in execution with a particular meaning at runtime. Especially, *assignments* to an object's field indicate a certain behavior, since state changes in object-oriented programs are generally represented by values of object members.

2.4.3 Means of Specification

All AOP approaches studied in the preparation of this thesis offer a separate (pointcut) language for specifying properties of joinpoints. These pointcut languages differ in syntax, expressiveness and the supported joinpoint model, but they all provide similar means for selecting, filtering, and combining properties of joinpoints.

Figure 2.7 gives an idea of the variety of syntactic differences in present pointcut languages. The first pointcut is defined in the AspectJ syntax, using two pointcut designators, `call` and `withincode`, combined with the logical `&&` (and) operator. The second pointcut is defined as XML-based path description using an XQuery-based approach for specifying pointcuts [24]. It navigates from the root node of an abstract syntax tree (`all`) over a `class` with the name "B", to a `method` named "update" and returns all method calls (`invoke`). The last pointcut is defined in a logic programming syntax using the Alpha approach [72]. It expresses joinpoint properties as predicates. Some predicates are

Informal:	"Select any execution of all method calls located within method B.update( )"
AspectJ:	call(* *(..)) && withincode(* B.update())
XQuery:	$db:all/bat:class[@name="B"]/bat:method[@name = "update"]/bat:invoke

Alpha:	callWithin(ExprID) :-
	    within(
	        (_, calls((_, ExprID) , _, _)),
	        `B`,
	        `update`).

Figure 2.7: Same pointcut in different syntaxes of AspectJ, XQuery and Alpha.

composed of other predicates, such as the `within` contains a definition of the predicate `calls`.

All pointcuts describe joinpoint properties in a declarative way. Their expressions can be characterized in terms of *aggregation* and *completeness*, which are both of particular importance if a pointcut interferes with changes in the base program. We discuss both attributes in the following, together with inter-pointcut interference, which requires a *precedence* specification in case of multiple pointcuts share the same joinpoint.

2.4.3.1 Aggregation

Pointcut languages provide a means for aggregating individual expressions to a more complex specifications. An aggregation can be defined either by direct nesting of expressions or through logic operations, such as *and* (&&) or *or* (||). The evaluation of an **aggregated expression** will resolve any (nested) expression within the aggregation before their results are used to resolve the aggregated expression. This dependency between pointcut expressions can directly reflect a dependency to anchor properties. If any specification of an anchor property is specified by subexpressions of an aggregated expression, then anchor dependencies are directly reflected by the structure of the pointcut, even for recursively nested expressions. This reflections of anchor dependencies is of particular importance if a refactoring affects an anchor expression which is used within other expressions.

For example, consider the different syntactic definitions of the pointcut shown in Figure 2.7. Each pointcut specifies the same joinpoint properties, but aggregates pointcut expressions in a different way. Figure 2.8 shows the evaluation dependencies between the expressions of each pointcut. The *call* expressions are highlighted as every pointcut selects executions of method calls as joinpoints. The calls are discriminated by a containment-based scope. The containment property is the only identifier that characterizes this particular set of joinpoints, hence, the anchor expressions defining the scope give the pointcut its meaning.

The Figure 2.8 also illustrates the nesting level of each expression within the pointcuts. An evaluation of expressions in *level 0* depends on the evaluation of any connected expression in higher levels. Expressions of the highest level (e.g., *level 4*) can be evaluated independently, but, in turn, are the foundation for the evaluation of (all) other expressions. If we consider the nesting level as indicator for an expression's importance in

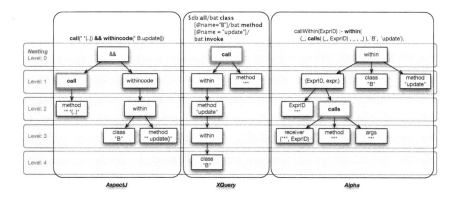

Figure 2.8: Three different way of describing the joinpoint properties.

terms of the evaluation result, then expressions of higher levels should specify anchor properties on which properties specified at lower levels depend on.

For example, the &&-expression of the AspectJ pointcut depends on all other expressions (level 0), whereas the name-based expressions (method, call) can be evaluated independently (level 3). It also indicates that any modification of method update() or class B could entirely disguise the containment property for any call, while a removal of a single call "just" removes any execution of that call.

A comparison with the other pointcut definitions in Figure 2.8 shows that the XQuery-based pointcut also reflects this anchor dependency, even in a less cluttered way. The Alpha pointcut, however, indicates no dependency from the containment scope, in fact, the pointcut's structure leaves much room for ambiguous interpretation. For example, it is not clear from the structure how the three parts of the within expression depend on each other.

2.4.3.2 Completeness

Since pointcuts are specifications of properties they can describe a property more or less completely. The incompleteness is mostly introduced by dependencies of *signature patterns*.

Most pointcut languages provide a means for specifying the signature/name of types, methods, constructors and fields. Such a pattern consists of several parts that specify a particular information of a signature. For instance, a method signature pattern consists of modifiers, return type name, declaring type name, method name, and a list of parameter type names. Every part in the pattern can be completely omitted, i.e., specified by a wildcard "*", or partially specified through a string of characters, e.g., "set*", "get*" or "test*". The list of parameter types can be partially specified by ".." (any), ".., int" (last parameter is of type int), or "int, .." (first parameter type is int).

The combination of partially specified signature patterns with other pointcut expressions obviously makes the composed expression less complete. For example, consider the following AspectJ pointcuts:

```
1 pointcut strictCmt(): call(* *(..)) && withincode(void CustomerTest.testInit());
2 pointcut partialCmt(): call(* *(..)) && withincode(* CustomerTest.testInit *(..));
3
4 pointcut strictCtrlFlow(): call(* *(..)) && cflow(call(void CustomerTest.testInit()));
5 pointcut partialCtrlFlow(): call(* *(..)) && cflow(call(* CustomerTest.testInit *(..)));
```

The first two pointcuts select all executions of any method call contained within a certain method. The pointcut `strictCmt()` explicitly specifies the method through its complete signature, while the `partialCmt()` pointcut only defines the characters of a method name. Even if both result in the same selection, the pointcut `strictCmt()` is more specific and leaves no room for selecting similar methods as anchors in future versions of the program.

The second pair of pointcuts shows that a partial signature pattern can affect the completeness of almost any other pointcut expression.

2.4.3.3 Precedence

In cases where multiple pieces of advice are bound to the same joinpoint, an aspect has to provide a so-called **advice precedence**. A precedence clause defines in which order different advice declarations are executed at a *shared joinpoint*. The execution order is a partial definition that neither defines a subsequent execution nor an execution dependency, i.e., a second advice can be executed, even if the first advice did not.

Since a refactoring can cause additional joinpoints to be matched, it also can introduce an additional sharing of joinpoints. If no advice precedence is defined, the refactoring tool can inform the developer of the newly shared joinpoints. A computation of a specific proposal, however, would be impossible, because a thorough understanding of the associated aspect behavior is required. A pure detection of newly shared joinpoints can nonetheless be useful to the developer. It is a crucial information that affects the developer's decision making, even if "cancel the refactoring" is the only concrete action that can be proposed.

2.5 Preservation of Behavioral Composition

Refactoring tools for object-oriented programs seek to preserve the program behavior through explicit checks that detect violations of syntactic and semantic properties of a program. If a refactoring violates such a property, the tool either performs additional changes to keep the property valid, e.g., for overriding methods, or informs the developer that the refactoring (if performed) cannot be prevented from altering the program behavior [70, 75].

Refactoring tools for aspect-oriented programs additionally have to check the joinpoint properties specified by pointcuts. Any change effect on a specified property have to be detected and either the corresponding specification adjusted or the developer informed on potential effects on the invocation of advice code.

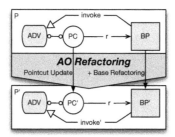

Figure 2.9: Aspect-oriented refactorings that preserve the invocations of advice code.

The general goal of the aspect-aware refactoring approach developed by this thesis is depicted in Figure 2.9. Any base code refactoring that changes the base program BP into BP' is extended with an analysis to detect change effects on aspect oriented modules in the program. Aspect-oriented refactorings are defined as extensions to base code refactorings that control the change effects on the composed program P while producing the refactored version P'. These refactorings infer adjusted pointcuts PC' from changes in the base program BP', so advice ADV is bound to a semantically equivalent set of joinpoints ($invoke'$). The joinpoints selected in the execution of BP' are semantically equivalent to joinpoints of BP in terms of the properties used for their identification, i.e., an adjusted pointcut specifies the same properties of the same program representations as before the refactoring, but uses property values of the refactored program BP'.

The differentiation between the attributes of joinpoint models and pointcut languages described above, allows us to discriminate the following change effects on pointcuts and to reveal the concrete challenges for adjusting the specifications of joinpoint properties.

2.5.1 Change Effects on Pointcuts

A pointcut specifies properties of program representations that represent the implementation or execution of the base program. Refactorings are program transformations, that modify the base program and inherently affect these program representations, because they are created from the program code. Program transformations change programs at the level of program elements, they can modify (e.g., rename, move), add, or remove a program element. In this section, we give an overview of the kinds of changes that can affect pointcuts and discuss the effects that can be observed.

2.5.1.1 Affecting Changes

A program transformation can either be behavior-preserving, causing only a modified structure of the program, or non-behavior preserving, causing an altered program behavior. In the context of pointcuts, the impact on the program representations that are referenced by pointcuts can be additionally considered and the following changes be distinguished.

An *unrelated behavioral change* can modify the behavior of the base program in a way that no property specified by a pointcut is affected, but a pointcut still results in a different set of joinpoints. Such a transformation would not affect any specified property, but alter the number of selected joinpoints that occur at runtime and thus affect the composed program behavior.

A *change of a dynamic property* can affect a specified dynamic property of a join-point, i.e., a particular program behavior is affected, that is specified to recognize individual joinpoints. This behavioral change would result in joinpoints with a modified (dynamic) property at runtime, which does not match the specified behavior. Thus, the change would alter the set of captured joinpoints.

An *unrelated structural change* can modify a certain program element that is not referenced by a pointcut. Since the program behavior is not affected, the same joinpoints occur at runtime. The composed program has the same behavior as before the change.

A *change of a static property* can affect the program's structure and modify a static property of joinpoints that is specified by a pointcut. Such a change would lead to a different selection of joinpoint shadows, and thus to an altered set of joinpoints.

A *change of an anchor property* can modify a static or dynamic property that identifies a pointcut anchor, a so-called anchor property. This would alter the set of selected anchors and thus affect the selection of joinpoints whose properties are specified using it.
Every specification of a property that refers to the changed anchor was defined under the assumption that the anchor exhibits the original property. The change of the anchor alters not only the resulting set of joinpoints, but also the assumptions under which other specifications were made. Such a change would therefore modify the semantics of these property specifications, which is also known as the fragile pointcut problem [56].

2.5.1.2 Change Effects

Any of the changes described above can have different effects on the selection of join-points. In general, we can discriminate the changes by the affected kind of element selected by a pointcut, like joinpoint, shadow or anchor, or by the quantity of modified matches (partial or complete). The following four kinds of change effects can be distinguished:

Even if no specified property is affected, a behavioral change can affect the *number of joinpoints* that occurs during an execution. This would impact no element in the program selected by the pointcut, but the number of executions of joinpoint shadows that occur at runtime. The behavioral change of the base program caused different invocations of advice, and hence an alteration of the composed program behavior.

A program transformation can cause additionally matching joinpoints for pointcuts that have not selected any joinpoint before. Such transformations often change a program element into a matching shadow or anchor. The transformation causes a *complete addition of shadows or anchors*.

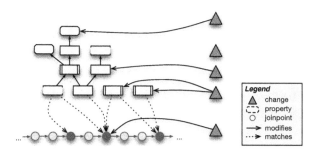

Figure 2.10: Change effects on the meta-level interface.

Also the opposite case can happen particularly if a shadow or anchor is modified or removed from the system. Such a transformation would cause a **complete loss of shadows or anchors** and therefore a loss of all dependent joinpoints.

Especially for pointcuts with incompletely specified shadows or anchors, a transformation can cause a **partial addition or loss of shadows or anchors**. For example, incompletely specified name patterns match several elements in the program. A modification of one matching element affects only a partial set of selected joinpoints, other joinpoints still remain in the pointcut selection. Also joinpoints selected by dynamic properties, such as `cflow`, can be split by a transformation. A specified control flow-based scope can be reduced by behavioral changes affecting the specified control flow.

2.5.2 Challenges in Refactoring Aspect-oriented Programs

Changes in the program's source code can cause various effects on existing pointcuts. If we consider the different attributes of joinpoint models and pointcut languages described above the following challenges for aspect-oriented refactoring can be identified.

2.5.2.1 Detection of affected Pointcuts

A refactoring can affect the program representations that exhibit properties of joinpoints. Some pointcuts in the system can specify these properties and select therefore an altered set of joinpoints in the execution of the refactored program. These pointcuts are called **affected pointcuts**, because the refactoring interferes with their evaluation results.
The detection of affected pointcuts is influenced by the *granularity of joinpoints* and the analyzability of specified properties. The more fine-grained the joinpoint model, the more execution-related properties can be specified. Static properties of statements, such as location and order, are directly related to a particular program behavior. In addition, statement-level joinpoints can be directly associated with runtime values, which is not possible for operation-level joinpoints at all.
This interacts with the *analyzability of specified properties*. Static properties can be represented by program representations that reflect the structure of the program code,

while dynamic properties are represented by program representations that reflect the execution of a program. Refactoring tools employ static program analysis, therefore all referenced dynamic program representations have to be approximated by a static representation. Such a static representation of dynamic properties is a conservative approximation, i.e., it can contain more joinpoints with a particular property as actually occur at runtime. Depending on the particular dynamic property specified by a pointcut, an approximated representation can be exceptional expensive to compute and also very imprecise so that differently specified properties cannot be discriminated.

Another kind of interference is the *introduction of joinpoint sharing* between multiple advice declarations. Even if a refactoring does not interfere with a specified property, it could alter the set of selected joinpoints, and introduce shared joinpoints. Such cases require an interaction analysis considering the approximated joinpoints of every pointcut defined in the system.

2.5.2.2 Assessing the Change Impact

In case a refactoring tool detects affected pointcuts, the tool has "just" recognized pointcuts with (possibly) altered sets of joinpoints. Since pointcuts select points in the execution of a program, a refactoring tool cannot simply include missing or exclude additional joinpoints. It rather has to rephrase the specifications of their properties to adjust a set of selected joinpoints. Moreover, a pointcut can specify properties of joinpoints more or less completely, which can intentionally or unintentionally capture an altered set of joinpoints in future program versions. Some pointcuts may also intentionally match newly added or changed elements. For these reasons the effects on pointcuts need to be further analyzed, before a refactoring tool can infer an update decision.

The analysis can assess the ***impact on a pointcut*** in various ways. It can determine which parts of the pointcut are affected, what kind of properties are used by these parts and how complete the affected properties are specified and also how many joinpoints are approximately affected.

Multiple of the attributes of pointcut languages discussed above influence such an impact analysis. The analysis can determine which parts of the pointcut are affected. As stated before, effects on joinpoints, shadows, and anchors can be distinguished. Effects on a selected shadow or anchor are considered more crucial, because they can prevent any recognition of specific joinpoints at all. In particular, unmodified pointcut anchors are a fundamental prerequisite for the evaluation of joinpoints. They represent *dependencies* in evaluating specified properties of the joinpoints. The degree of dependency should be directly inferred from the *aggregation* level of affected pointcut expressions in some pointcut languages. The more an expression is nested in the pointcut, the more the evaluation of the complete pointcut depends on its matching elements. As discussed above, in some pointcut languages these dependencies between properties are not reflected by their syntax.

Furthermore, the *completeness* of expressions that specify an affected property can be taken into account. A completely specified signature, for example, indicates that the pointcut refers to a single declaration element in the program, which, if modified, can cause the loss of all captured joinpoints. Whereas, weakly specified properties can be an indicator for unimportant elements. The completeness a property specification can be used by a refactoring tool to differentiate specifications that exactly select "these" elements from specifications that select "some of those" elements.

In addition to the specification completeness, the *meaning of a property* can be an indicator for the relevance of selected elements in the program. In Section 2.4.2.3 we differentiated several kinds of scopes. Each of them is to some extent connected to a particular program behavior. The more a property of these scopes is connected to the program behavior, the more meaningful is its specification in terms of behavioral semantics. Changes that affect meaningful properties are more likely to alter the base program behavior, rather than just its structure. Hence, it alters the behavior some advice is attached to, and are therefore considered as more crucial than changes of meaningless properties.

Also, the *analyzability of affected properties* definitely influences this impact assessment. For dynamic properties that cannot be statically determined, the impact can hardly be assessed. The *symmetric joinpoint models* that also allow aspects to adapt the execution of other aspects makes the assessment of the change impact even more difficult. An aspect that adapts another aspect is indirectly invoked at a behavior that itself is indirectly invoked at a third behavior. These dependency chain of indirect behavior execution includes additional modules in this analysis, but generally requires the same mechanisms. However, if an AOP approach would provide additional properties more specific to the execution of advice code, the analysis is also required to consider these additional properties.

2.5.2.3 Behavior Preservation in AO Refactoring

An advice is invoked at a set of joinpoints, i.e., at executions of elements. Pointcuts can select all executions of a set of program elements, but also restrict the selection to specific executions. Pointcuts that select a set of joinpoints only through static properties, restrict the selection to any execution of specific joinpoint shadows. A refactoring tool can *preserve the program behavior* for such pointcuts, simply by ensuring that a change does not alter the set of selected shadows. The tool can either propose to adapt the specification of shadows or to cancel the refactoring. For pointcuts that additionally specify dynamic properties, every referenced runtime representation has to be statically approximated, in order to detect violations of dynamic properties.

Pointcuts can select joinpoints by specifying *intrinsic properties* which refer only to elements that exhibit the property. A change of these elements can only alter the resulting selection, but not the means of their identification. Consequently, the semantics of pointcuts that specify only intrinsic property cannot be changed by refactoring.

Specifications of *extrinsic properties* are anchored to other program elements that do not exhibit the specified property, but represent the context in which an extrinsic property can be recognized. A refactoring has to preserve the specifications of the anchor properties in order to retain the identifier of the selected joinpoints. Otherwise, the joinpoints could not be recognized by the specified property, which would change the specification's semantics. Explicit checks that detect violations of anchor properties require a seizable specification. Since pointcuts can select any program element (shadows and anchors) with very few, unspecific and highly dynamic information, the determination whether a program element is considered essential for the pointcut can be exceptionally difficult. Furthermore, the preservation of the pointcut semantics differs from the preservation of joinpoints that exist at runtime. While the latter would preserve the program behavior, the former may accept additional matches or lost matches, which can intentionally be modified to lose a specified property. This introduces a new situation to refactoring, in which a developer expects the tool to accept a modification even if it alters the composed program behavior. In aspect-oriented programs, refactorings have to distinguish illegal from intended behavioral changes.

2.5.2.4 Adjustment of Invalidated Pointcuts

In cases where a refactoring tool aims at adjusting an affected specification, it tries to ascertain the replacement that restores the original pointcut semantics. Single extensions of a pointcut, which simply exclude unintentionally added capture or include accidentally lost captures, are an insufficient solution. Multiple updates of the same pointcut would *bloat its specification*, making it unrecognizable and incomparable to its original appearance. In addition, updates of incomplete property specifications may cause a selection of other unwanted joinpoints. Hence, the only applicable solution seems to directly replace the smallest affected parts of the pointcut with an update that is sufficiently complete to capture only joinpoints of the original selection. Such an replacement is particularly difficult to compute for imprecisely specified properties or references to highly dynamic program representations that do not communicate the properties meaning to a refactoring tool. The intention behind those pointcuts remains to a large extent in the developer's mind or in program's runtime states. No tool would be able to distinguish unintended from intended captures.

Furthermore, the kind of change, such as rename, remove or create, needs to be considered, when update proposals are computed, e.g., a lost set of joinpoints cannot be restored if it is caused by removing a pointcut anchor.

2.6 Summary

In this chapter, we have investigated the reasons for evolution problems of AOP with a particular focus on tool-supported refactoring and identified several characteristics of existing pointcut languages as the reasons for this evolution problems.

Refactoring changes the program code which inherently affects the program representations used by pointcuts to select the joinpoints at which the aspect behavior is invoked (cf. Section 2.3). Hence, refactoring tools for aspect-oriented programs have to detect any interference between a refactoring and existing pointcuts, and ideally also support the developer in adjusting affected pointcuts.

However, the ways in which pointcuts can be expressed by current pointcut languages lead to several problems. In Section 2.4, we have described the attributes of joinpoint models and pointcut languages that significantly influence reliable refactoring support for AOP.

Pointcuts can describe properties of program representations that represent runtime conditions of a particular program execution. Since refactoring tools use static program analysis some of these conditions cannot be statically represented and, thus, not be checked by a refactoring tool. Furthermore, pointcuts can specify joinpoint properties more or less precise, e.g., if similar behavior is added in the future, the corresponding joinpoints should be intentionally adapted by aspects. Such pointcuts do not necessarily state such an intention explicitly. In addition, specifications of particularly extrinsic properties can depend on specifications of other properties. These dependencies cannot always be recognized from the pointcut structure.

These attributes of pointcuts are the primary reasons for unpredictable effects on the program behavior which often cannot be solved by existing program analysis approaches. Even if an analysis detects interferences with a pointcut it could be impossible to determine whether a pointcut has to be adjusted, because of an imprecise or statically not determinable specification.

Refactoring tools for AOP have to face a new challenge in preserving the behavioral compositions defined in aspect-oriented programs (cf. Section 2.5). They deal with specifications of meta-level properties and have to determine whether an alteration of the program behavior is intended or has to be prevented. In addition, the adjustment of invalidated pointcuts is not only about the replacement of simple values, it is about rephrasing a specification of a particular program behavior.

These problems in the detection of change effects on pointcuts, determination of invalidated pointcuts, and the generation of pointcut updates have been in the focus of multiple research works, which are surveyed in the next chapter.

Chapter 3

State of the Art

This chapter analyses the literature in a number of fields. We begin by surveying existing work in aspect-oriented refactoring (3.1), evolution-specific tool support (3.2) and aspect-aware mechanisms on programming language level (3.3). In Section 3.4 we review the state-of-the-art in these three fields and conclude that most existing refactoring approaches concentrate on the identification or automation of new refactorings for AOP, but neglect the meta-programming nature of AOP in their attempts to preserve the behavior.

Furthermore, we present some recent work that recognizes the lack on proper treatment of pointcuts in tool-supported refactoring. Part of the problem is that techniques are needed to assess the impact on pointcuts and to narrow the intention behind such specifications in an automated way.

3.1 Aspect-oriented Refactoring

Various approaches to aspect-oriented refactoring have been developed and presented in recent publications [8, 39, 41, 46, 66, 78]. They comprise the identification of new, AOP-specific refactorings, the development of tools supporting these new refactorings and the investigation of behavior preservation issues specific to aspect-oriented language mechanisms. In this section, we survey the most influencing work in systematic documentation of manual step-by-step guides for aspect-oriented refactorings, tool support for the extraction of crosscutting concerns, and the introduction of aspect-awareness to existing refactoring approaches.

3.1.1 Extension of existing Refactorings

Ramnivas Laddad developed several guidelines to ensure a safe manual execution of refactorings for the extraction of crosscutting concerns into aspects [58, 59]. Along with these guidelines he identified a collection of refactorings that widely vary in level of abstraction and scope of applicability.

Besides some refactorings that are specific for crosscutting concerns in J2EE applications, such as *Extract Concurrency Control*, *Extract Contract Enforcement*, he also proposed refactorings for transforming more general implementations into an AOP solution, including *Extract Interface Implementation*, *Extract Method Calls* and *Replace Override with Advice*.

In addition, he identified bigger refactorings which belong to the category "Refactoring to Patterns" [51], such as *Extract Worker Object Creation*, *Replace Argument Trickle by Wormhole*. Those refactorings are based on the design patterns for AspectJ presented in the book "AspectJ in Action" (cf. [60] p.247, p.256).

All his work is very practically grounded on concrete implementations problems and, in general, focussed on aspect-oriented programs implemented in AspectJ.

Also **Monteiro et al.** developed a collection of aspect-oriented refactorings covering both the improvement of an aspect module's structure and the extraction of crosscutting concerns. All refactorings are specific to the programming language AspectJ. They are described in a pattern-like form, as common for "traditional" refactorings [28], and are systematically documented within a catalogue [67].

In addition to manual step-by-step guides, the authors also tried to motivate every refactoring through code smells. They reviewed existing code smells for object-oriented programs, considering the aspect-oriented modularization concept and proposed new smells indicating more AOP-specific weaknesses code smells [68, 66]. For example, Monteiro et al. discovered that *Divergent Change* ([28], p.79) can be a sign of code tangling and that *Shotgun Surgery* ([28], p.80) and *Solution Sprawl* ([51], p.43) often indicate code scattering. More AOP-specific code smells, such as *Double Personality*, *Abstract Classes* and *Aspect Laziness*, are proposed for identifying crosscutting concerns in existing base code as well as structural weaknesses within an aspect's implementation itself. Whereas the former motivate refactorings for extracting a crosscutting concerns into aspect-oriented implementations, the latter indicate refactorings to improve the code within an aspect module. The developed catalogue of refactorings depicts 27 aspect-oriented refactorings [67], which target these code smells, i.e., guide the developer in manually improve the design of aspect-oriented programs.

These extensions to existing refactorings mainly focus on improved modularizations gained from AOP. They extend existing procedures for manual refactoring and developed new procedures for AOP-specific refactorings. Even if some guidelines have been proposed for dealing with behavior preservation issues, no new concepts were developed, which take the nature of AOP language constructs into account to cope with the AOP-specific evolution issues, such as the fragile pointcut problem [56].

3.1.2 Tool-supported Extraction of Crosscutting Concerns

Refactoring crosscutting concerns into a well modularized aspect-oriented implementation is one of the most popular research goals in aspect-oriented refactoring. Various approaches propose different workflows and tool support to automate the selection of a crosscutting implementation, generate the basic aspect module structure and move the selected program elements into the aspect. Recent publications have shown two major potentials for automating such refactorings: (i) the identification of candidate aspects in a given program (aspect mining) [13, 63, 93, 96], and (ii) the semantic-preserving transformation of object-oriented code into an aspectized implementation (automated refactoring). In the following, we focus on approaches for tool support in the second field, which is more related to this work.

Binkley et al. developed an *AOPMigrator* that automates the extraction of crosscutting concerns into aspect-oriented implementations [8]. The authors propose a small number of semi-automated refactorings which extract marked fragments of a given program into aspects. The tool can automatically migrate all marked fragments to aspects and produces a semantically equivalent aspect-oriented implementation of the program. To this end, a specific refactoring workflow is proposed that encompasses the following steps:

- *Refactoring discovery:* Determination of applicable refactorings for a marked code fragment.

- *Transformation:* In case a selected fragment cannot be extracted through existing refactorings, behavior-preserving object-oriented transformations are suggested, such as Extract Method, to make an extraction into aspects generally feasible.

- *Refactoring selection:* The selection of an appropriate refactoring is guided through a hard-wired prioritization scheme refactoring.

- *Refactoring execution:* Fully automated generation of aspect stub code, move of marked fragments, and creation of necessary pointcuts and advices.

The *AOPMigrator* supports the described process for the extraction of class members and statements into aspects. For every extracted program element it generates a single pointcut bound to a single advice which contains the extracted element.
The approach was evaluated using a medium size (40,000 LoC) case study, the JHotDraw application framework [47]. In the case study the originally scattered UnDo functionality was successfully migrated to an AspectJ implementation. The tool applied 151 refactorings for extracting the UnDo concern and has shown that a large fraction of the code could be automatically extracted [8].

Hannemann et al. developed a similar approach for extracting crosscutting concerns into aspects [41, 40]. Their approach particularly focuses on an automated migration of design patterns, implemented in Java, to an implementation in AspectJ. The proposed workflow comprises the following steps:

- *Refactoring selection:* Let a developer choose a certain refactoring from a library of so-called crosscutting concern (CCC) refactorings.

- *Mapping definition:* Tool-guided mapping of program elements to specific roles of a design pattern implementation.

- *Refactoring configuration:* A program analysis identifies alternative decisions in the refactoring process and provide the developer with tradeoff information, like name clashes, newly introduced matches to existing pointcuts. The developer is requested to decide how to resolve every case.

- *Refactoring execution:* Automatic transformation of the program according to the abstract introductions defined by the chosen refactoring (incorporating the developer's decisions). The transformations create new program elements, move methods from classes to aspects and may remove obsolete interfaces.

The approach was developed focussing on the migration of design pattern implementations, but it can also be used for restructuring other, more general CCC. It basically assumes some crosscutting structure that can be mapped to an abstract description of the aspect-oriented target implementation. This mapping is the key activity of the approach and the major focus of provided tool support.

Both approaches target a tool-supported workflow for configuring semi-automated refactorings. The major goal of this research is to investigate how a particular program transformation can be defined for every marked program element and which information is required to automate such transformations. The developed tools guide a developer in the selection and configuration of program transformations, rather than in resolving unexpected conflicts or evolution problems in general. A sophisticated analysis of the impact of applied changes on existing program elements (classes and aspects) is not the primary research goal, just as the generation of robust and maintainable pointcuts.

3.1.3 Behavior Preservation in Aspect-oriented Refactoring

In tool-supported refactoring, the behavior of a program is preserved by preventing a refactoring from changing specific properties of a program, which are known to most likely affect the program behavior. Such properties are related to fundamental concepts of a programming language and were originally introduced for the refactoring of object-oriented programs by William Opdyke [70].
Not much work can be found, which tries to identify such properties for aspect-oriented programs and extend existing constraints for object-oriented refactorings to make them aspect-aware.

Hanenberg et al. investigated the interference between refactoring and aspect-oriented adaptation mechanisms, and observed that transforming aspect-oriented programs inevitably leads to a modification of joinpoints to which aspects might be bound [39]. As result, well-known refactorings are no longer behavior-preserving and existing tools cannot be used to restructure the base program, unless they become aspect-aware.
The authors identify that the interference between aspects and existing refactorings is essentially influenced by the joinpoint model and the pointcut language of an AOP approach. They, therefore, see a thorough understanding of how joinpoints can be specified as basic prerequisite to determine (and solve) the conflicts between traditional refactorings and constructs of AOP languages. In the paper, the authors discuss the dependencies between name patterns and rename refactorings by example and conclude the interference can be resolved, though it is unlikely more difficult for pointcuts which depend on much more information of a program.
For simplifying the interference analysis, Hanenberg et al. propose a categorization of joinpoints, considering the information that a pointcut has specified to select a joinpoint.

The authors distinguish three categories: *lexical* (name patterns), *structural* (code containment) and *behavioral* (dynamic values). Based on this categorization they observed that joinpoints of a particular category are interfered by specific refactorings, e.g., *Rename Method* can affect lexical joinpoints and *Extract Method* can conflict with structural joinpoints.

In order to introduce aspect awareness to existing refactorings, the authors extend the approach of Opdyke, who identified program properties of object-oriented programs which represent fundamental concepts of the underlying programming language (cf. [70], p. 26). Existing refactoring tools prevent a refactoring from changing such properties, because this would very much likely alter the program behavior. Hanenberg et al. suggest the following additional constraints for preserving adaptations defined by aspects:

- The quantity of joinpoints referenced by a particular pointcut must not change.

- All joinpoints which are referenced by a particular pointcut have an equivalent position within the program's control flow in comparison to the state before the refactoring.

- The information available at a joinpoint are not decreased.

The additional constraints were evaluated by refactoring a small AspectJ application with a *Rename Method*, an *Extract Method* and a *Move Method* refactoring. For every refactoring, they describe by example how it is made aspect-aware and how it deals with the impact on bound joinpoints.

Initial ideas on how to treat pointcuts within a refactoring workflow are described using the additional refactoring constraints. In doing that, every refactoring tries to reestablish the previous program behavior by updating any affected pointcuts. Nonetheless, neither a general workflow for refactoring aspect-oriented programs, nor a concrete extension for the discussed refactorings is proposed.

Hanenberg et al. also developed a refactoring tool that seeks to support the proposed approach for refactoring AspectJ programs. They state that only a tool is able to provide a developer with the particular reasons for violations of a property specified by a pointcut. Moreover, the authors see a developer-centric workflow as essential, which supports the visiting of all violated information specified by a pointcut, proposed an update and requests for the developer's confirmation. All other parts, such as the creation of new elements and the modification of existing code could be automated as long as the program provides the same behavior. The refactoring tool developed by the authors, however, never reached the maturity to meet these requirements.

Rura and Lerner present in [77, 78] a framework for refactoring aspect-oriented programs, which advances the initial work of Hanenberg et al. They highlight the special need for understanding what comprises behavior preservation in all aspect-oriented programming languages, as basic foundation for introducing aspect awareness to known refactorings. Furthermore, the authors identify pointcuts as the language construct with the most fundamental impact on what changes are behavior-preserving.

The developed framework is basically an extension of the framework for refactoring object-oriented programs developed by Opdyke [70]. Rura and Lerner adapted the fundamental program properties identified by Opdyke for aspect-oriented programs and developed a set of AOP-specific constraints for atomic refactorings. They argue that any refactoring constructed of these atomic refactorings is behavior-preserving, if the following constraints are ensured:

1. *Language requirements* (name conflicts, sub-typing violations, method signature conflicts, type safety violations);

2. Preserving *sub-type relationships* (type inheritance, method overriding, dynamic binding, method dispatch);

3. Preserving *semantic equivalence* of references and operations;

4. *Pointcut pattern equivalence.*

Opdyke originally considered a subset of the programming language C++, so Rura and Lerner translated his constraints to the specific language constructs of Java, before they could extend them for AspectJ.

The *language requirements* are very low-level and prevent a refactoring to introduce basic problems, such as name conflicts, sub-typing violations, method signature conflicts and type safety violations. These requirements were extended to meet the specific requirements of the AspectJ programming language features, such as inter-type declaration, pointcut (definition), and advice. For example, locally introduced members or declared super types through an inter-type declaration are checked when changing names or inheritance relationships.

The preservation of *sub-type relationships* restrict the transformations to those that preserve inheritance relationships at class and method level. This guarantees that dynamic binding resolves to the same types before and after a refactoring, limiting the effects of a change upon sub-types. Such constraints are extended to preserve sub-typing and method overriding relationships that are introduced by inter-type declarations. Refactorings that modify non-private class members are additionally constrained to change super-types introduced by aspects in order to ensure that sub-typing relationships are preserved.

The constraints that preserve the *semantic equivalence* allow for, e.g., simplification of expressions, removal of dead (unreachable) code within a method or unreferenced variables, change of a variable's type, and replacement of references to a field or a method. The same refactorings for class code are also possible in AspectJ-like aspects, thus the code in aspects must be analyzed for references to classes, methods, and variables. In addition, code in advice is examined for semantic equivalence, since it can also be a target of AO refactoring.

The extensions so far target the constructs of the AspectJ programming language itself, for the preservation of the specified joinpoint properties Rura and Lerner introduce a separated so-called *"pointcut pattern equivalence"* constraint. This new constraint reduces the idea of "every advice must apply at semantically equivalent joinpoints" after a refactoring to a more simple determinable but stronger requirement "signature patterns used in a pointcut must match semantically equivalent program elements". In particular, the authors point out that there are several ways to argue that a refactoring is behavior-preserving with respect to advice elements: (i) by showing that the advice is bound to semantically equivalent joinpoints (advice binding preservation, similar to method lookup), (ii) by preserving the meanings of pointcuts, or (iii) by ensuring that the signature patterns used in a pointcut match semantically equivalent program elements. The authors further state that it seems intuitive that a refactoring should ensure each pointcut is left with either the same joinpoints or semantically equivalent joinpoints to those it referenced before the refactoring, however, some pointcuts cannot generally be determined statically, including `cflow`, `if`, `this`, `target`, and `args`.

As result, Rura and Lerner propose the most restrictive constraint, ensuring that every single signature pattern selects an equivalent set of program elements. This is a stronger requirement, as to require a pointcut to select an equivalent set of joinpoints, because individual patterns may match many more elements than their combination in the resulting pointcut. As major advantages, the authors mention the possibility to statically determine matches of patterns and that it is intuitive to treat name patterns in a similar way are references to program elements. Moreover, they highlight that updating a pattern is not always necessary to preserve the program behavior (e.g., for empty selections), but it preserves the intentions of the programmer (who may not be certain if the method is called or not), i.e., a preservation of the selected set of joinpoints requires only to change the pattern if the method is actually called.

In cases, where signature patterns do not match the same elements as before the refactoring, it is proposed to broaden/narrow the pattern in a way that lost/new matches are prevented. The inclusion/exclusion of matches is proposed in any case where the set of matching elements is altered. This makes, on the one hand, pointcuts unrecognizable and worse readable, and, on the other hand, it does not consider the programmer's intention behind a pointcut.

3.2 Tool Support for Software Evolution

Besides pure refactoring tools there are other but closely related kinds of tools that are built to support the evolution of software in general. Some specific program analysis approaches aim an automated change impact classification to distinguish different kinds of change effects. Moreover, tools that support the verification of existing pointcuts by comparing pointcut matches against an automatically generated verification turn out to be successful in determining accidentally matching joinpoints. Also, the generation of pointcuts from a given set of joinpoint shadows is an issue that a refactoring tool must deal with, if invalidated pointcuts should be adjusted.

3.2.1 Change Impact Analysis

In addition to refactoring tools that detect the effects of predefined transformations on specific program properties, also program analysis approaches that focus on arbitrary program edits can be used to detect alterations of the program behavior. Such approaches often qualitatively analyze the impact of changes, either by comparing different program versions, or by analyzing the applied changes and their dependencies. Two different kinds of analyses are of particular interest, the analysis of effects on pointcuts in aspect-oriented programs and the analysis of change effects on the program behavior of object-oriented programs.

A few analysis *approaches for aspect-oriented programs* have been developed to cope with fragile pointcuts. In general, they provide tool support for detecting the change effects on pointcuts by comparing two program versions [1, 85].

Störzer et al. present an approach for detecting differently bound advices in two program versions in [56, 85]. They coined the term *fragile pointcut problem*, as silent change of a pointcut's meaning and illustrate how renaming, move, addition or deletion of classes, fields, and methods affect pointcuts. Furthermore, the authors point out a general distinction between refactoring and evolution. Refactoring could detect effects on pointcuts and avoid breaking them in some cases, whereas the evolution of aspect-oriented programs is more problematic in general, e.g., addition of new methods, class, or packages due to new functionality.

For that reason, Störzer et al. propose a *pointcut delta analysis* that approximates the bound joinpoints for every pointcut by so-called pointcut matches. The analysis calculates the pointcut matches for two versions of a program, compares the resulting sets and creates a so-called *pointcut delta*. The delta is further analyzed to discover *new*, *lost* and *modified* (in terms of match quality) matches. The approach is generally feasible for any AspectJ-like pointcut language, where the set of matching pointcuts is (at least partly) statically computable. For uncomputable cases the matching is conservatively approximated and the resulting matches are accordingly marked with a quality label.

The authors developed a tool that implements the proposed analysis, called *PCDiff*. The tool requires the developer to make a snapshot of the code base in prior to the analysis. This snapshot simply stores all pointcut matches for the current program version. Afterwards, the tool can compute the pointcut matches for the changed program version and produce the pointcut delta between both program versions. The presented delta information is represented as tree which directly shows affected aspects, advices, pointcuts, and matches. This makes it easy to identify changes with no effects on any aspect (empty delta), but also trace differences back to the affected aspects. Also unexpected matches can be identified more easily and although it is no trivial task to find expected but not experienced matches, the developer only needs to search through a small delta, not through the entire program.

The identification of *causes for deltas* is possible but not directly supported by the tool. Nonetheless, the analysis approach considers all kinds of changes with effects on pointcuts: modifications at a pointcut itself, modifications at the aspect (removed or added advices), and base code edits. Since the analysis directly targets the actually occurred advice bindings (joinpoints) all these kinds of changes are generally covered and it is possible to infer what kind of change is responsible for a specific delta.

Some analysis *approaches for object-oriented programs* seeking for a qualitative assessment of change effects by analyzing the applied changes and their dependencies. **Ryder et al.** present in recent publications [73, 79, 84] a change impact analysis to find test cases that are potentially affected by a source code edit (set of changes). The goal of this research is to develop *change classifiers* for changes that are highly likely, highly unlikely, or somewhere in between to be failure-inducing.

The analysis approach divides a program edit into its constituent *atomic changes*, then identifies tests affected by the edit through correlating (dynamic) call graphs for the tests with the atomic changes, before it determines affecting (atomic) changes for each of these tests.

The proposed *atomic change model* captures program edits at a semantic level, i.e., only edits with a potential effect on the program behavior are represented, which makes edits more amenable to program analysis. The model captures program edits like add a class (AC), delete a class (DC), add a method (AM), delete a method (DM), change body of a method (CM), change virtual method lookup (LM), add a field (AF), and delete a field (DF). The analysis also computes syntactic dependencies between atomic changes, indicating that one change is a prerequisite for another one. These dependencies can be used to construct syntactically valid intermediate versions of the program that contains some, but not all atomic changes.

For the determination of *affected tests* a call graph that is constructed either using static analysis, or by observing the actual execution of the tests. The graph's edges corresponding to dynamic dispatch are labeled with a pair of the receiver object's runtime type and the method referenced at the call site. A test is determined to be affected if its call graph (in the original program) contains either a node that corresponds to a changed method (CM), or a deleted method (DM), or an edge that corresponds to a lookup change (LM). The set of *changes affecting a given test* can be computed by constructing a call graph for that test in the edited program. All atomic changes (including transitively prerequisite changes) for added (AM) and changed (CM) methods that correspond to a node in the call graph (in the edited program) and lookup changes (LC) that correspond to an edge in that call graph, affect the given test.

However, the absence of a syntactic dependence between two changes (A1, A2) does not imply the absence of a semantic dependence, if both changes affect a given test, i.e., program behaviors resulting from applying A1 alone, A2 alone, or A1 and A2 together may all be different. To this end, Ryder et al. developed different change classifications that indicate the likelihood of a change to be failure-inducing. Any classification categorizes affecting changes as test improving, test degrading, or test independent. For example, the most *Intuitive Change Classification* labels changes as follows:

- Green = a change that affects only improving tests;

- Red = a change that affects only worsening tests;

- Yellow = a change that affects both improving and worsening tests.

Other classifiers, such as the *Simple Change Classification* relies only on test results in the edited program and labels effects failing or crashing tests (Red), affected passing tests (Green), and all other (Yellow). More complex classifications try to combine this information to achieve a better classification of intermediate cases.

The work of Ryder et al. demonstrates that the introduction of atomic changes makes program edits more amenable to program analysis, simplifying the assessment of a change's impact. Moreover, their approach shows that change classification can effectively identify changes with a specific impact on the program behavior and be an enabler for assessing semantic dependencies between different changes. Empirical case studies provide quantitative measurement of the effectiveness of several classifiers on different kinds of programs.

3.2.2 Verification and Testing of Pointcuts

Tool support that automates the examination of existing pointcuts using an either automatically generated or manually defined model of pointcuts is another approach for detecting unintended pointcut matches. Very few work has been published for verifying or testing pointcuts in aspect-oriented programs. In the following, two approaches are presented with initial ideas on tool-supporting the comparison of selected joinpoints with the developer's intention.

Zhang et al. propose an *Aspect Refactoring Verification Tool (ARV)* as support for the automated extraction of crosscutting concerns into aspects [104]. The authors particularly focus on the extraction of method calls from a class into an advice. The ARV supports a developer to restore the original call flow by capturing the calling context of that call, i.e., its caller information or its control flow. The tool provides two verification views: the *specification view* and the *difference view* within a specific verification workflow:

- The developer selects a project and specifies the program elements to represent the functionality to be extracted into the aspect, using the "declare warning" construct of AspectJ (cf. [103], Appendix B, Static crosscutting).

- This specification represents the expected set of method calls, which alternatively can be gathered using an aspect mining tool.

- The developer manually refactors the program, extracting individual program elements in to newly created aspects and defines the pointcuts to bind the extracted functionality to its original callers.

- The ARV analyzes the program, collects elements matching the pointcuts and compares elements matching the "declare warning" constructs with elements advised by the aspect.

- The verification compares the original and the refactored program functionally, which involves a comparison of the advised elements and the logic contained in the advice.

- The results of this comparison are displayed in the difference view.

The comparison can produce three possible results: (i) *equivalence*, original and refactored programs are considered as equal, (ii) *under-refactoring*, some originally matching elements are not covered by the aspect's pointcuts, and (iii) *over-refactoring*, refactored aspects extend original functionalities at more elements as before the refactoring.
The ARV supports the identification of inequalities between original and refactored code. An reliable verification, however, needs to be performed through unit and integration tests. Over- and under-refactoring are compared by filtering out identical call sites captured by pointcuts from both sides of comparison. The equality between two call sites is evaluated, by determining whether they affect the same method, the exact locations of the call sites cannot be used by this approach.

Anbalagan and Xie built and *Automated Pointcut Testing Framework (APTE)* [4] for validating the correctness of pointcut expressions. The APTE identifies program elements that satisfy a pointcut expression and a set of nearly matching elements, which almost satisfy a pointcut expression. A predefined threshold value is used to define the maximum distance which other program elements can differ from an original pointcut but are still considered as near misses. The author's goal is to provide a developer with tool support that identifies unintentionally matching joinpoints, i.e., both including potentially missing and accidentally matching joinpoints.

To this end, APTE receives a threshold value, the program's source and the a set of target classes as input. The tool computes matching program elements for existing pointcuts in the target classes, including nearly matching boundary elements. In addition, the tool computes the distances for every nearly matching element. A developer can inspect these matching and nearly matching elements for correctness of the pointcuts.

The distance between matches and near matches is calculated using, a so-called Levenshtein algorithm, which is used to measure how many characters of on signature pattern have to be edited to correspond to another signature pattern. The result of this algorithm is an integer value that signifies the number of transformations (i.e., insertions, deletions) that should be performed on a nearly matching pointcut to transform it into a matching pointcut. Then the APTE tool identifies boundary matches by comparing the distance of nearly matching pointcut to the user-defined threshold value.

Both approaches demonstrate that a determination of whether a joinpoint unintentionally matches a pointcut can at least to some extent be automated. The developer, however, needs to express is expectations in a way that a tool can verify it.

3.2.3 Generation of Pointcuts

Pointcuts in aspect-oriented programs can refer to properties of various program representations. Their specification requires a developer to have detailed knowledge of many program parts, to be able to select the properties which are most suited to identify desired joinpoints. This difficult task can be supported by tools, e.g., using techniques for *inductive logic programming* (ILP) to derive a pointcut definition from joinpoint examples. Some approaches are already known in the field of pointcut generation in general [10, 11] and within aspect-oriented refactoring [38, 95].

Braem et al. have developed an approach for generating pointcuts from any structural property available in a static joinpoint model [10, 11]. They propose the use of inductive logic programming for automatically generating pattern-based pointcuts. Since the model is restricted to properties of static program representations, dynamic properties, such as runtime values or cflow, are generally not supported.

Logic induction is a technique that returns a logic query that, by using conditions drawn from background information on a set of examples, satisfies all positive examples while not including any negative examples. The authors use ILP to generate a pattern-based pointcut as follows:

Positive examples: A number of positive examples is taken as input, i.e., for pointcuts a set of joinpoint shadows whose executions should be captured by the pointcut. This set can either be selected manually or automatically using for example an aspect mining technique.

Negative examples: All other joinpoints are defined as negative examples for the ILP algorithm, which are used to ensure that the derived rules never cover these shadows. Negative examples effectively force the algorithm to use other information of the background in the induced rules.

Background information: Another input to ILP is background information on the example shadows, such as information associated with the joinpoints, i.e., predicates in the pointcut that have to evaluate to true for the expected joinpoints. In fact, a tool constructs a logic database consisting of the information that is available from static program representations, such as the abstract syntax tree or static type inheritance.

Logic induction: The logic rules are based on the positive examples and constructed in an iterative process. Starting from an empty rule, in each step of the process, the rule is extended with a condition drawn from the background information which decreases the number of negative examples covered by the rule. This is repeated until the rule describes all positive but no negative examples. The added conditions are generalizations of facts in the background information, by adding logic variables.

The algorithm will induce a pointcut that captures exactly the joinpoints currently in the program that should be captured (the positive examples), and none of the others (the negative examples). The authors claim that it is reasonable to expect, though not guaranteed that the induced pointcuts are non-fragile, because the induction process generalizes the conditions before adding it to the rules.

Tourwe, Kellens and Gybels have presented in earlier publications the use of a very similar approach for generating pointcuts within an aspect-oriented refactoring process [38, 95]. The authors show how pointcut definitions and refactoring interfere with each other in a negative way and argue that this is due to the fact that pointcuts are very tightly coupled to an application's structure. To overcome these problems they propose the notion of *inductively generated pointcuts*.

The authors use ILP to transform extensional definitions of pointcuts, enumerating all program elements whose executions are selected as joinpoints, into intensional pointcuts. They state that such pointcuts allow a developer to work with pointcuts at high-level of abstractions, and argue that it is more easy to assess the impact of particular source code changes and update affected pointcuts automatically, since the resulting pointcuts are automatically generated from abstract properties. Moreover, ILP techniques uncover common properties of program elements that should be adapted by an aspect. Hence, the specifications of these properties are generalized and complete. The background knowledge base essentially required for such the ILP techniques can be automatically produced, and consists of predicates, such as `classImplements`, `superclassOf`, `subclassOf`, and `senderOf`.

The authors claim that an inductive pointcut model enables a refactoring tool to:

- Generate pointcuts automatically and manage them during evolution;

- Consider alternative pointcuts and to generate the most precise pointcut that includes the provided examples and no other element of the program;

- Detect an impact on existing pointcuts and the recompute appropriate adjustments; and

- Treat references to properties of program elements in a way as "symbolic" references.

Both approaches have shown that inductive logic programming can be an enabler for generating pointcuts from a given set of joinpoint shadows. They demonstrated that specifications of common properties can be generalized, which makes multiple updates of a pointcut within a refactoring process much less intrusive.

3.3 Aspect-aware Declarations

Several approaches try to tackle the evolution problems of aspect-oriented program at language level. Some approaches propose the use of annotations instead of enumeration-based pointcuts, particularly for heterogeneous aspects. Other approaches demonstrate that a conceptual model as middleman between pointcuts and the targeted program code simplifies evolution or introduce a complete aspect-aware interface, which expresses a verifiable specification along with each pointcut.

3.3.1 Meta-level Annotations

Annotations of program elements such as introduced by Java and C# allow to augment an element with metadata, i.e., properties that do not belong to the program, but can be used by tools, such as debuggers or runtime environments. Some AOP languages, like AspectJ, are able to access such annotations, also for binding an advice to program elements with a certain annotation. Some work can be found in the literature that investigates the integration of meta-level annotations into existing pointcut languages.

Eaddy and Aho present an approach for combining statement-level annotations and pointcuts to support the advising of instances and statements [20]. They propose an extension to AspectJ's pointcut language and argue that annotation-based pointcuts are more robust and reusable, especially for heterogeneous concerns, such as logging and exception handling. The use of statement-level annotations for augmenting individual statements with "semantic" properties is particularly beneficial, claim the authors, if these statements have not many structural properties in common. They further argue that pattern-based pointcuts are tightly coupled to the implementation details of the base program and are incomprehensible and fragile, in particular for such heterogeneous concerns.

Annotations, as proposed by Eaddy and Aho, require intrusive changes to the base program and do not completely encapsulate a crosscutting concern, but allow a developer to "name" any statement in a method body in a declarative fashion. They can be used to expose "hidden" joinpoints or to perform fine-grained (instance- and statement-level) advising. The authors further argue that annotation-based pointcuts are more robust because they only depend on meaningful annotations, rather than on the underlying structure of the code. That's why annotation-based pointcuts are more robust than enumeration-based pointcuts, which are likely to break if the underlying code changes.

Kiczales and Mezini also compared annotations and pointcuts in a recent paper [55]. They investigated how well meta-level annotations, pointcuts and advice can be used for separating concerns in source code. To this end, they define a characterization in which each is seen as making a different kind of binding:

- Annotations bind attributes to program points;

- Pointcuts create bindings between sets of points and descriptions of those sets;

- Named pointcuts bind attributes to sets of points; and

- Advice bind the implementation of an operation to sets of points.

In this characterization, they use the term *attribute* to denote a property which is identified by a certain name and the term *point* to designate either program elements or its executions.

From comparing examples implementing the same concern using each technique the authors inferred guidelines for how to choose among the mechanisms. These guidelines clearly suggest only to use annotations to mark elements when it is difficult to write a stable property-based pointcut to capture all elements, when the name of the annotation is unlikely to change, and when the meaning of the annotation is inherent to the elements rather than context-dependent. In other cases, Kiczales and Mezini, suggest to use enumeration-based pointcuts (when a stable property-based pointcut is difficult and element set is relatively small), or a property- or pattern-based pointcut (when a stable property/pattern is shared, or element set is relatively large).

In general, the authors distinguish between bindings that make a specific property explicit and local (named pointcut) and bindings that make it explicit and non-local (annotations). This observation leads to several more concrete evolution issues with annotation-based pointcuts:

Named pattern-based pointcuts capture the decision which operation is executed, as well as a specification of program elements that are considered to trigger this operation. Thus, any renaming, moving or removing of this operation, as well as of the program elements targeted by the specification affect pattern-based pointcuts.

Annotations are generally not affected by renaming or moving of attached elements, that is why they are often considered as more robust. However, disabling a functionality, that is triggered by annotations requires editing all the methods to remove the particular annotation and also an addition of a related class or method requires to edit all new elements that could correspond to an annotated-property. Which requires a high effort for managing the consistency between annotations and program elements, even in simple evolution scenarios.

3.3.2 Model-based Pointcuts

An approach which directly tackles the fragile pointcut problem through an abstract structural model as middleman between base code representations and pointcuts is proposed by **Kellens et al.** [50, 49]. They identify the tight coupling of pointcuts with the base program's structure as primary cause for the fragility of pointcuts and propose so-called *model-based pointcuts* to decouple pointcuts by referring to conceptual properties of the program. Model-based pointcuts are defined in terms of a conceptual model of the base program, rather than referring directly to the implementation structure of it. The model classifies program elements and imposes high-level conceptual constraints on those elements, which render the conceptual model more robust towards evolutions of the base program. As result, model-based pointcuts capture joinpoints based on conceptual properties instead of structural properties of the base program elements. Potential evolution conflicts can be detected at model level, and are solved by changing either the model or its mapping to the program's source. Existing model-based pointcuts can remain untouched.

The authors argue, that this decoupling of pointcuts from implementation details makes pointcuts significantly less fragile to evolution of the base program, because the classifications of the conceptual model are more evolution robust. They claim that as long as the conceptual model classifies all accessor methods correctly, the pointcuts remain correct. All evolution issues are treated by a mechanism of the model that automatically verifies the correctness of the classifications in the conceptual model. To this end, the model defines design constraints that need to be respected by all source-code elements. The mechanisms checks these constraints and detect two different situations:

- *Unintended capturing* of elements for a conceptual property, which do not satisfy all constraints of that property, such as misclassified elements.

- *Accidental misses*, i.e., elements that do not belong to a conceptual property but satisfy at least one of its constraints. Such elements could belong to the set of elements with the conceptual property.

Such situations can be caused through misclassified elements that should be removed from the set of elements holding the property, a constraint that no longer applies and thus needs to be modified or removed, or elements that accidently satisfy a constraint and should be adapted.

Kellens et al. admit that not all issues of the fragile pointcut problem can be detected or resolved by this approach. They point out that the constraints imposed by the conceptual model are the most crucial part in detecting missing or unintentional captured elements. The more constraints are defined, the lesser is the chance that some inconsistencies keep unnoticed. They propose further research on methodological guidelines to design the conceptual model such that it provides sufficient coverage to detect violations of the design rules.

If a developer wants to adopt the model-based pointcut approach she needs to describe a conceptual model of the program and its mapping to the program code. The authors argues that this should be seen as an explicit and verifiable design documentation of the implementation, which is valuable for the evolution of the software system in general. Such a manual definition of explicitly expressed and verifiable design rules is required for any adoption of the approach.

Kellens et al. have shown that model-based pointcuts can simplify the evolution of pointcuts along with base code change significantly. However, a solid description of the verifiable design rules is not easy to produce and its soundness difficult to assess.

3.3.3 Aspect-aware Interfaces

A recent approach for supporting the modular reasoning in aspect-oriented programs and also the evolution problems is the introduction of aspect-aware interfaces [15, 35, 54]. Such an interface between aspects and targeted program tackles the obliviousness problem in AOP and defines a clear, sometimes even verifiable, expectations from an aspect's point of view.

Griswold et al. propose an approach for defining aspect-aware interfaces called *XPI* [35]. An XPI is an interface between an aspect and the base program. The authors claim, that XPIs help to separate the aspect code from the details of advised code, and make the overall conceptual design clearer. In fact, it exposes joinpoints consistently using pointcuts to define contract like design rules as abstract interface constructs.

An XPI has four elements: a name, a scope over view the XPI abstracts joinpoints, one or more sets of abstract joinpoints (verifiable pointcuts), and a partial implementation. Each set of abstract joinpoints is expressed as a pointcut definition declaring a name and exposed parameters. Furthermore, it comprises a semantic specification stating preconditions that must be satisfied at each point where an advice can run (provided clause) and postconditions that must be satisfied after an advice runs (requires clause).

A partial implementation of an XPI contains (for each set of abstract joinpoints) a pointcut matching the corresponding concrete joinpoints, a before, after, or an around designator, and a corresponding set of constraints (design rules). The constraints prescribe how code must be written to ensure that all and only the desired points in the program execution match the given pointcut. The rest of an XPI implementation is in the code's conformance to the stated design rules.

"An XPI, like an API, abstracts changeable and complex design decisions and operates as a decoupling contract between providers and users. Unlike an API, an XPI abstracts a crosscutting behavior rather than a localized procedure implementation" [35]. Griswold et al. state that XPIs modularize crosscutting design decisions that are complex or likely to change. An XPI is not implemented by providing a procedure implementation, but by writing pointcuts and shaping code to expose specified behavior through joinpoints matching the given patterns.

Developers need not to know about specific aspects, argue the authors, but they must decide which abstractions have to be to exposed as XPIs to facilitate aspect development and evolution. A developer can specify 'how the code has to look like' which is associated with a specific behavior, like 'transition A has occurred in state B of Class Foo'. The XPI then provides a named pointcut by which aspects can advise all such transitions without depending on the underlying source code. In addition, an XPI constraints the developer to implement all abstract state changes in a way that matches the pointcut patterns. A developer defining an XPI provides a pointcut including a verification indicating whether actually matching joinpoints are expected to match. In this way, an XPI guides the implementer in choosing names for methods and in making other decisions that can influence the matching of pointcuts.

The approach has been evaluated in an experiment using common AOP methods to improve the design of a medium-sized Java application (300 classes, 50,000LOC) called

HyperCast. It has shown that effects of apparently innocuous changes or extensions to the code base are indicated as violations to the defined constraints.

3.4 Critical Analysis

Most of the research on refactoring and AOP is driven by the idea of having a "Refactor"-button which automatically extracts a crosscutting concern into an aspect. The work of *Binkley et al.* is one step in this direction showing that only a few new automated refactorings are required which can be composed of behavior-preserving program transformations [8]. Their work and the work of *Hannemann et al.*, however, also demonstrates effectively that powerful tool support is essential for configuring such refactorings, similar powerful as for big (object-oriented) refactorings of the category "Refactorings to Patterns" [51]. In fact, they rely on a specific technique, called aspect mining, which helps to automate the selection of the program elements that belong to a crosscutting concern. Moreover, even if all elements comprising a certain crosscutting concern are selected, it seems still a complicated task to configure such refactorings. For every element a particular transformation has to be chosen, and the tool has to ensure that such transformations have no undesired impact on other elements in the system.

Especially the tool support for solving such conflicts, including inter-aspect interference and the impact on existing pointcuts, seems hard to achieve for present AOP approaches. *Binkley et al.* claim to preserve the original behavior, while modularizing the code of the crosscutting functionality, but even if the supported refactoring process can be used in an iterative way, they seem not to consider effects on pointcuts that may already exist in the system. Their approach may be able to deal with changes that impact pointcuts generated by the tool, but a more thorough analysis for other kinds of pointcuts, such as proposed by *Störzer et al.*, is not provided. In fact, even if integrated with this analysis approach, the tool would still not be able to assess the impact sufficiently concrete that reasonable pointcut updates could be proposed. Also *Hannemann et al.* mentioned in their approach an impact with basic mechanisms for detecting name clashes and newly matching elements for existing pointcuts, but more complete support for adjusting affected pointcuts or the planned changes seems not to be provided. In particular, both approaches neglect non-obvious effects on existing aspects, such as a changed semantics of existing pointcuts, treatment of under-specified joinpoints, and adjustment of responsible program transformations at all.

Most of the presented refactoring approaches ensure that the planned changes have no undesired effect on the program behavior, but almost all of them neglect that AOP is meta-programming. Hence, the definition of behavior preservation, as used for object-oriented programs, cannot be used for AOP. Just as standard refactorings for OOP are not valid in the presence of Java-like reflection mechanisms or C-like macros. A new notion for behavior preservation in aspect-oriented refactoring needs to be defined, which considers meta-level properties specified by pointcuts in a similar way as it is done, e.g., for C-like macros [31, 32]. Only *Rura and Lerner* tried to address this issue to some extend with their "pointcut pattern equivalence" constraint.

Finally, a refactoring tool must be able to adjust pointcuts in a proper way. Most refactoring tools for aspect-oriented programs, however, just generate enumerations of program elements whose executions are considered as joinpoints. A generation of more generalized property-based pointcuts, such as proposed by *Braem et al.*, could lead to pointcuts with an actual meaning, even if the computation of reasonable names seems not possible for pointcuts at all. Of a similar importance is the generation of pointcut adjustments, i.e., a refactoring tool must be able to adjust a pointcut multiple times without making it completely unrecognizable to its original developer. The preservation of the pointcut's meaning during such updates is completely ignored by all presented refactoring approaches.

In summary, existing refactoring approaches may automate an initial extraction of a crosscutting concern into aspects to some extent, but they fail to provide a proper notion for behavior preservation in AOP as foundation for an automated but controlled refactoring process. In the following sections, we discuss more concrete open issues specific to the approaches surveyed above, regarding the evolution of aspect-oriented programs.

3.4.1 Expressing the Pointcut's Intention

Joinpoints are points in the execution of the program, or more technically they are executions of program elements. They neither have a unique name nor can somehow be directly selected. A developer defines a pointcut to specify some of their (static or dynamic) properties, in a somehow complete way. The fact that this specification can be incomplete and some of its information cannot be statically determined leaves much room for interpreting the original intention behind a pointcut. This room makes it exceptionally difficult to detect accidentally new and lost pointcut matches in an automated fashion.

Also more abstracts pointcuts as proposed by *Kellens et al.* seem just to defer this problem to another level, even if their design rules can be adjusted more simply than pattern-based pointcuts. An authoritative verification of pointcut matches using unit and integration tests [104] is an insufficient and incomplete solution. Testing only shows the presence of bugs and can never prove their absence. Moreover, test failures do not explain the failure reason and have to be further analyzed to actually track down the bug. Finding the failure inducing code modifications is especially hard for pointcuts, since every changed part of the system can be responsible.

A more promising alternative is an explicitly expressed expectation that can be automatically verified [35]. *Griswold et al.* propose an aspect-aware interface to expose joinpoints through verifiable pointcuts. It facilitates the detection of unintentionally matching joinpoints caused by addition or removal of program elements, but it still can negatively be affected by simple rename or move refactorings, particularly since the developer's expectation is expressed using joinpoint properties as well.

Such a verifiable specification of the developer's intension could be even more interesting for aspect-oriented refactoring if it is combined with a distance measure as proposed by *Anbalagan and Xie* [4]. Their approach for computing boundary joinpoints, which are almost intended, is of particular help if a refactoring causes a loss of still almost matching elements. Such nearly matching elements are especially hard to find [85]. *Anbalagan and Xie* however consider only signature patterns in their distance measure. Pointcuts, specifying other properties of joinpoints, are not handled by this approach. Nonetheless, a generalized distance measure for all joinpoint properties could be used to automate the finding of potentially intended joinpoints.

3.4.2 Analyzability of Pointcuts

The pointcut delta analysis approach by *Störzer et al.* has effectively shown that it is particularly difficult to detect change effects on all kinds of properties specifiable by AspectJ-like pointcuts. Their analysis employs a specific model for representing joinpoints as pointcut matches to discover new, lost, and changed matches. The matches of different program versions can be compared, but it seems not possible to automate the inference of change reasons.

Moreover, this research demonstrates how dynamic properties, can be statically approximated to detect change effects through static program analysis. An approximation of certain dynamic properties, like runtime values, can lead to very poor analysis results. A threshold indicating the quality of an approximation could be an important indicator for the analyzability of dynamic properties. Such a threshold could be used as concrete boundary indicating for which kind of dynamic properties a static approximation still makes sense.

In addition, there is no concrete notion for program edits that are responsible for a particular pointcut delta. An atomic change model, as presented by *Ryder et al.* [84] could make program edits more amenable to program analysis. This could enable a tool to distinguish potential effects of different kinds of changes, e.g., rename versus remove, and infer different actions for a refactoring. A proper classification of change effects would allow for automating the decision making, whether caused effects on pointcut can be made undone or have to be accepted.

3.4.3 Behavior Preservation in AOP

AOP is meta-programming. Existing approaches to preserving the behavior in tool-supported refactoring cannot "simply" be extended for AOP. However, almost none of the presented refactoring approaches tries to preserve meta-level properties specified in pointcuts, rather than seeking for possibilities to restore the program's behavior before the refactoring.

Ramnivas Laddad proposed along with his best practices in refactoring aspect-oriented programs, the use of AspectJ's declare error mechanism for verifying whether two different pointcuts capture exactly the same set of joinpoints [58, 59]. Such a "workaround" is of some help, if no tool support for finding new or lost matches of existing pointcuts is available. However, it offers no support for deciding whether such a match is intended, and can end up in long debugging sessions.

Hanenberg et al. propose new constraints introducing aspect awareness to refactoring, but they do not consider in their approach that a pointcut may intentionally select additional joinpoints after a refactoring. They even neglect that joinpoints are points in the program execution which must be statically approximated to enable an analysis of change effects. As much as their constraint "the quantity of joinpoints referenced by a particular pointcut must not change" [39] may seem obvious on first sight, its verification is barely possible. Since the number of joinpoints occurred during the execution depend on the program parts that were executed, it is impossible to statically determine all joinpoints.

Rura and Lerner introduce a pointcut pattern equivalence constraint, which ensures the same set of program elements matching all signature patterns within a pointcut. This is a more restrictive requirement, than ensuring the same set of joinpoints captured by the pointcut, and it is statically determinable. It ensures that every single signature pattern matches the same set of elements, even if the resulting combination of signature patterns in the pointcut does not select a single joinpoint. If a matching program element is changed, *Rura and Lerner* always propose to update the pointcut. Such a more restrictive approach can be achieved with existing refactoring tools and seems more reliable than preserving a selected set of joinpoints. But in fact it has a number of disadvantages. First, it does not distinguish signature patterns that select specific program elements from those that select elements of a certain kind. For example, consider the following AspectJ pointcut:

```
1 pointcut allMethods(): execution(* *.*(..))
```

It would select all methods in a program, including methods that will be added in the future. Every addition of a new method would cause an exclusion of this method, following the approach of *Rura and Lerner*. This is obviously not intended by the pointcut. Second, the effects of different kinds of changes are not distinguished. An inline refactoring completely removes a program element from the system entirely. Whereas for move or rename refactorings one could say, it removes an element with certain properties (location, name) from the system, but adds the same element with changed properties to the system at the same time. Hence, some effects of pointcuts can be made undone, and others have to be prevented at all. Third, the approach considers only change effects on signature patterns, however, a pointcut's selection can also be affected by changes to other parts of the program. For example, consider the following (AspectJ) pointcut for the code piece presented in Figure 3.1:

```
1 pointcut set(* int Foo.num)
2          && withincode(public void Foo.bar())
```

The figure illustrates the change effects of an *Encapsulate Field Refactoring*. The refactoring is performed on the field `num` in class `Foo`. The right side of the figure shows the source code after the refactoring. The refactoring moves the assignment of field `num` in method `bar(int)` to the newly created method `setNumber(int)`, which has no effect of the signature pattern "`* int Foo.num`", but causes a loss of all matching joinpoints. Changes to statements or expressions, like method calls or field accesses, are not covered by this approach. Fourth, the introduced patterns for extending/narrowing pointcuts in a way that new and lost captures are prevented, represent a straight extension of an existing pointcut. The pointcut is extend by enumerations of new or lost pointcut matches, which, on the one hand, makes pointcuts unrecognizable and worse readable, and on the

```
                                   1  class Foo {
                                   2     private int num = 0;
                                   3     public void bar(int count) {
                                   4        setNumber(count);
                                   5     }
                                   6     public void setNumber(int num) {
1  class Foo {                     7        this.num = num;
2     public int num = 0;          8     }
3     public void bar(int count) { 9     public int getNumber() {
4        num = count;              10        return this.num;
5     }                           11     }
6  }                             12  }
```

Figure 3.1: Example program before and after the *Encapsulate Field Refactoring*

other hand, it does not consider the developer's intention behind the pointcut. Fifth, the approach is not supported by a tool.

3.4.4 Generation of Pointcuts

The generation of a pointcut from a given set of example elements (joinpoint shadows), as described in Section 3.2.3, is an important part within an aspect-oriented refactoring process. Since almost every change caused by a refactoring can affect existing pointcuts, it is obvious that aspect-aware refactorings will have to adjust pointcuts frequently. Multiple updates of the same pointcut, however, can lead to so-called pointcut bloating. The *"pointcut pattern equivalence"* constraint, as introduced by *Rura and Lerner*, would add an extension to an affected pointcut, which includes lost matches and excludes new matches simply by enumerating them [78].

Inductive logic programming techniques for generating pointcuts as presented by *Braem et al.* have demonstrated its usefulness in generating specifications that define all common properties of examples shadows. This technique can be used to abstract from the enumerated elements and infer a property-based pointcut that specifies more structural properties than just names. This can prevent pointcut bloating, but can also make the pointcut unrecognizable.

Since the properties specified by the original pointcut are not considered by this approach, it is possible that the resulting pointcut is not bloated but uses a different set properties to identify the joinpoints. Also, a developer could under-specify a set of joinpoints, in order to accept newly added elements. Such specification would be completed by the proposed approaches, neglecting the original intention behind the pointcut.

It seems as particularly important that a refactoring tool adjusts only affected parts of a pointcut with the same level of completeness and abstraction when a pointcut is updated. In doing so, a refactoring minimizes the changes to a pointcut, which makes it recognizable and preserves most of the original intention behind the pointcut without a need for its analysis. All existing approaches to the generation of pointcuts do not address the preservation of the developer's intention behind a pointcut in that way.

3.5 Summary

In this chapter, we have surveyed the work in a number of fields and discussed various approaches for solving evolution problems of aspect-oriented programs.

Refactoring tools are responsible for detecting behavior-affecting changes and for adjusting program elements that reference the modified program parts. In the presence of aspects both tasks are significantly more complicated and require a completely new approach for refactoring. Existing refactoring tools check a predefined set of syntactical and semantical program properties [70] to prevent a refactoring from altering the program behavior.

Pointcuts in aspect-oriented programs can specify properties of static and dynamic program representations imprecisely and incompletely, hence, a stronger verification is required that is independent of this specification quality. Refactoring tools deal with distinct and known changes, they can simply be made aware of the original and the refactored program version.

A comparison of the program elements that are referenced by pointcuts in both program versions will reveal any change effect on specified properties, regardless the quality of their specification. This can be done in a similar way as the approach by Störzer et al. [85].

Some properties of joinpoints, however, depend on a context, i.e., other pointcut anchors, like the declaring type or enclosing package. These so-called extrinsic properties cannot be recognized if the context in which they are identified is changed. Therefore, we need to extend the model of Störzer et al. to represent effects on all program elements that are referenced by a pointcut.

A comparison of statically approximated references to these elements would reveal any effect on existing pointcuts. However, even if alterations can be detected it is still difficult to decide whether they are intended or just accidental. The work of Kellens et al. [50] and Störzer et al. effectively demonstrates this problem, and also Anbalagan and Xie address issues arisen by almost matching elements [4]. As one result of their work, we know that the question whether differently matching elements are intended or accidental needs a qualitative answer.

Qualitative heuristics can classify the specification of any affected property in terms of the change impact. Only if the refactoring tool is aware of the affected elements and the quality of matching specifications, it would be able to propose reasonable adjustments.

Furthermore, a refactoring tool has to consider the kind of changes that affects the elements that are referenced by pointcuts. A proper classification of change effects would allow for automating the decision, whether caused effects can be made undone or have to be accepted. The work of Ryder et al. [84] has demonstrated that a concrete notion for program edits can enable a tool to differentiate effects of different kinds of changes.

The generation of proper adjustments for affected pointcuts causes various problems in the context of refactoring. All existing approaches to the generation of pointcuts do not address the preservation of the developer's intention behind a pointcut. Basically, they can generate a pointcut from given examples but the appearance of resulting pointcuts cannot always be predicted. A refactoring tool must be able to adjust a pointcut multiple times without making it completely unrecognizable. Hence, we propose an approach for replacing the smallest affected pointcut expression, which provides the possibility to preserve both the pointcut's appearance and its specification quality (precision and completeness).

To summarize, an aspect-aware refactoring tool has to detect all change effects on point-cuts and bound advice. This can be done by statically approximating references to program elements, so-called property matches, and comparing these matches for the program before and after the refactoring. Such a comparison reveals every new and lost match of specified properties, and allows for an separated assessment of the change impact on affected pointcut expressions. A heuristic-based approach can provide a qualified answer whether altered matches of incompletely and/or imprecisely specified properties should be accepted. With a predefined range of "acceptable" values for these heuristics a refactoring tool can be enabled to automate the inference of update decisions. Finally, a classification of changes that can be caused by refactorings enable a differentiation between repairable and broken pointcuts. Based on this information a refactoring tool can compute valid pointcut updates.

Chapter 4

An Aspect-aware Refactoring Process

Aspect-aware refactoring additionally has to consider change effects on structural and behavioral composition mechanisms. While structural composition mechanisms can be treated in the same way as object-oriented mechanisms, constructs for behavioral composition need a conceptually new approach. Our refactoring approach integrates a change impact analysis for pointcuts into a tool-supported refactoring workflow and provides two additional refactoring steps: (i) to assess effects on advice code, and (ii) to update invalidated pointcuts.

In this chapter, we present our aspect-aware refactoring process and describe the additional process steps in detail (4.1). For each refactoring step, we illustrate what the developer can expect from the tool. In Section 4.2, we describe the additional change information that is computed for each refactoring in order to make the effects on program representations (used by pointcuts) more explicit.

This chapter can be seen as the description of the process framework for the following two chapters, which present the two most important process steps, the pointcut impact analysis, and the pointcut update computation, in more detail.

4.1 Extending Tool-supported Refactoring

Refactoring tools are an integral part of current IDEs, like the Eclipse JDT [21] or IntelliJ IDEA [44]. They assist the developer in refactoring a program, rather than perform a refactoring automatically. Such a refactoring capability offers a user-controlled and highly interactive workflow. In this section, we describe the most commonly provided refactoring workflow and present our extension for the refactoring of aspect-oriented programs.

4.1.1 Standard Workflow for Tool-supported Refactoring

Most modern IDEs provide two kinds of automated refactorings: wizard-based and dialog-based refactorings. Simple refactorings, like rename refactorings, are usually realized as dialog-based refactorings. They usually require just a single user input, and do not need nor provide many configuration possibilities, thus the complete user interaction can be performed in a single step.

More complex refactorings, on the other hand, are often provided as wizard-based refactorings. For example, the *Pull Up Method* refactoring as provided by the Eclipse JDT can pull up multiple collaborating methods. For this purpose, it offers additional options for resolving conflicts. The effects of particular decisions can be reviewed and adjusted in different configuration steps. Such a step-wise configuration allows for immediate feedback on each configuration step before the refactoring is executed.

In general, a tool-supported refactoring workflow consists of three major steps: input gathering, change preview and problem review, before the code is transformed:

Refactoring input — The developer is requested to input information for one or more parameters of the refactoring, that is, the information required to execute the refactoring. For example, the *Pull Up Method* refactoring in Eclipse provides one step to gather the methods and fields to be pulled up, and another one to define which methods and fields in subclasses are obsolete and thus can be deleted.

The user can navigate between these steps using the *Next* or *Back* buttons. After any required information has been provided, the *Finish* button carries out the refactoring without previewing the results, while the *Next* button leads to a preview of the changes.

Change preview — If the developer selects the preview an additional dialog shows the expected changes of the refactoring. In Eclipse, a compare view is provided, which shows the original and the refactored source code side by side to simplify the comparison of the refactoring's changes. *Back*, *Next* and *Finish* buttons allow for navigating between the input gathering step(s) and the refactoring execution.

Problem review — If an error is detected during the precondition checks, a separate problem review step presents the problems of the refactoring. A dialog indicates if there are suspected, potential, or definite problems with the refactoring. Problematic changes are directly shown in the program's source code. From this problem review step the developer can press *Finish* if there are not any fatal problems to perform the refactoring, *Next* to preview the refactoring results, or *Back* to modify the refactoring's configuration.

4.1.2 Additional AOP-specific Computations

Existing refactoring tools analyze the program source code to determine whether the selected refactoring can be safely performed for its target(s) and the given parameter input. They (most often) use static program analysis to for this evaluation. After the input data was checked the tool evaluates the preconditions of the selected refactoring to determine whether it would affect the behavior of the program. This second analysis step is targeted by our extension for integrating aspect-awareness into standard object-oriented refactorings.

Our aspect-aware extension aims to detect change effects on pointcuts, and to reveal additional and lost matches of any affected pointcut. In addition, it targets the assessment of the change impact on pointcuts in order to support the update decision making, and the proposition of pointcut updates. To this end, we add three additional analysis steps which support the developer in recognizing effects on the aspect behavior and to create valid pointcut updates:

Detection of affected pointcuts — An aspect-aware refactoring tool can be enabled to statically compute all program elements that are selected by a pointcut. Such a *pointcut selection* is a conservative approximation, i.e., it possibly contains more program elements than are actually selected by the pointcut at runtime. Refactoring tools have access to the original program and can virtually produce the refactored program, e.g., for previewing planned changes. We take advantage of this functionality and compute the pointcut selection for both program versions.

A further comparison of the pointcut selections reveals all new and lost matches of any specified joinpoint property. This so-called *pointcut selection delta* contains all altered matches of any specified joinpoint property, and, thus, the complete effects on every pointcut and bound advice[1].

In Chapter 5 we describe the complete analysis approach for assessing the change impact on pointcuts in detail. The particular analysis for detecting affected pointcuts is described in Section 5.5, together with an example illustrating the computed models.

Change impact assessment — A change impact assessment determines whether every new or lost match should be accepted or has to be prevented. Pointcuts can imprecisely and even incompletely specify joinpoint properties, therefore we employ a heuristic-based approach for this assessment. The set of heuristics is used to measure how precise every altered match is specified by the corresponding pointcut expression, and how important is the match to the evaluation result of the complete pointcut.

In addition, we classify the changes that can be caused by refactoring into changes that modify a particular property, remove program elements, or add newly created elements. This classification enables the tool to differentiate between repairable and entirely broken pointcuts.

The change impact assessment is presented in Section 5.6 where each impact measure is defined and described in detail.

Proposition of pointcut updates — A predefined range of acceptable values for the heuristics is used to automate the inference of update decisions. Basically, new matches of sufficiently specified expressions are accepted, unless the expression is too relevant for the pointcut, i.e., too many other expressions depend on its evaluation result. Lost matches are only accepted if the corresponding expressions are not relevant for the pointcut and incompletely specified. In any other case, our set of heuristics proposes to adjust the pointcut or to cancel the refactoring (if it completely removes elements).

The final analysis step computes a pointcut update based on this information. In this computation we locate the smallest affected pointcut expression, and try to replace it. Such a replacement would preserve the pointcut's appearance even after

---

[1] A pointcut selection is likely to contain false positives (i.e., elements that are not selected at runtime), because it is a static approximation of the set of elements selected at runtime

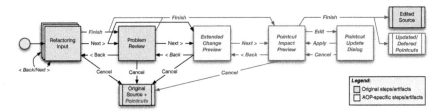

Figure 4.1: Extended workflow for automated refactoring aspect-oriented programs.

multiple updates. If it is not possible to replace the affected expression, the point-cut is extended with explicit exclusions for unintended matches as well as explicit inclusions for accidentally lost matches.

In Chapter 6, we describe the analyses for computing update decisions and generating pointcut updates in detail. The heuristics for the update decision making are completely defined in Section 6.2, together with the ranges of their values which lead to a particular decision. In Section 6.3, we explain how pointcut updates are constructed in general, and present our algorithms for generating the least intrusive pointcut update.

4.1.3 A Workflow for Refactoring Aspect-oriented Programs

The additional analyses for handling of pointcuts can be integrated into any standard refactoring workflow. Based on the results of our pointcut analyses we extend the existing change preview and add two additional refactoring steps that support the developer in dealing with change effects on pointcuts. Figure 4.1 shows our extension of a standard refactoring workflow.

In the aspect-aware refactoring workflow, we perform our pointcut impact analysis after every refactoring input parameter has been entered. At this point, we enforce the preview mode to ensure that the refactoring computes the virtual refactored program version. After both program versions are available, we perform our pointcut analyses. They compute the pointcut selection delta, assess the change impact, compute an update decision and generate pointcut updates for invalidated pointcuts.

Following our pointcut analyses, an *extended change preview* additionally shows the change effects on advice declarations of existing aspects. For each aspect it presents the effects on its advice declarations, showing every planned change together with affected program elements that are referenced by pointcuts. This additional change information states what will happen with the referenced elements if the refactoring is carried out.

The extended preview allows the developer to estimate what effects on the program behavior are to be expected. For instance, in cases of unimportant behavior, such as a logging aspect, the developer could just perform the refactoring immediately and leave the remaining decisions to the refactoring tool (cf. Figure 4.1).

Two additional refactoring steps support the developer in cases where more crucial aspect behavior is affected by the refactoring. The *pointcut impact preview* shows the concrete results of our pointcut impact analysis. It previews the change impact on existing pointcuts, highlights invalidated pointcuts, and presents proposed update decisions. The developer can review proposed updates (if any) and modify update decisions.

The *pointcut update dialog* provides the possibility to customize proposed pointcut updates or even to completely rephrase any affected pointcut.

4.2 Extending Refactorings with Change Information

Refactorings are program transformations that can modify a program in various ways. The modifications can range from a renaming limited to the local scope, to the introduction of a design pattern. Bigger refactorings are generally composed of several smaller refactorings. A refactoring tool utilizes this fact and realizes the automation of any refactoring by performing a composition of program transformations. Every possible change that can be caused by a refactoring is achieved through a particular sequence of transformations. Also, the preservation of the program behavior is argued in terms of these program transformations.

In this section, we illustrate very briefly how automated refactorings are composed of low-level transformations and how resulting changes can be made more amenable to program analysis.

4.2.1 Composition of Refactorings

William Opdyke defined in his Ph.D. thesis [70] a framework for automating the refactoring of object-oriented programs. He identified several big refactorings for restructuring object-oriented frameworks and defined them as compositions of smaller refactorings. For each of these low-level refactorings, he specified preconditions that guarantee the preservation of the program behavior. The low-level refactorings capture creation, deletion, change and move of program elements. Each of these categories contain refactorings for different program elements, like classes, variables and methods (cf. [70], Chapter 5). For example, consider the *Rename Method* refactoring. It basically consists of three different parts:

$$RenameMethod(m, n) := RenameMethodDeclaration(m, n)$$
$$+ RenameMethodCalls(m, n)$$
$$+ RenameOverridingMethods(m, n)$$

The $RenameMethodDeclaration(m, n)$ ensures that the method gets a new unique name. $RenameMethodCalls(m, n)$ ensures that every existing method call to this method uses this new name. $RenameOverridingMethods(m, n)$ finally performs the same renaming for every method declaration that overrides this method in subtypes of the declaring type[2].

Refactorings tools realize these individual parts of a refactoring by separating program transformations (cf. Eclipse Java IDE [21]). Any change effect of a refactoring can be

---

[2]Potentially overridden methods in supertypes are not considered by refactoring tools, because they perform the refactoring always for the topmost method within a type hierarchy.

represented by its constituent program transformations. The automated version of the
Push Down Method refactoring (cf. [28], p.328) from the example of Section 5.2 can be
represented by three low-level transformations:

$$PushDownMethod(m, t) := CreateMethodDeclaration(m, t)$$
$$+ MoveStatementList(l, m)$$
$$+ RemoveMethodDeclaration(m)$$

The $CreateMethodDeclaration(m, t)$ creates an empty method declaration with the
name of method m in class t while also making sure that the name is not already used.
The transformation $MoveStatementList(l, m)$ moves all statements l from within the
body of method m to the newly created method, and $RemoveMethodDeclaration(m)$
then removes the method declaration m.

4.2.2 A Model of Atomic Changes

The changes caused by different refactorings vary in extent and complexity, and can range
from a local text edit with no further effect, to huge adaptations that affect multiple
implementation modules. Similar to Ryder et al. in [73, 79], we have developed an
abstract change model that represents program edits through atomic changes.

An **atomic change** abstracts from program edits and represents the change through
program elements of an AST, covering any element from package down to expression.
Since our impact analysis compares the original and refactored program version, we are
only interested in changes that affect the existence of elements in the AST. We consider
only changes that cause the creation or deletion of elements, such as added type (AT),
deleted type (DT), added method (AM), deleted method (DM), added expression (AE)
and deleted expression (DE). Other changes, like rename or move, can be represented
by these atomic changes because the analysis is aware of the transformation that causes
an atomic change, e.g., the renaming of a method is represented through an AM (the
method with the new name) and a DM (the method with the old name). The resulting
representation of changes is tailored to the analysis of change effects on pointcuts and
reduces the effort for analyzing change effects significantly.

All changes caused by a refactoring are represented within the so-called **atomic change
model**. The atomic change model ACM can associate any affected program element
of P with the affecting atomic change AC and relate it to the responsible program
transformation T. Hence, changes caused by any refactoring can be represented by tuples
of affected elements, atomic changes and responsible transformations $\{P \times AC \times T\}$.

Since the atomic change model already consists of concrete change effects, we can further simplify the representation of change effects and introduce a *classification of program
transformations*, so-called **change reasons**. A change reason abstracts from the concrete transformation and describes its effect in terms of the program representations used
to specify properties of joinpoints (like program's name space, code containment, inheritance relationships and stack trace). Elements of these representations can generally be
created, removed, moved, and declaration elements can also be renamed. These kinds of
program transformations represent the particular change reasons for added or removed

program elements. For each kind we introduce a specific change reason: $CREATE$, $REMOVE$, $RENAME$, $MOVE$[3].

Using these abstract reasons, the change effects of every refactoring can be represented in terms of the program representations that are referenced by pointcuts:

> **Definition 4.1:** The *atomic change model* $ACM : \{P \times AC \times R\}$ represents all change effects on a program P as a triple, associating affected elements P with affecting atomic changes AC and their change reasons R (i.e., the kind of program transformation).

Any kind of transformation of $\{CREATE, \ REMOVE, \ RENAME, \ MOVE\}$ is a possible change reason R. With this more precise definition of change effects, we can rephrase our definition for program transformations:

> **Definition 4.2:** A *program transformation* $T(P, in) \longrightarrow \{P' \times AC \times R\}$ changes a program P for a given input in and results in a set of modified program elements P' associated with affecting atomic changes AC and the responsible change reasons R.

4.3 Summary

In this chapter we have introduced our approach for refactoring aspect-oriented programs. We have illustrated how the standard refactoring workflow can be extended and which program analyses can be used for providing a proper handling of pointcuts. In addition, we have shown that existing refactoring tools implement refactorings as compositions of lower-level program transformations and how the analysis of change effects can be simplified by computing additional information for every refactoring.

The standard tool-supported refactoring workflow consists of three refactoring steps: user input gathering, change preview, and problem review. Our aspect-aware refactoring workflow extends the change preview step, also showing change effects on aspects, and provides two additional refactoring steps, a pointcut impact review, and the pointcut update customization. The former allows the developer to review proposed update decisions. The latter provides the possibility to customize proposed pointcut updates.

Such an additional refactoring support requires a powerful program analysis which detects all alterations of matching program elements and provides enough information about the affected pointcut expressions so that the developer is able to validate the automated update decisions.
Since these pointcut analyses in particular evaluate properties of static and dynamic program representations, we propose a change classification that simplifies the analysis of change effects on pointcuts. This classification differentiates between four kinds of program transformations: rename, move, create, and remove. For every performed refactoring the kinds of its constituent transformations are determined and associated with a simplified change representation, so-called atomic changes. The resulting atomic

---

[3]A move transformation changes the physical location in the program code and can also alter the position inside a type hierarchy.

change model contains for any lost or newly matching element the particular transformation kind as the change reason. Based on this model of change effects, we can give a definition for the program transformation that is more suitable for describing change effects on pointcuts.

Chapter 5

A Change Impact Analysis for Pointcuts

Refactoring tools use static program analysis for detecting behavior-affecting changes. They check a set of preconditions that preserve specific program properties to reveal effects on the program behavior. For aspect-oriented programs additional preconditions have to be checked to detect change effects on the behavior defined by aspects.

In this chapter, we describe our program analysis approach for detecting change effects on pointcuts. In Section 5.1 we give an overview of our impact analysis approach, describing every analysis step of the overall analysis process. In Section 5.3 we illustrate the program representations that are used to statically represent dynamic properties of joinpoints. In addition, we describe the algorithms for constructing these representations and for evaluating the dynamic properties. Furthermore, we present each analysis step in detail, depict our static representation of joinpoint sets by examples, and define their semantics. At the end of the chapter (Section 5.6), we present our impact measures for classifying the change impact and discuss the results expected from their application.

5.1 Analysis Approach at a Glance

Our analysis approach uses several advanced program representations and different algorithms to compute them. This section gives an overview of the whole analysis process, states its goals and presents known limitations. The remaining sections of this chapter present the here outlined analysis steps in more detail, including mentioned program representations, algorithms, and expected results.

5.1.1 Concrete Goals

Pointcuts refer to program representations that can be affected by several refactorings. A refactoring tool should be able to detect these effects and to adjust pointcuts if they reference changed program representations, in a similar way as it is done for symbolic references. The primary goal of the analysis approach is to assess and classify change

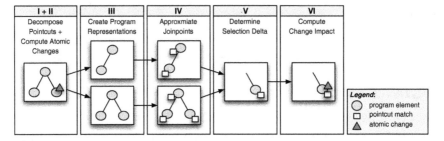

Figure 5.1: Overview of the impact analysis process.

effects on pointcuts in aspect-oriented programs, as well as to compute adjustments for affected pointcuts, making these effects undone. From this general goal more concrete objectives can be derived:

- *Detection of differently bound advice code.* The analysis can compute the joinpoints that are supposed to be selected by a pointcut and identify additional or lost joinpoints when the program is refactored. It exposes the affected pointcuts as well as the altered invocations of advice code.

- *Identification of the impact reason.* The tool can automatically reveal the particular program transformation that is responsible for the change effects on a pointcut.

- *Assessment of the change impact.* The analysis enables the refactoring tool to determine whether a specific change impact has to be undone and also if it can be undone. Further recommendations to the developer, such as *Cancel Refactoring* or *Update Pointcut*, will be computed from distinguishing these cases.

- *Inference of updates for invalidated pointcuts.* The analysis can propose adjustments for invalidated pointcuts to restore their original semantics. These adjustments should be as less intrusive as possible, so that pointcuts can be updated several times and are still comparable to its original appearance.

5.1.2 Analysis Process

The impact analysis comprises *six* analysis steps, which are sequentially processed. The Figure 5.1 gives an overview of the process and illustrates the information gained from every analysis step.

5.1.2.1 Decomposition of Pointcuts (I)

One major objective of the analysis approach is the recognition of change effects on specified joinpoint properties as well as the assessment of effects on their specifications. The analysis would benefit from a pointcut representation that makes the specification of every single property explicit, i.e., the pointcut directly states which part of the specification addresses which property of the joinpoint. Since present AOP environments do not provide such a representation, we construct a so-called **pointcut model** which provides a distinct specification for each addressed property.

A pointcut fractionizer decomposes existing pointcuts into elementary pointcut expressions. A **pointcut expression** refers to a single joinpoint property, or to be more precise, to a property of an element of a program representation that is used to represent the joinpoint's property. For every property of a program representation, a specific pointcut expression is provided, such as for signature patterns ($method()$, $field()$), code containment ($within()$, $contains()$), static type hierarchy ($supertypes()$, $subtypes()$) and the program execution ($cflow()$, $args()$). Furthermore, the fractionizer determines all evaluation dependencies between the expressions of a pointcut, and computes every partial aggregation of expressions. The resulting pointcut model represents a pointcut as tree of pointcut expressions, using nodes to represent expressions (a leaf node indicates an independent expression) and directed edges to represent evaluation dependencies. A more detailed description of the pointcut model and illustrating examples can be found in Section 5.4.

5.1.2.2 Computation of Atomic Changes (II)

The impact analysis considers program transformations that change a program by modifying elements of an abstract syntax tree. We can therefore introduce a specific granularity of change, a so-called **atomic change**, that is particularly suited to represent effects on matching program elements. Atomic changes are a simplified representation of possible changes, such as added type (AT), deleted type (DT), added method (AM), deleted method (DM), added expression (AE) and deleted expression (DE). All other changes are either represented by these atomic changes or omitted, e.g., the renaming of a method can be represented through an AM (the method with the new name) and a DM (the method with the old name). Such a simplified representation of changes is tailored to an analysis of change effects on pointcuts and significantly reduces the effort for analyzing a change.

Our analysis computes the **atomic change model** for every performed refactoring after the refactoring tool has performed the refactoring's transformations virtually to produce the refactored program version. The atomic change model was already defined in Section 4.2 of the previous chapter. An example that illustrates the model is presented in Section 5.2.

5.1.2.3 Creation of Advanced Program Representations (III)

Joinpoints are points in the execution of a program, i.e., they have no direct representation in the program's source. A refactoring tool needs, particularly for dynamic properties of joinpoints, a statically available representation. The analysis computes an abstract syntax graph (ASGs), representing containment, inheritance and usage relationships, and partial call graphs (CGs), representing call dependencies, of the program.

Which program representations are actually computed depends on the joinpoint properties specified in existing pointcuts, i.e., the types of pointcut expressions contained by the pointcut model. In section 5.3, the advanced program representations and their computation is described in more detail.

5.1.2.4 Approximation of Joinpoints (IV)

Our impact analysis uses the advanced program representations to evaluate the pointcut expressions. This process is called **pointcut matching** and evaluates every partial aggregation of expressions following the evaluation dependencies defined by the pointcut model. A pointcut resolver computes the program elements that correspond to the properties specified by the expressions, or to be more precise, the nodes of the employed program representation which represent the program elements. Every program element that matches an expression is called **property match**. Program elements that match the root expression of a pointcut model are called **pointcut matches**. A pointcut match corresponds to all properties specified by a pointcut, and is therefore the static approximation of a joinpoint.

The pointcut resolver produces for every pointcut (model) a so-called **pointcut selection**, which is a static program representation that represents all program elements that are referenced by a pointcut. A pointcut selection contains all (property and pointcut) matches of a pointcut model within a given program. Every node of a pointcut selection represents a (property or pointcut) match, and is connected to other matches through a dependency relationship. This relationship reflects the evaluation dependencies in the pointcut model and denotes a directed dependency between matches of associated pointcut expressions.

The impact analysis computes such a pointcut selection for every pointcut in the program, the so-called **pointcut selection model**. This model represents any (property and pointcut) match for every pointcut in the program and is used to detect inter-pointcut interferences. See Section 5.5 for examples and more details on the pointcut selection model.

5.1.2.5 Determination of the Pointcut Selection Delta (V)

This analysis step aims to compare two pointcut selection models for different program versions. To this end, the impact analysis computes such a model for the original and the refactored program version, and compares both selection models to produce the so-called **pointcut selection delta**. This delta contains all new and lost matches for the refactored program version, and thus represents the direct impact of a refactoring on pointcuts in the program.

This delta, however, may still contain spurious effects (in both program versions) of the same program transformation. The actual delta is determined by locating every program transformation that causes new or lost matches of a pointcut expressions. For every lost match in the refactored program the analysis tries to locate a corresponding added match in the same version (caused by the same program transformation). Those corresponding matches are removed from the pointcut selection delta. As result, only really new and lost matches remain in the impact representation for every pointcut.

In addition, the responsible program transformation is assigned to every pointcut expression with new and lost matches. The resulting **change impact representation** contains every pointcut expression that is affected by the refactoring and associates it with the change reason for the delta entry. Hence, it describes the impact on every specified joinpoint property that is modified by the refactoring in terms of change effects (new and lost matches), its specification (affected pointcut expression) and the change reason (responsible transformation).

Dynamic properties require a delta that reflects the nature of the corresponding program representation. For example, selections of a $cflow$ property are represented by a matching call path described as a tuple of start-trigger, end-trigger and path quality. A refactoring can cause new or lost match paths, or just an alteration of a path's quality. The pointcut selection delta for $cflow$ properties is defined as the set of new, lost and changed (in terms of path quality) property matches. This representation of the change effects enables a static program analysis to assess the change impact on the dynamic property $cflow$.

The impact representations for static and dynamic properties and the detailed impact measures are described in Section 5.6.

5.1.2.6 Computation of Change Impact (VI)

The change impact representation contains all information necessary to assess the extent of the impact. Four different kinds of information are used for this assessment: (i) the change reason, (ii) the impact kind, (iii) the specification quality of pointcut expressions and (iv) the impact's extend.

The **change reason** is represented by the program transformation that is responsible for a particular impact on the pointcut. It is obvious that a refactoring tool has to propose different actions if the lost matches were caused by a remove and not by, e.g., a rename transformation. Lost matches cannot be recovered if the matching elements were removed from the program.

The **impact kind** distinguishes between new and lost matches. The occurrence of lost matches is considered to be more serious than occurrences of new matches. A refactoring tool cannot allow a refactoring to remove elements that match precisely specified properties, whereas it could allow newly matching elements.

The **specification quality** of an affected pointcut expression indicates how complete a property is specified. Such a completeness measure is required, because most joinpoint properties can depend on partially specified signature patterns. A low quality denotes a weakly specified signature, whereas a high quality is an indicator for a complete specification. A low quality states that not much information is required to match a pointcut, therefore it can be an indicator for "bad" pointcuts. The opposite, however, is not always true, i.e., a "good" pointcut takes more as completely specified properties.

We uses two impact measures as indicators for the **extend of an impact**. The number of altered matches, indicates how many matches for a specific pointcut expression are affected by a change. It is used to provide the developer with a quantified assessment of the effect in terms of the selected joinpoints. The nesting level of the affected expression, indicates how many properties specified by the pointcut are affected by the change. It quantifies the effects in terms of the specification.

The refactoring tool uses these four kinds of information as input for computing update proposals for affected pointcuts.

5.2 A Running Example

In this section, we introduce a small example program to illustrate the purpose of the program representations described in the following sections. The program is implemented in AspectJ. Listing 5.1 shows its source code, which is refactored performing the *Push Down Method* refactoring (see [28], p. 328).

Listing 5.1: Source code of the example program.

```
1  package p1;
2  public aspect A {
3      pointcut posChanged(): set(int *);
4      before(): posChanged() {
5          System.out.println("Changing_position");
6      }
7  }
8
9  package p1;
10 public class B {
11     int pos;
12     static void main(String[] args) {
13         C c = new C();
14         c.setPos(1);
15         c.update();
16     }
17     void setPos(int pos) {
18         this.pos = pos;
19     }
20 //  will be moved during the refactoring
21     void update() {
22         pos = pos + 10;
23     }
24 }
25
26 package p1;
27 class C extends B {
28 }
```

5.2.1 Behavior of the Example Program

The program consists of two classes B, C and one aspect A. The class C extends class B, but with no further implementation. The class B implements an update mechanism for a field named pos. The main method in class B creates a new instance of class C, sets the value of field pos to 1 by invoking C.setPos(int) and calls the method C.update() to increase the field pos by 10.

The aspect A defines a pointcut that selects every field assignment to any field of type int. In this program the pointcut intercepts executions of any assignment to field pos.

The bound advice prints some status information to the console before the field `pos` is modified.

5.2.2 Push Down Method Refactoring

The program is modified using our aspect-aware version of the standard Java *Push Down Method* refactoring (cf. [28], p. 328). It is applied to method `B.update()` in order to move it to the subclass `C`. By moving the `update()` method also the contained joinpoint shadows are transfered to a new place.

Using our atomic change model the change effects of the refactoring can be represented as an added method (AM) in the target class, a deleted method (DM) in the original class (associated with the same reason), and an added/deleted expression (AE/DE) for every contained expression that is moved along with the method:

$$PushDownMethod(P, \{m, t\}) \longrightarrow$$
$$\bigcup \{\{m', AM, MOVE\}, \{m, DM, MOVE\},$$
$$\{e1', AE, MOVE\}, \{e1, DE, MOVE\}, \{e2', AE, MOVE\}, ...\}$$

The association of any atomic change with its responsible reason allows us to distinguish added/deleted elements from the appearance/disappearance of changed elements, e.g., caused through rename or move. The refactoring tool creates the atomic change model during the refactoring process and attaches the computed changes to every changed element and its enclosing parents. Furthermore, it associates affected elements with the change reason. For the example, the change model in Figure 5.2 shows the removal of method `update()` in `class B` and the addition of the method in `class C`. The associated reason indicates that both changes are caused by moving of the same method from `class B` to `class C`.

In combination with the property matches from the pointcut selection model, the effective change impact on existing pointcuts for every changed program element can be determined.

The standard Java refactoring is neither aware of the pointcut nor of the effects on the composed program behavior. In the following sections, we present how the standard Java refactoring influences the pointcut of `aspect A`, how this can be determined by a our program analysis approach, and how our refactoring tool can calculate whether the pointcut needs to be updated.

5.3 Static Approximation of Dynamic Properties

The developed impact analysis determines pointcut matches via static program analysis, i.e., a joinpoint is represented through elements of the program representations that are used for specifying its properties. This approximation of joinpoints is particularly difficult if properties of dynamic program representations are used to select a specific set of joinpoints.

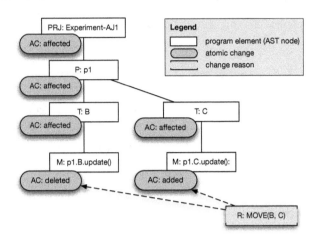

Figure 5.2: Atomic change tree for Example of Section 5.2.

In this section, we present multiple background information on dynamic program representations and their properties that are used by several AOP approaches for selecting joinpoints. We also describe selected properties and how these properties can be approximated through equivalent static program representations. Furthermore, we present several examples, discuss important attributes of approximated representations and point out the limits of static program analysis for the evaluation of dynamic joinpoint properties, in general. ,

5.3.1 Dynamic Program Representations

Pointcut languages of existing AOP approaches allow a developer to specify several runtime properties. Two dynamic program representations, the object graph and the execution history, are used by the most powerful pointcut languages found in the literature. Both representations are described in more detail, since we are using them later to construct a model for detecting a change impact on dynamic properties.

5.3.1.1 The Object Graph

An object graph is a program representation that represents objects (instances of classes) and their dependencies in the execution of a program. The graph represents objects as nodes and their references as edges. An object graph is a directed graph, i.e., a reference between two objects indicating that one object references the other, but it does not show the inverse relationship.

An object graph can contain different objects and references at every point in the execution of the program. The nodes it consists of and also its structure can change during runtime. The number of nodes in the graph is altered through instantiations of new objects or by removing the last reference to an object. The graph's structure can be changed through several operations, such as assignments of new objects to fields. After such an assignment the field refers to a new object, which causes an additional or changed edge in the graph.

At every point in the execution of the program a certain part of the object graph is directly accessible. The so-called *execution context* defines which objects can be directly accessed. An execution context is, e.g., the method body in which the execution currently invokes statements. It provides variables, such as the actual parameters of the method, field members of the enclosing object at which the method was invoked, or locally defined variables. The currently available execution context defines the entry points into a call graph, i.e., the initial objects from which the graph can be explored.

An illustrating example that depicts the general structure of object graphs and their changes during the execution can be found in Appendix A.1.

5.3.1.2 The Execution History

The execution history, often also called execution trace, represents a sequence of events that occur during runtime until a considered point in execution. Various levels of abstraction can be considered when representing events during the execution of a program. The most concrete level would consider every single instruction in the byte-code level for a Java virtual machine or in machine-level code level. A suitable abstraction level for representing joinpoints would obviously consider any execution of a program element. Since executions of program elements are no single point in the execution history, it would represent every occurrence of an entry and exit to the execution of a program element as joinpoint. At this abstraction level every joinpoint occurs as single event within a sequence of runtime events. The execution history can represent any sequence of joinpoints happened during runtime in its precise order of occurrence. The Figure 5.3 shows such a sequence of joinpoints for one possible execution of a small example program.

5.3.2 Properties of Dynamic Program Representations

Within these program representations several dynamic properties can be specified by selecting specific executions of program elements as joinpoints. We describe some properties in more detail to give a better understanding of their individual nature, which we consider as essential to comprehend the impact of affecting changes.

In general, two kinds of dynamic joinpoint properties are distinguished: single trigger and multi trigger properties. A node of a dynamic program representation that contains a specified property is called **trigger**, and the program element represented by the node, accordingly *trigger shadow*. A **single trigger** property is an independent property of a single node in the representation, whereas a **multi trigger** property comprises properties of several nodes. For example, a property denoting an "occurrence of joinpoint *jp1* before a joinpoint *jp2*" is considered as multi trigger property, because it is not intrinsic to the nature of joinpoint *jp2*. A multi trigger property depends on a context, and is therefore an *extrinsic property* (see Chapter 2). The context of a multi trigger property,

```
 1 public class Main {
 2    private int field;
 3
 4    public static void main(String[] args)
         {
 5       boolean runtimeValue = args == null
 6          ? true
 7          : (args.length % 2) == 0;
 8
 9       Main obj = new Main();
10       if (runtimeValue) {
11          obj.m1();
12       } else {
13          obj.m2();
14       }
15    }
16    private void m1() {
17       int var = field;
18       m2();
19    }
20    private void m2() {
21       field = 5;
22    }
23 }
```

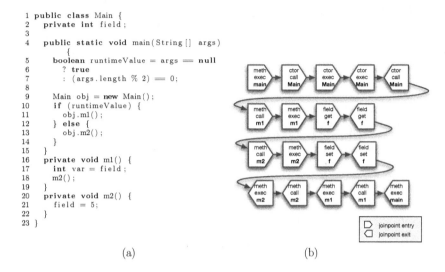

(a)   (b)

Figure 5.3: Example program (a) and its execution flow (b) for illustrating the execution
          history.

however, is dynamic and may differ for every individual execution. Hence, we consider
multi trigger properties as a specific kind of extrinsic properties.

Any occurrence of a specified property in a dynamic program representation is called
trigger, regardless if it is an occurrence of the complete property or just a part of it. For
multi trigger properties we further distinguish, partial matches of the property, called
start-triggers, and complete matches, called **end-triggers**.

In this section, we only describe properties of the execution history in more detail and
illustrate it by examples. Examples for typical properties of object graphs are presented
in Appendix B.1.

5.3.2.1 Execution History Properties

The execution history is a program representation that represents a (partial or complete)
chain of events that occurred during runtime until a considered point in execution. This
representation can be used by pointcuts to identify joinpoints which are either located
in a particular control flow, or occur after a specific execution sequence.

Control Flow Containment (Cflow). The so-called *cflow* property denotes that a
joinpoint (end-trigger) is located within the control flow of another joinpoint (start-
trigger). It uses the stack trace of a program execution, which can be seen as a simplified
representation of an execution history. A stack trace represents joinpoints directly as

executions of program elements (triggers). The start-trigger defines the control flow in which any occurrence of an end-trigger is considered as selected joinpoint. The start- and end-triggers can be selected through other properties. For example, consider the program in Figure 5.4 (a) and the following AspectJ pointcut:

```
1 pointcut exampleCflow():
2    cflow(execution(void Example.m3())) && execution(void Example.m9())
```

The control flows of the methods are depicted in Figure 5.4 (b), showing which control flow contains which method invocation. The pointcut selects every execution of a method with the signature `void Example.m9()` that occurs in the control flow of a method with the signature `void Example.m3()`. Several executions of method `m9()` lead to joinpoints with different cflow properties, as illustrated by Figure 5.4 (c). The first execution of the method `m9()` is contained in the control flow of method `m3()`, and thus selected by the pointcut. In the remaining execution of the program, other invocations of method `m9()` occur, but outside the control flow of method `m3()`, and, hence, are not selected by the pointcut. Similar to the specification of a particular containment, it is also possible to exclude specific control flows. A negated *cflow* property denotes that any execution of a certain method is selected by the pointcut, except those that occur within the specified control flow.

Execution Sequence.   More advanced approaches introduce specifications of specific execution sequences for selecting joinpoints. As an example, we present here an extension to AspectJ by Allan et al. called *tracematches* [3] and an extension to the language JAsCo of De Fraine et al. called *Stateful Aspects* [99]. Both approaches employ a formal model for representing execution sequences by Douence et al. [19]. This model represents joinpoints within the execution history as entries and exists of executions of program elements, e.g., every occurrence of a method entry in the history is a joinpoint. In the execution history, joinpoints are not the program elements represented by the nodes, they are events that occur during the execution of a program element. This difference in the representation of joinpoints allows a more precise specification of runtime events; much closer to the actual execution of programs. An illustrating example for an execution sequence property is presented in Appendix A.2.

Both properties denote a particular program behavior at runtime, but differ significantly in their meaning. The cflow property denotes the containment of a partial execution history. It spans the control flow of a particular joinpoint $jp1$ and considers any joinpoint $jp2$ as selected, regardless where, when, and how often it occurs in this very control flow. The execution sequence property denotes a particular sequence of events that can occur anytime during the program execution and can even be incompletely specified. It represents a temporal relationship denoting joinpoint $jp2$ occurs after joinpoint $jp1$. These temporal relationships are not restricted to a certain part of the program.

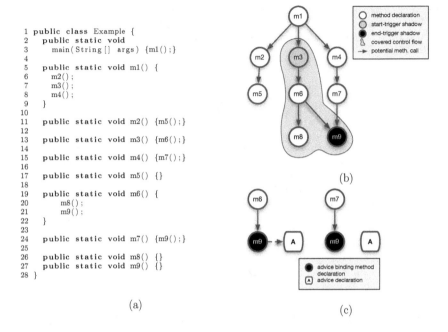

```
 1 public class Example {
 2    public static void
 3       main(String[] args) {m1();}
 4
 5    public static void m1() {
 6       m2();
 7       m3();
 8       m4();
 9    }
10
11    public static void m2() {m5();}
12
13    public static void m3() {m6();}
14
15    public static void m4() {m7();}
16
17    public static void m5() {}
18
19    public static void m6() {
20       m8();
21       m9();
22    }
23
24    public static void m7() {m9();}
25
26    public static void m8() {}
27    public static void m9() {}
28 }
```

(a)

(b)

(c)

Figure 5.4: Example program (a), visualized control flows (b) and caused advice bindings (c)

5.3.3 Static Representation of Dynamic Properties

Static properties of joinpoints are directly represented by the program representations that can directly be obtained from program code. Source code changes affect these static representations directly, thus effects on static properties of joinpoints can be simply inferred. For dynamic properties, however, a model of all possible program executions needs to be constructed, to be able to recognize the executions in which a dynamic property occurs. Such a model of the program execution approximates various runtime representations and allows for an identification of change effects on dynamic properties.

5.3.3.1 A Static Model for Cflow Properties

In Section 5.3.2.1 we described the *cflow* property as execution dependency between two joinpoints. An end-trigger of the property binds the advice to a joinpoint, if it occurs in the control flow of the property's start-trigger. A concrete joinpoint is located within the control flow, e.g., of a method, if it occurs after the execution entered the method and before it returns from the method.

A static model for representing a *cflow* property, needs to consider all possible program executions, for identifying any potential occurrence of this property. For such a static model we use a *call graph* for representing an approximation of all possible control flows in the execution of the program. A call graph is the standard representation for the approximation of execution dependencies. We consider every potential start-trigger of any specified *cflow* property as entry points for its computation, i.e., we compute a call graph for every joinpoint shadow that is a potential start-trigger.

Principal Algorithm. The call graph is basically computed as combination of all possible control flows considering the execution dependencies of method declarations and method calls. If the start-trigger shadow is a method declaration, then all possible control flows of its body represent the first level of the graph. For method calls, the first level is computed from the bodies of their corresponding declarations. Any further level is computed in the same way and attached to already existing control flows. We proceed with the computation as long as there are additional method calls in a method body. In case, the start-trigger is a call then we directly add the call to the computed control flow. In this way, we compute the control flows for every level, which constructs a static representation of any possible control flow for every shadow of a start-trigger.

In this static representation, we can locate every shadow of an end-trigger specified by the *cflow* property. If such a shadow is located within a corresponding control flow of the computed static model, then we can consider this particular execution of the shadow as a joinpoint of the associated *cflow* property. Such a static model contains various details which are not particularly needed for representing *cflow* properties. Since *cflow* properties just denote the containment within a control flow, the temporal order within a control flow can be omitted.

Basic Call Graph Representations. A call graph is a directed and possibly cyclic graph that represents execution dependencies as directed edges. A node in the graph represents a method declaration, whereas edges indicate a potential method call, i.e., the graph contains a directed edge from m1() to m2() if there is a possibility during runtime that method m1() calls m2(). The reason for possible cyclic paths in a call graph is language support for defining directly or indirectly recursive invocations.

Such a basic call graph, however, has a number of limitations which make it insufficient for representing *cflow* properties. It only considers method declarations, so executions of other elements, such as individual method calls or field accesses, are not represented. Most pointcut languages allow developers to select also other elements as start- or end-trigger for a *cflow* property, which could not be evaluated using such a call graph. Moreover, the particularly use of control flow statements has to be considered in order to detect change effects on the execution likeliness. For example, an addition of a control flow statement could alter a definite execution dependency to a conditional dependency, or an added loop statement could introduce a multiple execution of call graph nodes. Basic call graphs also do not contain parallel edges, i.e., multiple invocations of the same methods are represented by a single edge.

Multiple invocations, however, have to be considered when evaluating cflow properties, because every occurrence of an end-trigger within the start-triggers control flow invokes bound advice code. In addition, a special treatment of cyclic paths is required when analyzing the graph. Cycles in graphs can lead to an unlimited number of different paths, which would make a deterministic path analysis impossible.

A Call Graph Representation for Cflow. A basic call graph has to be improved in several ways to be a more suitable representation for evaluating properties of joinpoints. For representing expression-level execution dependencies additional nodes are inserted into the call graph, e.g., method declarations that are not considered as an end-trigger shadow, but contain shadows of end-triggers. Multiple invocations of the same methods are represented through parallel edges, i.e., several edges can connect the same pair of nodes. Figure 5.5 illustrates the improved call graph with an example.

A specific annotation of edges is introduced to qualify the likeliness of an execution. Such an annotation denotes how likely and how often an occurrence of an end-trigger can lead to a joinpoint of the specified *cflow* property. Two nodes with a direct execution dependency, are connected through edges annotated as "*definite*". Edges that represent a conditional execution, e.g., introduced through dynamic binding or if-else constructs, are labeled as "*conditional*", and annotated with the condition that guards the execution. These annotations add, e.g., the number of possible branches to a condition and the individual condition to a branch. In this way, different alternatively executed nodes can be distinguished in the static representation. Multiple executions, e.g., nodes that are contained in loops, are connected with multi-edges. A multi-edge is annotated with a label "*multiple*", that indicates the possibility of multiple executions.

Since a program can contain directly or indirectly defined recursive invocations, the resulting call graph can contain cyclic paths. These cycles can be treated as other statements for multiple execution, such as loop statements. Does a path between the shadows of a start-trigger and an end-trigger contain a cycle, then it can be considered as a several times executed path, just as loops. End-trigger shadows within a cycle are considered as the same situation, however if start-trigger shadows in cycles have a different meaning. A multiple execution of a start-trigger shadow cannot lead to multiple cflow joinpoints. A cflow property selects a joinpoint only if the end-trigger occurs.

All cycles in the graph are represented as single node with outgoing edges that are labeled as multi-edge.

Approximation of Cflow Properties. A computation of an enhanced call graph allows reasonably approximated representations of cflow properties. The enhanced call graph is computed for every start-trigger shadow and results in a set of all possible call path for any combination of start- and end-trigger shadows. The annotation process labels every edge in a call paths and allows for a distinction between definite, conditional, and multiple paths. The qualification of a path depends on the edges it comprises and is computed as follows:

- A *definite path*, is a path that exclusively contains definite edges and indicates a certain occurrence of the cflow property.

- A *conditional path*, is a path that contains at least one conditional edge, but no multi-edge. It denotes a potential occurrence of the cflow property.

- A *multi-path*, is a path that contains at least one multi-edge and it is an indicator for multiple occurrences of the cflow property. The actual number of occurrences depends on the concrete execution of the program, and can therefore not be computed.

In addition, a special treatment of conditional paths ensures that the number of definite and conditional paths is not counterfeited. Conditional executions can mutually exclude each other, e.g., if an `if-then-else` construct calls in its `if`- and `else`-branch the same method. Such a path is actually a definite path, even if it contains conditional edges, since the same method is located in mutually excluded branches.

As result, for every program a number of definite, conditional, and multiple paths is computed for every specified *cflow* property (in combination with shadow pairs of start- and end-triggers). The Figure 5.5 shows the source code and a visualization of a conditional multi-path. For this example the *cflow* property was specified, using method `st()` as shadow for the start-trigger and method `et()` end-trigger shadow.

```
 1 public void st() {
 2    m1();
 3 }
 4 public void m1() {
 5    if (condition) {
 6        m2();
 7    }
 8 }
 9 public void m2() {
10    while (condition) {
11        et();
12    }
13 }
14 public void et() {}
```

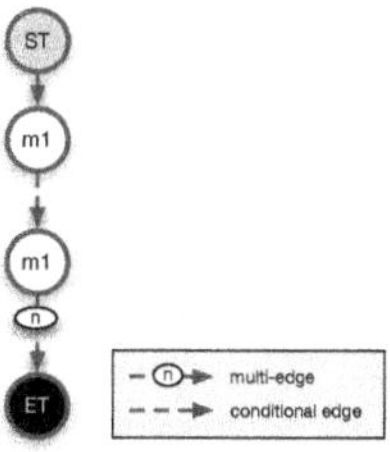

Figure 5.5: Source code and visualization of a conditional multi-path.

The extended call graph allows a static program analysis to evaluate a specified cflow property within all possible executions of a program. Segments that correspond to the cflow property are represented by call paths, which does not contain any variable values yet. A representation that considers the values of conditional paths, would be a more precise approximation of the actual execution. Such a representation, however, cannot entirely be computed. Even very small programs can have a huge space of possible program states and transitions. Also infinite state spaces can simply be produced. The evaluation of the program state, however, is necessary for determining variable values, which makes the use of variable values in pointcuts to a property the cannot reasonably be approximated.

5.3.3.2 A Static Model for Execution Sequence Properties

Similar to the cflow property the execution sequence is a multi-trigger property. Its triggers, however, are points before and after a joinpoint, such as entries and exists of a method. In Section 5.3.2.1 we already gave examples for concrete execution sequences.

A particular sequence is specified by a regular expression. If an executed sequence of triggers matches the specified sequence, the current trigger is the end-trigger, which leads to a selected joinpoint.

A static evaluation of execution sequences requires a representation for all possible executions of a program, similar as for the cflow property. Such a representation of an execution sequence, however, is much more complex. A *cflow* property addresses very small segments of a control flow and in these segments also just a few specific information. A specified execution sequence is a much more precise requirement to a particular control flow, which needs more detailed control flow information of almost the complete program. A cflow property selects a specific set of start- and end-triggers which only requires a static representation of all possible control flows between the shadows of these triggers. An execution sequence is specified using regular expressions, which makes it much more difficult to determine all pairs of start- and end-trigger shadows.

A suitable program representation for a static model of execution sequences is the *control flow graph*. A control flow graph represents all possible executions of a program, and comprises any information needed to identify start- and end-trigger of a specified execution sequence. In addition, it represents temporal dependencies which allows for a distinction between concrete execution sequences.

Control Flow Graphs.   Several approaches to program analysis use a control flow graph as static representation of the program execution. It is often used for analyses within compilers to optimize the compiled code (cf. Section 9.4 or Chapter 1 in [2]). A control flow graph describes all possible executions of a program, i.e., all different execution paths including all possible sequences of statements.

The fundamental element is a so-called ***basic block***, a kind of atomic segment of statements which are executed all at once. An execution of the block's first statement is always followed by an execution of all other statements of this block. Moreover, a jump to a basic block addresses always the block's first statement, all other statements cannot be reached from outside.

A control flow graph represents basic blocks as nodes, which are connected by edges, denoting in which order the blocks can be executed. In contrast to a call graph, an edge does not represent call dependencies, but denotes which basic block can be executed after another basic block (loops can also cause edges to the same block).

The graph is recursively constructed following all possible executions until a basic block does not call others blocks and the program execution would stop. For programming languages with function calls, procedure calls or method calls as direct language constructs, at first a partial control flow graph is computed for every body of their declarations. These partial graphs are then composed with the control flow graph of the program using a pushdown automaton. The pushdown automaton is used to determine the correct basic block for every jump to method calls and in particular from method returns.

Limitations of Control Flow Graphs.   There are two general disadvantages when control flow graphs are used to represent the property execution sequence as used in AOP [3, 99]. On the one hand, the graph can only represent the property partially, and on the other hand, the recognition of specified properties within a control flow graph tend to be exhaustive. Often the complete graph has to be analyzed for detecting a specific execution sequence. If the identity between objects at different points in execution should also be evaluated, the graph additionally has to contain instantiations of objects and the variable values that store these objects. A standard control flow graph does not contain such information. Other but similar control flow analyses for the optimization compiled code (cf. [2], Section 10.3) use data flow analyses to compute such information. An analysis of the data flow could probably solve these issues, but is considered as out of the scope of this thesis.

Static Evaluation Issues. In general, an execution sequence could be represented in a similar way as the cflow property, except of using a control flow graph to represent corresponding paths. The paths could be annotated in the same way for indicating the likeliness of an execution, distinguishing definite, conditional, and multiple edges. A specified cflow property is detected in a call path, if two or more subsequently occurred triggers can be found. A specified execution sequence can be detected in a control flow, by matching the specified regular expression. The use of regular expressions, however, allows for unlimited possible sequences of trigger shadows. Even if the possibilities within a specific control flow are limited, the set of possibilities can be very huge.

A static evaluation of execution sequences is much more complex, but it is not impossible, even if regular expressions are used for specifying a particular sequence. *Model checking* approaches, for example, have provided solutions for such evaluation problems in other programming languages, e.g., the language C [14]. This tool was developed to detect safety-critical program states in C programs, which are described through regular expressions. An exact definition of the safety-critical segments in a control flow graph, however, is in this work not presented. Hence, we cannot claim that an execution sequence can be statically evaluated, and also if such a solution would sufficiently perform in daily work with refactoring tools. Nevertheless, we have found several indicators that make it really hard to think of such a solution. Especially, if the most computation effort needs to be spend during that refactoring process.

5.3.4 Static Evaluation of Cflow Properties

As foundation for the evaluation of cflow properties we use the enhanced call graph as described in Section 5.3.3.1. The evaluation computes for every call path between start- and end-trigger shadows a possible matches of a given cflow property. A single cflow match is again a path, a so-called **match path**. The computation of match paths determines dynamic dependencies under which an end-trigger can occur in a call path, which would lead to an advice invocation. The resulting match paths are the starting point for the following detection of change effects on the cflow property.

The evaluation process comprises three major phases. In the first phase, all start- and end-trigger shadows are determined. In the second phase, all irrelevant shadows are filtered, i.e., all start- and end-trigger shadows with no potential call dependency are ignored for the further analysis. This filtering of irrelevant shadow pairs is the major reason for computing the call graph. Finally, the third phase computes the qualified match paths, i.e., every match path is annotated with its execution likeliness: definite, conditional or multiple. The last two phases of this evaluation process are described in more detail.

5.3.4.1 Filtering Start- and End-trigger Shadows

All possible call graphs are constructed between any shadow of a start- and an end-trigger. These graphs are computed using the so-called Class Hierarchy Algorithm, or CHA algorithm [18]. Using the CHA algorithm the shadows of irrelevant start- and end-triggers can be filtered directly during the graph construction. The computation starts from every shadow of a potential start-trigger and results in a set of graphs, whose roots are represented by start-trigger shadows. In a next step, every graph is searched for cycles, which are marked and combined to a single node. Since any cycle is removed, all partial graphs can be decomposed into separated call paths. In the final step of this phase, the set of call paths is filtered to remove all any that cannot that does not connect a shadow of a start- and an end-trigger. The resulting set of call paths represent the set of unqualified match paths for the specified cflow property.

Partial graph construction. All partial graphs are constructed with the CHA algorithm, using a *Depth-First Search*, or DFS (cf. [17], Section 22.3). The primary advantage of this algorithm is that the detection of cycles can be prepared during the graph's construction. Every graph is completely constructed, i.e., every edge is created until the last single leave. If we construct for every edge its inverse edge at the same time, the graph is already prepared for the detection of cycles.

Cycle detection. In each graph, cycles are detected and combined to a single node. This transforms a directed cyclic call graph into a directed acyclic call graph; an essential requirement before separated call paths can be extracted. The cycles are identified through detecting strongly connected components (SCC) within a graph. A strongly connected component is a partial graph in which every node of the graph can be reached from any other node. The employed detection algorithm, originally developed by Tarjan [90], is able to detect SCCs in linear time. It is based on the numbering of nodes during their exploration, produced by the DFS algorithm, and it requires the inverse edges (cf. [17], Section 22.5). Every discovered SCC is combined to a single node.

Filtering of irrelevant paths segments. The directed and acyclic graphs still contain several segments that cannot be part of a path between the shadows of start- and end-triggers. We remove these segments by using the algorithm described in Figure 5.6. Starting from a start-trigger shadow the graph is traversed using the DFS algorithm (lines 3 and 4). Every edge that leads to a node which is neither a shadow of an end-trigger nor has subsequent nodes, i.e., it is a leave node, is removed from the graph (lines 5, 6 and 7). In this way, all successors of the start-trigger shadow are removed, which cannot lead to a valid end-trigger shadow. After their removal, the graph either still contains some successors or it is no successor left. The former case indicates that the current shadow is part of a valid match path between the start-trigger shadow and one

shadow of an end-trigger. In the latter case, the node will be removed if it is no shadow
of an end-trigger.

PRUNE(v)

1   v mark visited
2   **for** each successor s from v
3   **do if** s is not visited
4   **then** PRUNE(s)
5   **if** s is not an end-trigger-shadow or has no successors
6   **then** remove v as predecessor from s
7   remove s as successor from v

Figure 5.6: The algorithm for removing irrelevant call paths.

An illustrating example. The example depicted in Figure 5.7 will help to illustrate
the first phase of the computation of match paths. Figure 5.7 (Step (A)) shows a call
graph directly after its creation. It contains all call paths for a start-trigger, named (ST).
The nodes, labeled (ETx), represent shadows of end-triggers or their enclosing method
declaration. The SCCs in the graph are indicated through underlying gray areas, which
indicate the cycles in the graph.

Figure 5.7 (Step (B)) shows the graph after the SCCs were detected and combined to
single nodes. In this step, parallel edges are added to the graph, which are labeled with
the number of two parallel edges.

The final step, illustrated in Figure 5.7 (Step (C)), represents the result of the pruning
algorithm. The graph now contains only edges, which belong to a valid match path,
between shadows of a start- and an end-trigger.

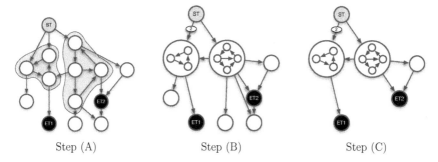

Step (A)   Step (B)   Step (C)

Figure 5.7: The individual steps of *Phase 1* in the creation of match paths.

We already explained in Section 5.3.3.1 that a basic call graph cannot sufficiently represent cflow properties. The representation of match paths created in this phase possesses
some of the required information (e.g., resolved cycles), but it is still to rough in terms

of execution likeliness. Mutual exclusions of different paths as well as the likeliness of a
path execution cannot be obtained from this representation.

5.3.4.2 Calculation of Qualified Match Paths

In *Phase 2* of the evaluation process the computed match paths are extended with information indicating the likeliness of their occurrence. We focus here on control flow statements (branches and loops) that enclose method calls and consider whether a method
call can be dynamically bound. This information is particularly necessary for detecting
change effects on cflow properties which alter the likeliness of their occurrence during
runtime.

To this end, we annotate the edges of a match path with additional attributes. Every
node of a match path is revisited, and enclosing control flow statements as well as possibilities for dynamically bound methods are identified. This step only considers method
calls that are represented as edges by the graph. Every edge in the graph is annotated
with this information, from which the execution likeliness of the complete match path
can be inferred.

Branches. For every control flow statement in a match path a unique identifier is created, the statement's type is determined and the number existing branches is ascertained.
Moreover, the maximum number of blocks that can possibly be executed for different
evaluations of the conditions is computed. For any of these blocks a unique identifier
is created, so different blocks at every branch can be distinguished. Also method calls,
whose method can be dynamically bound to different implementations, get a unique
identifier. The number of method bodies that can possibly be bound to the method call
is determined, and any of these methods gets a unique identifier.

With this information every execution possibility and the likeliness of its occurrence can
represented in the call graph. Moreover, for every edge in the graph an attribute is computed from this information. The attribute consists of an identifier, number of possible
branches and the identifier of the block or method which contains a (specific variant of
a) method call.

The programming language Java provides three different control flow statements (cf.
[33], Chapter 14). In this work, we discuss the treatment of `if-else` and `switch` statements in more detail. The `try-catch`, or `try-catch-finally`, construct and the related
`throw` statement is ignored within this thesis. Also directly defined jumps to labels are
not considered in this work. The developed prototype shows the feasibility of the analysis
approach, an additional treatment of these control flow constructs would make it more
complete, but is not necessarily required for a prove-of-concept prototype.

- The `if` statement introduces a conditionally executed block, i.e., one additional
  block, but two possible cases during execution. The `if-else` statement[1] even
  allows for mutually excluded blocks, i.e., it contains two blocks, which represent a
  separate execution behavior each. Moreover, `return` statements within these blocks

---

[1] The "? :" construct is another representation of the `if-else` control flow statement. It is treated
in the same way.

require a special treatment. The source code that follows a `return` statement is considered as an `else`-block, since it is only executed if the control flow does not follow the `return` statement.

- In `switch` control flow statements, the individual blocks (`case`, `default`) are selected by a specific value. The number of execution possibilities is defined by the number of contained blocks. Similar to `if` statements, these blocks need a special treatment regarding `break`, `return` and `continue` statements. The number of execution possibilities and mutual excluded paths are determined in the same way as for `if` statements.

Loops and Recursion. The representation for loops and recursion abstracts from the actual number of executions, as described in Section 5.3.3.1. All edges that belong to a loop statement or a recursive block are marked as *multiple edge*. In the programming language Java, three different loop statements are provided `while`, `do-while` and `for` (cf. [33], Chapter 14). It is obvious, that blocks of these loop statements can be treated in the same way. Every corresponding edge is marked as multiple edge, and annotated with the loop's identifier.

In the previous *Phase 1*, SCCs were already detected and specific nodes created that mark recursive parts in the graph. Every outgoing edge of these SCC nodes is marked as multiple edge and annotated with the SCC's identifier. Such identifiers enable a distinction between different multi-paths in the presence of mutual exclusive match paths.

Partitioning of Partial Graphs into in discrete Match Paths. After all edges in the partial graphs were annotated, the graphs still contain overlapping paths, i.e., every graph has a single start-trigger shadow as root but several end-trigger shadows as leaves. In order to spilt each graph into a set of separated match paths, we traverse the inverse graph starting from the end-trigger shadows. For every end-trigger shadow a separate path is constructed.

The concrete algorithm for partitioning the graphs consists of two functions, $\text{SPLIT}(E)$ and $\text{GETPATHSET}(v)$. Both are described in Figure 5.8 using a pseudo code notation. The first function $\text{SPLIT}(E)$ gets as input the set of all end-trigger shadows E for one partial graph. Starting from the shadow of the first end-trigger the graph is partitioned for every shadow e in E into separate match paths using the function $\text{GETPATHSET}(v)$.

The function $\text{GETPATHSET}(v)$ recursively creates the path for every node. If it is performed with a node that has no predecessor, it creates a new path and adds it to the resulting set of match paths. Since every partial graph is traversed using the DFS algorithm, this happens only if the start-trigger shadow is reached. It is the only node in the graph without a predecessor (see lines 3 and 4). Is there a predecessor node, then every path that was constructed for the predecessors is extended with the current node and the paths of the predecessors are combined to a set of paths for the current node and returned (see lines from 6 to 10).

The algorithm visits all possible paths and adds every time it arrives the start-trigger shadow a new match path to the resulting set. This set of match paths corresponds the *cflow* representation, as described in Section 5.3.3.1. For every path the execution

Split(E)

1   $F \leftarrow \emptyset$ ▷ Partial graphs with end-trigger shadow as root.
2   **for** each end-trigger-shadow e from E
3   **do** $F \leftarrow F \cup \{\text{GetPathSet}(e)\}$
4   **return** F

GetPathSet(v)

1   $R \leftarrow \emptyset$ ▷ Set of resulting paths.
2   **if** v has no predecessors
3   **then** $P \leftarrow \{v\}$ ▷ Create new path from v.
4            $R \leftarrow R \cup \{P\}$
5   **else**   ▷ Add v to paths of predecessors.

6   **for** each predecessor p from v
7   **do** $PS \leftarrow \text{GetPathSet}(p)$
8   **for** each P from PS
9   **do** $P \leftarrow P \cup \{v\}$
10                             $R \leftarrow R \cup \{P\}$
11 **return** R

Figure 5.8: The algorithm for splitting all partial graphs into a set of separate match
          paths.

likeliness can directly be determined. Only for paths with conditional edges, it can be
necessary to compare the edges' attributes in all paths possessing these edges, in order
to determine if the path is a conditional or a definite path.

5.4 The Pointcut Model

Our analysis approach uses a specific model for evaluating the properties specified by
pointcuts for a particular program. This so-called *pointcut model* is built for every pointcut defined in the program. It abstracts from the concrete syntax of the employed pointcut language and represents every single specification of a property through a separate
pointcut expression. A *pointcut expression* (PCE) refers to a single joinpoint property,
or to be more precise, to a property of an element of a program representation that is
used to represent the joinpoint's property.
Such a representation of property specifications leads to two major advantages: (i) every
expression refers to a single program representation and (ii) every expression holds the
specification of a single property. This significantly simplifies the detection of program
elements that correspond to a single property and allows for a distinct assessment of
change effects on single part of a pointcut.

The pointcut model is created by parsing the concrete syntax elements of a pointcut language and a subsequent decomposition of every partial specification into a tree of pointcut expressions. The model represents pointcut expressions as nodes and the evaluation dependencies between different expressions as directed edges. In general, the pointcut model provides a separate set of pointcut expressions for program representations that are most commonly used in AOP, such as the program's name space, code containment, static type hierarchy and the program's call graph. Pointcuts of every pointcut language, that specifies properties of joinpoints in a declarative way, can generally be translated in such a pointcut model. The model was evaluated for the pointcut language of AspectJ.

5.4.1 Notation Remarks

In the following sections, we use a simple textual representation of the model to illustrate what properties are specified by pointcuts, how the specification is represented and which parts of the specification are affected by a change. The textual representation comprises the following syntactical elements:

- *Property* – A single term with a capitalized first letter denotes a type of a joinpoint property.

- *VARIABLE* – A completely capitalized term denotes a free variable parameter for an arbitrary string.

- *< Property >* – Terms within brackets denote a list of nodes. The list is ordered and every contained node is of the specified type.

- *expression*(*Property*) → *Property* – Pointcut expressions are specification that may get parameters (or list of parameters) and denote a single property of a program representation.

5.4.2 Static Properties

The pointcut model provides separated set of expressions to specify properties relating to element names, code containment, usage and inheritance relationships. The underlying static program representations are directly obtained from the program code.

5.4.2.1 Name-based Properties

The program's name space contains all named elements of a program, i.e., all declaring elements. Such elements are e.g., packages, types, constructors, methods, and fields. The pointcut model provides expressions that take an element's signature as input and return a name-based property that can be matched with elements of a program representation:

$method(< Modifier >, \ TypeProperty, \ NAME, \ < TypeProperty >) \rightarrow$
$MethodProperty$
$field(<Modifier>, \ TypeProperty, \ NAME) \rightarrow FieldProperty$
$type(<Modifier>, \ NAME) \rightarrow TypeProperty$
$package(<Modifier>, \ NAME) \rightarrow PackageProperty$

The free variable parameter $NAME$ denotes the element's simple name and also allows wildcards for specifying partial names. All name-based expressions refer to the program's name space, which makes them fragile against every change with effects on declaring elements.

5.4.2.2 Usage-based Properties

Usages of a declared program element, or references, cannot be selected by a name, because they do not possess a unique name. Among these elements are obviously method calls, field accesses, constructor invocations, but also other elements such as the block of methods, constructors and initializers are accessed by usage-based expressions. In general, all usages of any declaring element can be selected from the program's AST, using, e.g., the following expressions:

$call(MethodProperty) \rightarrow Property$
$get(FieldProperty) \rightarrow Property$
$set(FieldProperty]) \rightarrow Property$
$staticinitializer(TypeProperty) \rightarrow InitializerProperty$

These pointcut expressions take a set of declaring elements as input and return a set of program elements.

5.4.2.3 Containment- and Inheritance-based Properties

The access to other static program representations such as code containment and the static type hierarchy is provided by expressions like:

$within(Property, Property) \rightarrow Property$
$contains(Property, Property) \rightarrow Property$
$subtypes(TypeProperty) \rightarrow Property$
$supertypes(TypeProperty) \rightarrow Property$

The *within* expression gets two sets of program elements and returns any elements of the second set that is contained by an element of the first set. The *contains* expressions indicates the opposite containment relationship. The type inheritance related expressions return either all sub types or all super types for every type in the input set.

5.4.3 Dynamic Properties

The pointcut model also provides pointcut expressions for specifying dynamic properties, such as relating to dynamic typing and an execution's stack trace. These specifications do not actually select a node within the dynamic program representation, we use approximations of these representations instead. Every selected node is a conservatively approximated representation of an element with the specified runtime properties, i.e., we select more elements for a specified property as actually occur during runtime.

5.4.3.1 Dynamic Type-based Properties

The dynamic type of a program element is approximated using static type inheritance relationships. We provide expressions to specify the type of the element currently under execution ($this$), of the element targeted by the flow of control ($target$) and the parameters ($args$). Every expression returns a set of possible type, rather than the actual dynamic type:

$$this(TypeProperty) \rightarrow Property$$
$$target(TypeProperty) \rightarrow Property$$
$$args(<TypeProperty>) \rightarrow Property$$

These expressions receive a single type (or a list of types) and return an approximation of all statically possible types.

5.4.3.2 Cflow Property

The cflow property specifies a required containment of a specific stack trace. We use a specific call graph as approximation of any possible stack trace (cf. Section 5.3.3.1). The cflow property can be specified as follows:

$$cflow(Property, Property) \rightarrow Property$$

A $cflow$ expression receives two sets of expressions and returns $true$ if there exists at least one possible match path (cf. Section 5.3.4) in the call graph from an expression of the first set ($start$-$triggers$) to an expression of the second set (end-$triggers$).

5.4.3.3 Conditionals

Conditionals in pointcuts express execution conditions by utilizing application runtime values. Since our pointcut model is based on static program representations, we conservatively approximate every conditional expression with $true$:

$$if(*Expression) \rightarrow Property$$

Every specified conditional within a pointcut is represented by an if-expression, which always evaluates to $true$.

5.4.4 Logic Combinations

In addition, pointcut expressions can be composed through logical combinations of *or* (∥), *and* (&&), *not* (!) to specify more complex properties. The *and* and *not* expressions can be used to filter elements from a given element set:

$$or(< Property >) \rightarrow Property$$
$$and(< Property >) \rightarrow Property$$
$$not(Property) \rightarrow Property$$

The *or* expression combines any set of the given list of elements sets to a set union, whereas the *and* expression filters elements and return only elements that are contained in every set (intersection). The *not* expression denotes a specific set of elements that is excluded, particularly used in combination with *and* properties.

With these compositors, almost every pointcut can be decomposed into a representation of elementary expressions.

5.4.5 Examples

The developed pointcut model is an intermediate representation for pointcuts which can generally be used for any declarative pointcut language. In this section, we give a few more examples to illustrate how pointcuts can be decomposed into this representation. For example pointcut, we state the informal meaning, the specification within a concrete pointcut language and our intermediate representation. The pointcut model (PM) for each example pointcut is described in a corresponding textual representation.

The pointcut from the **running example** of Section 5.2 *"selects all executions of any field assignment to a field of type* `int`*"*. It can be represented by the pointcut model as follows:

AspectJ: set(int *)
 PM: $set(field(<..>, type("int"), "*"))$

The pointcut is fairly simple, but the pointcut model effectively demonstrates the dependencies of specified properties. The expression *type()* is the most nested expression, thus, any effect on its selection could affect the evaluation results of any other expression in the pointcut. In addition, the model indicates that the pointcut refers to expression-level and declaration elements using only the program's name space.

Pointcut: *"Select all executions of method calls contained in method* `setLastName-` `(String)` *of class* `Customer` *or its subclasses."*

AspectJ: call($*$ $*$(..)) && **withincode**($*$ Customer+.setLastName(String))
PM:
$within($
$\quad within($
$\quad\quad subtypes(type("Customer")),$
$\quad\quad method(<..>, type(" * "), "setLastName", <type(String)>)),$
$\quad call(method(<..>, type(" * ")," * ", <..>)))$

The decomposition, again, makes all referenced program representations explicit, i.e., program's name space, containment and inheritance relationships. In addition, any specified property and its direct dependencies are made explicit. A tool can easily determine that the pointcut above selects the `class Customer` only by specifying its name, whereas the method `setLastName(String)` is specified by its name, parameter type list, location in the source and its containment.

Furthermore, the model for this pointcut effectively demonstrates the employed scope for specified name patterns. The specified method name "setLastName" is scoped through an inheritance relationship and therefore depends on (the deeper nested) type name "Customer".

Pointcut: *"Select all method calls of* `foo(int, String)` *of any type with* `Test*`*, that are within* `MyClass.bar()`*":*

AspectJ: call(public $*$ Test$*$.foo(**int**, String)) && **withincode**($* *$ MyClass.bar())
PM:
$and($
$\quad call($
$\quad\quad within($
$\quad\quad\quad type("Test*"),$
$\quad\quad\quad method(<public>, type(" * "), "foo", <type("int"), type("String")>))),$
$\quad within($
$\quad\quad type("MyClass"),$
$\quad\quad method(<..>, type(" * "), "bar", <type(VOID)>)))$

This pointcut uses a name pattern "Test*" to specify a partial part of a type name. The pointcut model makes any other expression that depends on this partially specified property explicit. A refactoring tool can calculate matching elements and consider the completeness of an expression if one of these matching elements is changed.

Pointcut: *"Select any execution of all method calls located within method* `B.update()`*"*

XQuery: $db:all/bat:**class**[@name="B"]/bat:method[@name="update"]/bat:invoke
PM: $within($
$\quad type("B"),$
$\quad within($
$\quad\quad method(<..>, type(" * "), "update", <..>),$
$\quad\quad call($
$\quad\quad\quad method(<..>, type(" * ")," * ", <..>))))$

The pointcut specifies an containment path using the XQuery syntax. Our pointcut model directly maps the path to *within* expressions and just completes the representation with unspecified information. Both the XQuery pointcut and the pointcut model directly represent the dependencies between specified joinpoint properties.

Limitations.   One major limitation of the current realization of our pointcut model is a lack of support for unification. Unification allows for even more complex combinations and would require the introduction of identifiers for expressions. The current pointcut model could be extended as shown by the following pointcut:

LMP: ?jp matching reception(?jp, ? selector , <?arg, ?arg>)
PM: $and($
$execution(<..>, type(" * "), " * ", <v1, v2>),$
$same(v1, v2))$

The (LMP) pointcut specifies the identity of two successive arguments of an arbitrary method invocation of arbitrary objects. The identity is specified using a specific through unification. The pointcut model could provide an additional expression that indicates the identity of expression results (*same*). Generated *variables* would serve as identifiers, so the same evaluation results could be specified at several parts in the model. Unification in logic meta programming can additionally be used in nested expressions, which can make it in general difficult to represent evaluation dependencies. Since our pointcut model aims to represent dependent properties directly, we believe that more research is required to reveal concrete influences of unification on evaluation dependencies.

5.5 The Pointcut Selection Model

The *pointcut selection model* is the result of the pointcut resolution that evaluates all pointcuts for a particular program. It stores every program element that exhibits a specified property, i.e., elements that exhibit all specified properties (pointcut matches) as well as partially corresponding elements (e.g., pointcut anchors).

5.5.1 A Pointcut's Selection

A pointcut can specify several properties of joinpoints to select them for an interaction with an aspect. In fact, a pointcut specifies a single property that is composed from other properties, either through composition (the property uses others as parameter input) or by combination with logic operators. In the latter case, obviously the used logic operator represents the topmost property. The pointcut model is created for a specific pointcut and contains a so-called root expression that represents the specification of all addressed properties. All other expressions specify a partial set of properties and can again contain further expressions. A program element which corresponds to a partial property, i.e., a subset of the pointcut expressions, is called *property match*. Whereas a program element that corresponds to the root expression, i.e., all specified properties, is called *pointcut match*.

Pointcut expressions generally specify properties of nodes in program representations. Such nodes can either represent program elements whose executions are considered as joinpoints or other elements that are used to express a certain property. The former elements are called joinpoint shadows and represent a static projection of a joinpoint into the program code. The latter are called pointcut anchors, because they are used to specify a context in which a property can be identified. In the example, the pointcut `set(field(type(int), *))` refers to the fully qualified name of `type int`, any field declaration of type int, even if the actual joinpoint is located somewhere else. Every pointcut expression of the decomposed pointcut explicitly refers to the program representations that are used to describe the a joinpoint property.

Based on the distinction between property and property match we use the term pointcut selection as follows. A pointcut selection contains every element of a program that matches a (partial or complete) property specified by a pointcut. For every property match it maps the specification of the property (pointcut expression) to the matching program elements. In other words, a pointcut selection holds every program element, including pointcut matches, joinpoint shadows, and pointcut anchors, referenced by a pointcut via any program representation used to specify a certain property.

5.5.2 Computation of the Pointcut Selection Model

The pointcut selection is computed by a so-called pointcut resolver. The resolver receives a pointcut model that represents the dependencies between the pointcut expressions. It traverses the pointcut model and computes a stack of pointcut expressions representing the inverse order of dependencies. Every stack level contains a list of expressions that can either be independently evaluated or refer to results of already evaluated expressions (of a previous stack level).

Before the pointcut resolver processes every stack level, it computes an abstract syntax graph (ASG) for the program that represents the program's name space, code containment, usage, and static inheritance relationships. The resolver processes the first stack level, evaluating all specified static properties. In the last step, the resolver computes the call graphs for specified cflow properties and computes its match paths. Such a pointcut selection is computed for every pointcut defined in the program. The resulting pointcut selection model contains the pointcut selection for every pointcut in the program.

5.5.3 Static Properties

Static properties relate to a name, a containment, or an inheritance relationship. Such properties are completely comprised by a single program element, hence matches of the corresponding pointcut expression can be attached to the single element. For every matching program element a separate property match is created. The resulting *pointcut selection model* (*PSM*) contains one pointcut selection for every existing pointcut and is defined as follows:

Definition 5.1: The *pointcut selection model* (PSM) is defined as the tuple $PCM \times PCE \times PM$ of the set of matching pointcuts (PSM), the corresponding pointcut expressions (PCE), and the actual property matches (PM).

The pointcut selection model associates for every matching pointcut the matching pointcut expression (PCE) with the property matches (PM), the program elements that corresponds to the pointcut expression.

5.5.4 Dynamic Properties

A property match for dynamic PCEs differs from static matches as it has its selection in a runtime representation which cannot be directly mapped to the program code. In Section 5.3 we already stated which issues arise with the approximation of runtime representations. According to that, a statically approximated match of a dynamic property indicates only the possibility for an execution in which this selection exists.

A *cflow* property, for example, requires that a call, specified in the PCE as the start-trigger, must be on the stack trace before a potential joinpoint shadow (specified as end-trigger) really produces the joinpoint when executed. This means, that every program element that fulfills the static properties specified in the *cflow*'s end-trigger PCE is a potential *cflow* property match. A selection that only covers *cflow* end-trigger's would be the most conservative approximation. Such a representation would serve the purpose of detecting a change effects on cflow properties only in a very limited way. Only changes regarding the end-trigger PCE would be detectable. Handling the start-trigger PCE accordingly, would not improve the situation much. Changes to the stack trace containment, the meaning of a *cflow* property, are not reflected.

The aforementioned call graph can be used as a static approximation to obtain more precise results. The call graph is used as a basis for representing stack trace based containment, i.e., the existence of a path in this graph between a start-trigger and an end-trigger element indicates such a containment. Subgraphs for each combination of start- and end-trigger PCE matches are used to represent every possible path between the two elements. Any change to the program that can possibly affect the stack trace containment between two elements will be detectable in the subgraph containing an altered set of paths between start- and end-trigger elements.

Not only the number of paths, but also the quality of a path can be affected by a change. The fact that an end-trigger PCE match is located in the path of a start-trigger in both (original and refactored) program versions, does not always mean that the *cflow* property is unaffected. It is possible that a definite path for at least one execution in the original version is modified to a probably executed path in the refactored version. This could happen, if for example a call between the start- and the end-trigger is moved into an `if` control statement. Taking that into account, we define the property match for *cflow* properties as follows:

Definition 5.2: The *cflow match* PM_{cflow} can be defined as a tuple PM_{cflow} : $PM_{start-trigger} \times PM_{end-trigger} \times Q$, representing every permutation of start- and end-triggers including the quality (Q) that states whether an execution of

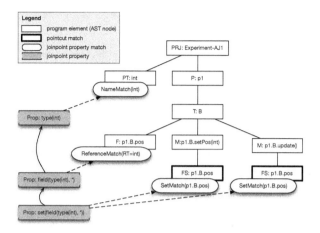

Figure 5.9: Pointcut selection for the unchanged program

a start-trigger will definitely ($DEFINITE$) or potentially ($POTENTIAL$) leads to an execution of an end-trigger.

The pointcut selection contains the cflow matches with the respective subgraph (possibly empty) for each pair of start- and end-triggers. Using the pointcut selection model we can define the resolution of all pointcuts as a function that receives all program elements (P) of a concrete implementation and the pointcut model (PCM) that comprises all defined pointcuts:

> **Definition 5.3:** The *pointcut resolution* is defined as function *resolve* : $P \times PCM \longrightarrow PCM \times PCE \times PM$ that evaluates all pointcuts in PCM for program P and in a pointcut selection model.

5.5.5 Example

Figure 5.9 shows the pointcut selection for set(int *) of our example program. It holds all program elements that are directly referenced by the pointcut, including their parent nodes, before the refactoring is applied.

5.6 Change Impact Classification

The change impact analysis computes an explicit representation of the impact, stating which kind of transformation causes new or lost matches for which expression of the pointcut. This representation contains any information about affected pointcut expressions and the changes that cause the effects. It can be used to assess the effects on the program behavior that is selected by a pointcut. Since this behavior is selected by a specification, we can distinguish changes that:

- alter the program behavior that corresponds to the specification

- modify properties of program representations that are used to recognize this behavior

Both kinds of changes cause a different set of selected joinpoints and, thus, affect the composed program behavior. The former alters the behavior of the base program (rarely achieved through refactoring), which changes how often a specified behavior occurs at runtime. The latter changes properties that are specified by pointcuts in order to recognize a specific behavior. The same behavior cannot be identified by the pointcuts, because they expect joinpoints with the original, unchanged, properties. This kind of changes alter the meaning of pointcuts for a given program, and, hence, affect the pointcut semantics. Such changes affect always properties of pointcut anchors (including joinpoint shadows), i.e., the assumptions under which the pointcut was defined.

In the presentation of our analysis approach, we do not consider the first kind of changes, because all pointcuts still select the joinpoints in the execution of the base program that are associated with the same properties, even if they occur more or less often at runtime. For the second kind of changes we developed an impact classification, that categorizes the impact on affected properties in terms of their specification.

A refactoring affects elements of program representations that are selected by properties. If it modifies a property of such a pointcut anchor, the refactoring tool has to determine whether affected pointcut expressions clearly state that the modified element is supposed to be selected. The most difficult part is to assess how much information needs to be specified that a pointcut expression clearly references an individual element.

Another important issue is the approximation of dynamic properties by static representations. The *analyzability of properties*, however, cannot be directly measured. We only distinguish three kinds of dynamic properties: runtime value-based, dynamic type-based and call graph based properties. Runtime values are considered as not analyzable, whereas dynamic types can be properly approximated by the corresponding static type hierarchy. Cflow properties are approximated with call graphs as described above. Any other property treated by our analysis approach is properly represented within our static representation.

In order to determine if an anchor selecting pointcut expression should be preserved or adjusted, we define the following indicators.

5.6.1 Specification Completeness

A pointcut can specify properties of a static or dynamic program representation more or less complete. Incomplete specifications were introduced to pointcut languages by signature patterns, which may only specify some parts of a signature and can also contain partial name patterns. We consider a joinpoint property as completely specified if all parts of every employed signature pattern are defined and no partial naming is used.

The *specification completeness* indicates how complete a matching property is specified by its corresponding pointcut expression. It measures the completeness of any signature

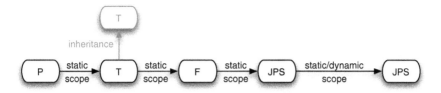

Figure 5.10: The scoping path for different kinds of program elements.

pattern that is used to specify the property. The specification completeness correlates the number of unspecified and partially specified parts to the number of expected parts of a signature pattern. We define the specification completeness SC of a pointcut PCE as the average completeness of all contained sub-expressions:

$$SC(PCE) = \frac{1}{|PCE|} \sum_{i=0}^{|PCE|} SC(e_i) : \forall e_i \in PCE$$

A property is completely specified (100%) if any part of employed signature patterns is fully defined. Incomplete parts, such as partial names or partial parameter lists, are counted with 50%, while undefined parts are considered with 0%.

For example, the expression $method(< .. >, type(" * "), "set * ", < type(" * ") >)$, would match the method signature of method `setLastName(String)` in class `Customer`. The specification completeness of the *method* expression would be 33%, because two of the three specification parts are partially defined[2]. We consider a particular match as more important for a set of selected joinpoints as more complete the corresponding expression is specified.

5.6.2 Match Scope

Another indicator for the importance of a matching element is the *match scope*. It indicates whether an affected pointcut expression is used to select a single or multiple elements. The match scope roughly approximates the path of (defined) scopes that leads to a selected program element. This path is illustrated in Figure 5.10. It can be compared with a fully qualified name, even if it may be incompletely specified and can lead to several elements. The figure depicts a path with kinds of program elements, like package (P), types (T), features (F) and joinpoint shadows (JPS). Shadows are any program element that can be contained by a feature (e.g., constructors, methods, fields), such as calls, field accesses, or method blocks.

The match scope measures the how many of these elements along the scoping path are specified by a pointcut. For example, consider a method call that is selected by a pointcut. The match scope indicates whether the pointcut restricts the location of the call (feature), its enclosing feature, the feature defining type and the type's package is

---

[2]The list of modifiers is ignored for the specification completeness as too unspecific information.

Classifier	Kind of scope	Focus	Measure
behavioral scope	control flow	statement	100
	inheritance	method	
	containment	operation	
lexical scope		type	25
		package	5
unscoped	no	no	0

Table 5.1: Definition of the execution semantics measure.

specified. We define the match scope as the relation of the number of specified path elements to the path length:

$$MS(match) = \frac{|PATH|}{len(PATH)} : match \in PATH$$

The match scope considers for static scoping expressions that define containment-based or inheritance-based scopes. However, inheritance-based scopes are ignored for the measure, because our representation does not distinguishes between different types of a type hierarchy. For the dynamic scope only cflow-based scopes are additionally considered between different joinpoint shadows.

The more a matching element is scoped by expressions of a pointcut, the more important is this very element for the pointcut.

5.6.3 Execution Semantics

A pointcut can specify properties with a different degree of behavioral meaning. There are properties with no behavioral meaning, like unscoped names, and properties with a particular meaning during the execution of the program, such as the cflow property. A more detailed differentiation and illustrating examples are presented in Section 2.4.2.

It is obviously not possible to measure the degree of a property's meaning by a single number. But we can at least distinguish properties that are connected with a certain behavior and properties that have no behavioral meaning at all. To this end, we introduce a distance measure that indicates how close the selected elements are related to a specific program behavior. The Table 5.1 shows the particular metric values. Selected names or elements that are restricted by a behavioral scope are counted as 100% and unscoped selections as 0% of behavioral meaning. The two values in between are low indicators to distinguish scoped elements from completely unscoped ones.

5.6.4 Degree of Dependency

The anchors of a pointcut represent the context in which an extrinsic joinpoint property can be identified. Pointcut anchors are also selected by a property, which again can be specified using other anchors. Every additional dependency level raises the need for that very anchor, because more properties depend on its existence. We use the evaluation dependencies between pointcut expressions in decomposed pointcuts as indicator for the anchor dependencies.

Nesting Level	0	1	2	>2
Measure	33	66	100	100

Table 5.2: Definition of the dependency measure.

The **nesting level** of a pointcut expression indicates the degree of evaluation dependencies. The deeper an expression is nested the more other expressions depend on its evaluation results. A comparison of the nesting in pointcuts of multiple AOP projects has given a strong indication, even without hard evidence, that expressions with a deeper nesting than level 2 can hardly be differentiated in their importance for the pointcut's evaluation result. We therefore distinguish the first three nesting levels in their importance, as shown in Table 5.2. Expressions at nesting level 0 specify the joinpoint shadows whose executions represent selected joinpoints. Any further nested expression specifies an anchor property. Expressions at level 2 (or deeper) tend to cause a complete loss of selected joinpoints, while expressions at level 1 have not always such significant effects on the set of selected joinpoints. The Table 5.2 shows the measurement that results from these observations.

Any aggregated expression is treated in this way, except of *OR expressions*. An *OR* expression denotes separated sets of joinpoints, thus any contained expression is considered as a separated specification of an individual joinpoint selection. Nested *OR* aggregations require an additional treatment, a so-called *normalization*. Any pointcut with nested *OR* aggregations is normalized into a disjunctive normal form (DNF), expressing commonly specified joinpoint properties within a logical formula combined by "||" operators. In this way, the *OR* expression are pulled up to the first nesting level, i.e., level 0. The impact analysis teats any constituent expression separately.

5.6.5 Match Impact

A refactoring can cause multiple added or lost joinpoints. Our analysis approximates joinpoints as pointcut matches within static program representations. The *match impact* indicates the effects on the pointcut matches (PM) in the program representations for the refactored program. It measures how many matches of the pointcut's root expression are affected by a certain refactoring, i.e., how many added and lost matches are caused. The match impact MI on a pointcut PCE is defined by the number of altered matches divided through the number of matches in both program versions:

$$MI(PCE) = \frac{|((PM_{org} \bigcup PM_{ref}) - (PM_{org} \bigcap PM_{ref}))|}{|(PM_{org} \bigcup PM_{ref})|}$$

The match impact computes the relationship between altered and total matches in both program versions. The more matches are altered by a refactoring, the bigger is the effect on the program behavior. A change of multiple pointcut matches can only be intended if the affected pointcut expression is completely specified.

5.7 Summary

In this chapter, we have presented our change impact analysis for pointcuts. We have given an overview of the complete analysis process in Section 5.1, describing each analysis step and its role in the process. Furthermore, we have presented an example program in Section 5.2 and illustrated the analysis model computed in every analysis step by this example.

A major part of this chapter (Section 5.4) investigates possibilities for approximating dynamic joinpoint properties. The characteristics of commonly used dynamic program representations, i.e., object graph and execution history, are compared and the properties that can be specified by existing pointcut languages are described. We have developed a model for statically representing properties of the execution history and discussed limitations of this model in particular for cflow and execution sequence properties.

We have highlighted especially the differences in computation effort and accuracy for static representations of these properties. While cflow properties can be statically represented by partial call graphs, execution sequence properties require a complete control flow graph that covers every possible program execution. In addition, we have pointed out that control flow graphs are more fine-grained. They consider all possible execution sequences of basic blocks as atomic segment of statements and not only call dependencies of program elements like call graphs. Control flow graphs are therefore not only inherently more expensive, an execution sequence property additionally requires the complete graph for any possible execution of the program. We have concluded that static approximations of execution sequence properties are too expensive (in terms of computation time) to evaluate during a refactoring, their static evaluation is too imprecise (in terms of false positives) particularly if they are specified by regular expression and invalidated specifications cannot be updated by a tool. For this reasons, we believe that effective refactoring support cannot be provided for execution sequence properties. Also potential alternatives for our static analysis approach, like model checking, are discussed in Section 5.3.3.

For cflow properties an extended call graph as static representation is presented in Section 5.3.3 and an algorithm for evaluating cflow properties on this graph. The algorithm not only detects cycles, but also computes cflow matches as qualified match paths. These paths indicate the execution likeliness of every cflow match (definite, conditional, or multiple) at runtime. This way, a refactoring is enabled to detected changes of the execution likeliness in addition to alterations of complete paths.

In Section 5.4 we have presented our intermediate representation for pointcuts. The representation is textually described and used for any following presentation of change effects. Our refactoring tool uses the intermediate representation of pointcut for the detection of change effects and computation of updates. We have described the model and highlighted two major advantages of this model: every joinpoint property is specified by a single pointcut expression and evaluation dependencies between properties are made explicit. Several examples are presented to how pointcuts can be decomposed into our intermediate representation.

The static evaluation of joinpoint properties determines all program elements that are referenced by a pointcut and results in our pointcut selection model. In Section 5.5 we have shown that the direct association of matching program elements and corresponding pointcut expression lead to several advantages. Since we detect change effects on point-cuts by comparing the matching elements for the original and the refactored program version, any associated expression represents the affected part of the pointcut. This association between code changes and affected pointcut parts is the key information that enables the assessment of the impact on the pointcut.

For the impact assessment, we have proposed five impact measures which classify the change effects in terms of the affected pointcut. The specification completeness indicates how complete an affected expression is defined. The match scope measures how precise an affected expression specifies an altered match. The execution semantics denotes how close a specified property is related to a particular program behavior and the degree of dependency indicates how many other pointcut expressions depend on an affected expression. Finally, the match impact is used to measure the number of altered matches.

The presented analyses, advanced program representations, and impact measures are used in the following chapter to infer update decisions and compute suitable adjustments for invalidated pointcuts.

Chapter 6

Computation and Generation of Pointcut Updates

The change impact analysis computes an explicit representation of the change effects, stating which transformation of the refactoring causes a new or lost match of which expression of the pointcut. Our impact indicators measure the change extent in terms of the pointcut and the set of selected joinpoints. However, they still need to be interpreted in oder to derive an update decision.

In this chapter, we define constraints for specific program transformations based on the impact measures and show how a tool can support the developer in deciding whether new or lost matches should be accepted or refused.

In Section 6.1 we give an overview of the update determination process describing how our refactoring tool SOOTHSAYER computes an update decision and how it generates the updated pointcut. In addition, we present the detailed decision criteria in Section 6.2 and explain how the impact measures are used to determine a particular decision. In Section 6.3 we present the algorithm for computing the least intrusive pointcut update and give illustrating examples.

6.1 Update Determination Process

Our refactoring tool determines pointcut updates in two phases. First, for each affected pointcut the tool determines whether the pointcut has to be updated. Second, the actual adjustment for the pointcut is computed. In this section we explain how affected pointcuts are distinguished from invalidated pointcuts and give an overview of the update determination process.

6.1.1 Invalidated vs. affected pointcuts

The joinpoints that are selected by a pointcut represent a particular program behavior. This target behavior is selected by a specification, i.e., every program behavior that corresponds to this specification is selected. Our program analysis approach approximates the target behavior through pointcut matches. Changes to the program behavior (even if rarely achieved through refactoring) do not affect the specification, they only alter how often it occurs at runtime. We consider a pointcut that matches a different set of joinpoints after a refactoring as affected, and define it as follows:

> **Definition 6.1:** A *pointcut is affected* by a refactoring if it matches differently in the original and refactored program version.

The change impact analysis computes the pointcut selection delta. If this delta contains additional or lost pointcut matches, then the tool regards a pointcut as affected. The delta can have entries because of a variety of reasons, which we have already discussed in Section 2.5. As a result, we distinguish changes that alter the set of selected joinpoints from changes that alter pointcut anchors. While the former results in affected pointcuts, the latter cause not necessarily a different set of selected joinpoints. Rather, it alters the assumptions under which the developer originally defined the pointcut, which may also lead to an effect on the pointcut's resolution result. We consider such a modification of pointcut anchors to be an alteration of the pointcut semantics which invalidates specifications of (extrinsic) joinpoint properties. We call such a pointcut invalidated and define it as follows:

> **Definition 6.2:** A *pointcut is invalidated* if it selects different anchors in the original and refactored program version.

Since joinpoint shadows are also anchors of the pointcut, we consider any pointcut with a changed program element in its selection to be an invalidated pointcut. A pointcut with an empty pointcut selection delta, i.e., with no altered match and no changed anchor, is considered as unaffected.

Pointcut anchors are also selected through specifications of their properties, which makes it difficult to determine whether a changed pointcut semantics is intended. The overall process for updating invalidated pointcuts is described in the following.

6.1.2 Process Overview

Figure 6.1 depicts the overall update computation process. For every pointcut in the change impact representation an update is computed, which proposes to keep the (original) pointcut, replace invalidated pointcut expressions, or extend the complete pointcut. As shown by Figure 6.1 the process consists of two phases. In the first phase the refactoring tool computes the *update decision* and in the second phase the actual *pointcut adjustment*.

Phase I: Update decision making. The update decision retrieves the change impact as computed by the impact analysis. If it contains any pointcut, the update determination process is invoked. It interprets the impact measures of invalidated expressions for new and lost anchor matches, and determines whether a modified anchor is supposed to be selected. This update decision making process is described in more detail in Section 6.2.

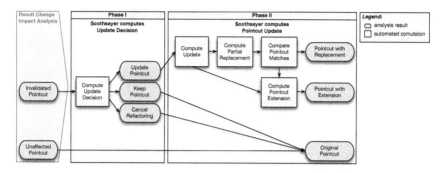

Figure 6.1: Overview of update determination process.

Phase II: Update computation. The update computation is performed for every point-cut that is marked as "to be updated", and results in an update proposal. In this phase, an algorithm tries to locate the affected pointcut expressions and also to compute a direct replacement. If such a partial replacement can be computed, the updated point-cut is evaluated again in order to ensure that this update causes no undesired pointcut matches. The resulting pointcut with the partial replacement is similar enough to the original pointcut that it is recognizable to its developer.

If no partial replacement can be computed or the evaluation of the updated pointcut fails, a verbose pointcut extension is computed. This extension explicitly includes lost or excludes additional anchor matches through a direct enumeration. The complete algorithm for computing adjusted pointcuts is described in Section 6.3.

6.2 Update Decision Making

Based on our impact measures we define two simple heuristics that provide different indicators for whether altered matches invalidate a pointcut. Both heuristics are used within a pointcut update decision table to automate the decision making.

6.2.1 Update Decision Criteria

Any invalidated pointcut causes additional and/or lost matches in the pointcut selection delta. Our analysis tries to determine for any of these matches if it should exist after the refactoring. To this end, we define two heuristics, the *specification quality* and *expression relevance*, which are used in the automation of the decision making.

Specification Quality. A program element can be explicitly selected by a pointcut or be just one of numerous matching elements. We use our *specification completeness* measure (cf. Section 5.6) to assess how complete the properties of a matching element are specified by a pointcut. In addition, we use the *match scope* measure to determine how much the selection of the corresponding expression is restricted to the matching element(s). Our impact representation associates any matching element with all corresponding expressions of a pointcut. The expression that specifies the most properties of a matching element is called ex_{max}, and its smallest sub-expression that is directly affected by the refactoring is called ex_{aff}. We define the specification quality as follows:

$$SQ(pm) = \frac{SC(ex_{aff}) \cdot \frac{1}{2}(100 + MS(ex_{max}))}{100}$$

with ex_{aff}, $ex_{max} \in PCE$; $pm \in PSM$

The heuristic is defined as a relation of specification completeness and match scope. The specification completeness is considered to be twice as important as the match scope, i.e., in the worst case a completely unscoped expression can reduce the value of the specification completeness by 50% .

The specification quality is computed for the directly affected expression (associated with the responsible transformation) using the match scope for the largest matching expression. The intention behind the heuristic is that fully scoped and completely specified matches are more desired by the developer than less precisely specified matching elements.

Expression Relevance. An affected pointcut expression can be more or less relevant for the evaluation of the complete pointcut. We define a heuristic as an indicator for this relevance using the *degree of dependency* and *execution semantics*. Both are defined in Section 5.6.

The *degree of dependency* uses the nesting level of an expression as the indicator for its relevance for the pointcut. The *execution semantics* indicates how close a specified property is related to a specific program behavior. Based on both measures we define the expression relevance as the zero-bounded difference:

$$ER(ex) = \begin{cases} DD(ex) - ES(ex) & \text{if } DD(ex) - ES(ex) > 0 \\ 0 & \text{if } DD(ex) - ES(ex) < 0 \end{cases} \text{ with } ex \in PCE$$

The relevance of a pointcut expression ex is defined by the degree of dependence of this expression minus its degree of execution semantics. Is the difference smaller than zero, then we just count it as zero. The intention behind this heuristic is that changes of behavioral properties are more likely to accept than changes of structural characteristics (like naming). However, the deeper an expression is nested in the pointcut the more unlikely can (amplified) effects on the resulting pointcut selection be intended.

6.2.2 Update Decision Procedure

With these heuristics we can automate the update decision making. Our decision making approach follows two general assumptions: (i) elements that match precisely defined expressions (high SQ) are wanted by the developer, and (ii) selections of deeply nested expressions must be preserved. For both heuristics we have defined an initial range that states how precise or relevant affected expressions have to be, so that they are considered as invalidated. We start with a quite conservative range, considering SQ 100% for precise, SQ 0% for unspecified and ER 60% for relevant.

Using these initial benchmarks we decide whether a pointcut PCE needs to be updated as follows:

$$SQ(m) = 0\% \rightarrow \begin{cases} NOUPDATE(ex) & \text{in any case} \end{cases}$$

$$0 < SQ(m) < 100\% \rightarrow \begin{cases} NOUPDATE(ex) & \text{if } ER(ex) < 60\% \\ UPDATE(ex) & \text{if } ER(ex) >= 60\% \end{cases}$$

$$SQ(m) = 100\% \rightarrow \begin{cases} NOUPDATE(ex) & \text{if added match} \\ UPDATE(ex) & \text{if lost match} \end{cases}$$

with $m \in PSM$, $ex \in PCE$

Using this table, our refactoring tool recommends to accept additional matches of unspecified or precisely specified expressions and to accept lost matches of (almost) unspecified expressions. Moreover, altered matches of expressions with an average precision are only accepted if the expression has a relevance of less than 60%.

6.3 Generation of Pointcuts

Pointcuts are specifications of properties, and thus, if these properties are changed, a new specification has to be generated. In contrast to general approaches to pointcut generation [10, 95], we can use for the generation of adjusted pointcuts the original pointcut and the change impact information. In this section we illustrate how pointcuts are updated and describe our algorithm for generating the least invasive pointcut update.

6.3.1 Pointcut Update Patterns

If the analysis has proposed to update an affected pointcut expression, the most straightforward approach would be to exclude unwanted or include lost matches. Our refactoring tool could extend the affected pointcut expression with an additional expression that specifies the exclusion or inclusion. Such a direct exclusion or inclusion of individual matches is proposed by other refactoring approaches for AOP [39, 78]. Following these approaches we can update an affected pointcut as follows:

$$pce(ap) = pce(ap) \parallel pce(ip) : ap \in PCE_{affected}, \; ip \in PCE_{incl}$$
$$pce(ap) = pce(ap) \;\&\&\; !pce(xp) : ap \in PCE_{affected}, \; xp \in PCE_{excl}$$

This explicit extension of pointcut expressions, however, leads to several disadvantages such as bloated pointcuts, which are already unrecognizable to the developer after only a few updates. A more sophisticated approach would check whether an affected pointcut expression can be replaced with a new expression. Such a replacement is possible in cases where all matches of the affected expression are altered (MI 100%) and the replaced expression captures comparable matches. This direct replacement of a pointcut expression can be defined as:

$$pce(ap) = pce(rp) : ap \in PCE_{affected}, \; rp \in PCE_{repl}$$

6.3.2 Update Computation Algorithm

In this section we describe the algorithm for determining whether an affected pointcut can be adjusted or if the refactoring needs to be canceled. Our algorithm tries to compute a replacement for the smallest affected pointcut expression. If this is not successful it creates an explicit extension of the pointcut. Figure 6.2 presents the algorithm in a semi-formal notation.

Update. Our update algorithm is performed with the computed impact representation, which contains the filtered pointcut selection delta of any affected pointcut. The invalidated expressions of these pointcuts have altered (property) matches and are labeled as "to be updated". The algorithm processes these pointcuts to produce valid pointcut updates.
It starts with an empty clone ex'_{root} (cf. Figure 6.2, line 1) and checks every expression ex in the original pointcut for whether it is invalidated. If so, then it is updated, whereas unaffected expressions are simply cloned. For invalidated expressions, the algorithm locates the smallest affected sub-expression, using the function FIND-SMALLEST-AFFECTED(ex, T).
This function recursively visits any sub-expression of ex and checks if it is associated with T. For the resulting ex_{small}, the algorithm determines the match impact (MI). If all matches of the expression are affected by the refactoring, the algorithm tries to replace the expression directly (line 6), using the function REPLACE. If not all matches are affected the algorithm cancels the computation of replacements and continues in line 12. Computed clones or replacements are inserted into the resulting pointcut ex'_{root}.
If invalidated expressions could be replaced, the algorithm compares the pointcut selections of the updated and the original pointcuts. If both selections contain the same set of unaffected and accepted altered matches (regarding the update decisions), the result of the algorithm is the updated pointcut. Otherwise, the original pointcut is extended with explicit exclusions and/or inclusions, using the function EXTEND.

Replace. The function REPLACE clones any expression of the given partial pointcut. Within this clone it locates the given invalidated expression and computes the affected part p of the this expression. If p is a simple parameter, p is replaced with the new value of T. Otherwise it is a nested expression and a more complex replacement is computed. The function CREATE-REPLACEMENT computes a new expression that completely specifies that signature of the matching element and is combined with a containment-based scope.

Extend. The function EXTEND clones all expressions of the given pointcut and locates any invalidated expression in the clones. For each invalidated expression, it finds the smallest affected sub-expression ex_{small}. For each of these, an explicit extension is computed using the function CREATE-REPLACEMENT.

This function uses the pointcut update patterns described in Section 6.3.1 to create an explicit exclusion for any additional match, and an explicit inclusion for any lost match.

6.3.3 Algorithm Issues

The algorithm benefits from the decomposed pointcuts (cf. Section 5.4). It can traverse every expression of our pointcut model and compute a replacement for any affected expression. Mutual interferences between different expressions can cause unexpected adjustments, e.g., if two directly nested expressions specify the opposite properties in the same program representation. For example, the expressions *within* and *contains* denote opposite relationships of the containment representation. The partial pointcut *contains(within(*
type(T), execution(method(ANY))), *call(method(m1)))* matches any method within type T that contains a call to method $m1$. If a matching method is moved to another type, the algorithm just replaces the *within* expression as the method still contains the specified calls.

Aggregated expressions (partial pointcut) can also be adjusted in this way if the directly affected expression can be ascertained. E.g., in the example above a move of the only matching method in type T to T2 would result in *contains(within(type(T2), execution(*
method(ANY))), *call(method(m1)))*.

Such a replacement can only be achieved if all matches of the affected expression are altered (MI = 100%). If only a partial set of matching elements is affected, the expression cannot be replaced because these matches would possibly be removed by the replacement. Thus, when the match impact differs from 100%, we always explicitly include or exclude altered matches.

If the algorithm proposes a direct replacement, we check the evaluation result of the updated pointcut before it is proposed. The expressions of a pointcut can be arbitrarily aggregated, or incompletely specified. They can also denote a dynamic property that is imprecisely approximated, hence the actual combination with replaced expressions can cause unintended pointcut matches. These matches are prevented by comparing the pointcut selection of the adjusted pointcut with the selection of the original pointcut.

The algorithm not only considers affected pointcuts. Every invalidated pointcut, i.e., "abstract" pointcuts which do not select a single joinpoint in the current program version, are also properly treated by our approach. As long as a refactoring causes an altered match of single pointcut expression, our approach can propose an update decision and (if proposed) compute a valid adjustment.

The actually implemented algorithm is slightly more complex than the algorithm presented in Figure 6.2. The presented algorithm illustrates the general idea of how we compute pointcut updates. It does not consider remove transformations, which can additionally require to cancel the refactoring if no adjustment can be computed. We have omitted the handling of remove transformations because it does not add anything relevant to the algorithm.

6.4 Summary

In this chapter we have described how a refactoring tool can be enabled to decide whether a given pointcut has to be updated, and how the least intrusive update can be computed. In particular, we have outlined the overall update determination process (Section 6.1) and presented its constituent phases. The first phase computes two heuristics to produce a qualitative update decision, the second phase determines the smallest affected pointcut expressions and tries to replace them.

In Section 6.2 we have defined both heuristics and described the update decision procedure. The first heuristic, specification quality, indicates how completely the pointcut expression defines the changed property and how much the expression restricts its selection to a specific scope. The second heuristic, expression relevance, indicates how much the specified property is execution related and how much the pointcut depends on the expression. Both heuristics use the impact measures that we have defined in the previous chapter and assess whether altered matches are accidental or intended. For this decision a predefined range is defined that suggests to accept new and lost matches of expressions that do not specify a property (SQ = 0%), and reject lost matches of highly specified properties. For specifications of an average quality it proposes to accept matches of less relevant expressions (ER < 60%), and reject them for more relevant expressions. This update decision is computed for each altered match and results in a set of invalidated pointcut expressions that are labeled "to be updated".

The computation of the actual pointcut updates is described in Section 6.3. In this section we have presented our algorithm for computing the least intrusive replacement, which is able to replace any invalidated expression whose matches are completely lost or new. The replacement specifies the same properties with the same completeness. If such a replacement is not possible, or only some matches are altered, then the algorithm instead proposes a explicit exclusion or inclusion of these matches. Any update restores the originally matching elements which were selected before the refactoring. If original matches cannot be recovered, e.g., because they were removed from the program, the algorithm proposes to cancel the refactoring.

We have also discussed limitations of the current version and highlighted a computation for incremental updates that narrow or broaden the scope of an update as the most crucial improvement for our algorithm.

Basically, our update decision algorithm proposes to accept effects on expressions that specify behavioral properties or expressions which are either precisely (new matches) or loosely (lost matches) enough specified. In any other case it tries to compute replacements for the smallest affected expressions, which restores the original pointcut matches and thus the original program behavior.

UPDATE(ex_{root}, T, P, P')

1   $ex'_{root} \leftarrow \emptyset$
2   **for** each sub-expression ex of ex_{root}
3   **do if** ex is invalidated
4   **then** $ex_{small} \leftarrow$ FIND-SMALLEST-AFFECTED(ex, T)
5   **if** $MI(ex_{small}) = 100$
6   **then** $ex' \leftarrow$ REPLACE(ex, ex_{small}, T)
7   **else goto** (12)
8   **else** $ex' \leftarrow$ CLONE(ex)
9   insert ex' in ex'_{root}
10 **if** RESOLVE(ex'_{root}, P', T) equals RESOLVE(ex_{root}, P, T)
11   **then return** ex'_{root}
12 **return** EXTEND(ex_{root}, T)

REPLACE($ex_{part}, ex_{invalid}, T$)

1   $ex'_{part} \leftarrow$ CLONE(ex_{part})
2   **for** each sub-expression ex in ex'_{part}
3   **do if** ex equals $ex_{invalid}$
4   **then for** each parameter p of ex
5   **do if** p is affected by T
6   **then if** p is simple parameter
7   **then** replace p with value of T
8   **else** $ex_{repl} \leftarrow$ CREATE-REPLACEMENT(p, T)
9   replace p with ex_{repl}
10 **return** ex'_{part}

EXTEND(ex_{root}, T)

1   $ex'_{root} \leftarrow$ CLONE(ex_{root})
2   **for** each sub-expression ex in ex'_{root}
3   **do if** ex is invalidated
4   **then** $ex_{small} \leftarrow$ FIND-SMALLEST-AFFECTED(ex, T)
5               $ex_{ext} \leftarrow$ CREATE-EXPLICIT-EXTENSION(ex'_{root}, ex_{small})
6   extend ex'_{root} with ex_{ext}
7   **return** ex'_{root}

Figure 6.2: The algorithm for updating invalidated pointcuts.

Chapter 7

Soothsayer: An Aspect-aware Refactoring Tool

Our refactoring approach is supported by an Eclipse-based refactoring tool called SOOTH-SAYER. The tool implements the proposed impact analysis, computation of update proposals and the generation of updated pointcuts. It extends the refactoring capability of the Eclipse JDT with the additional analyses and UI elements showing the analysis results and our impact visualization.

This chapter gives an overview of SOOTHSAYER's architecture and describes its constituent components implementing the impact analysis, static approximations, the pointcut adjustment and the impact visualization. In addition, we present important design decisions and describe how the developer is supported.

7.1 Architectural Overview

The presented refactoring approach has been implemented as extension to Eclipse. The developed tool, called SOOTHSAYER, consists of four different Eclipse-plugins and extends multiple Java refactorings of the Eclipse Java Development Tools (JDT) [22]. It provides an optimized structural representation of the source code and a call graph for approximating cflow properties. SOOTHSAYER implements the static resolution of pointcuts as presented in Section 5.5, the computation of the atomic change model (Section 4.2), and the proposed change impact analysis (Section 5.6). It also extends the JDT refactorings to detect affected pointcuts, to propose a pointcut update decision, and to compute an adjustment for invalidated pointcuts (cf. Chapter 6).

The Eclipse JDT is a well established IDE for the development of Java programs. It provides a plug-in concept that allows for almost arbitrary extensions of the JDT's data model, controls, and graphical user interface. Multiple development teams have used this plug-in concept to built different programming languages as extensions to Java.

One example is the tool support for the aspect-oriented programming language AspectJ. AspectJ extends Java with aspect-oriented development concepts and language mechanisms. Its developers are supported by the AspectJ Development Tools (ADJT) [1]. The

AJDT extends the JDT with core programming support for AspectJ and some advanced development tools. It provides an integrated compiler and build environment for compiling and deploying AspectJ programs. It supports the developer with a specific editor that highlights the AspectJ syntax elements and with an outline and cross references view that display the structure of aspect modules. In addition, advanced tools like the crosscutting view, markers, image decorators, and the aspect visualizer can inform the developer which parts of the program are adapted by an aspect and if a modification of an adapted part may influence the adaptation. Besides this general support for visualizing potential change effects on aspects, the AJDT provides no refactoring support.

The refactoring capability of the Eclipse JDT supports multiple refactorings for the programming language Java. They perform rename, move, extract, and inline transformations in a safe and automated way. The JDT provides a parser for Java source code that computes an AST as abstract representation. The refactoring support and also JDT extensions can access and manipulate Java source code by rewriting this abstract representation. A refactoring is carried out by performing program transformations that manipulate the program elements of the AST. Every transformation provides its change information, which can be used to predict what changes will be performed if a refactoring is carried out.

SOOTHSAYER extends the AJDT to make Java refactorings aware of their effects on aspects implemented in AspectJ. It uses an intermediate representation of pointcuts and bound advice declarations, so the prototype is not heavily interwoven with the AJDT and can be also used with tools for other AOP languages.

The implementation of the pointcut analyses depends on the Test and Performance Tools Platform (TPTP) [23]. The TPTP mainly offers support for dynamic program analyses, like runtime data collection, profiling, and testing, but it also provides support for static program analyses. In particular, the configuration, execution and result presentation of static analyses are well integrated in the Eclipse platform. The analysis process of SOOTHSAYER and the individual analysis steps are implemented using this part of the TPTP. Every step is realized as a so-called `AnalysisProvider` and is controlled by the an instance of the class `AnalysisProviderManager`. The TPTP executes every provider in a loosely coupled sequence, i.e., the analysis steps can be easily extended by adding new providers.

SOOTHSAYER consists of four different Eclipse plug-ins: REFACTOR, ANALYZE, DYNAMIC, and VISUAL. Figure 7.1 gives an overview of the general architecture of SOOTH-SAYER and depicts the relationships of every plug-in. The plug-ins on the bottom side are used by SOOTHSAYER and adjoin plug-ins exchange data with each other.

SOOTHSAYER::ANALYZE implements the basic infrastructure for all analyses. It creates static program representations, implements the static pointcut matches, and the change impact analysis.

Specific program representations, such as an ASG and a static type hierarchy are created for the evaluation of pointcut expressions. The pointcut matching evaluates each pointcut expression in its corresponding program representation and produces a set of ASG nodes that holds the specified property in this representation. For instance, inheritance-based properties are evaluated using the static type hierarchy for a certain class. If a

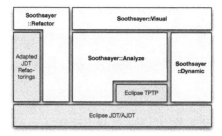

Figure 7.1: The components of SOOTHSAYER and their relationships (adjoin components exchange data with each other).

pointcut specifies such a property, SOOTHSAYER constructs the static type hierarchy for selected types and evaluates the expression.

The pointcut matching evaluates independent and aggregated pointcut expressions. To this end, all pointcuts are decomposed into our intermediate representation and all partial pointcuts are evaluated using the corresponding program representations. A pointcut matcher ascertains all elements of the ASG that corresponds to a specified property and associates each element with the pointcut expression. The resulting pointcut selection contains all matching program elements for every expression of a pointcut.

The change impact analysis uses the atomic change model (created by REFACTOR) and the pointcut selection to compute a pointcut selection delta by comparing the selections of the original and refactored program. Each delta entry (new or lost match) is assigned with the responsible program transformation.

SOOTHSAYER::REFACTOR creates the atomic change model to store every atomic change and change reason for each program transformation that is performed by a refactoring. The resulting atomic change model associates atomic changes with affected program elements and the responsible transformation. The REFACTOR plug-in uses the results of the change impact analysis to compute a pointcut update decision and (if proposed) an update for every affected pointcut. In addition, it extends the refactoring workflow and UI elements for supporting the additional refactoring steps.

SOOTHSAYER::DYNAMIC implements the approximation of dynamic program representations and the evaluation of their properties. It creates statically approximated representations in which dynamic properties, such as the cflow property, can be evaluated with static program analysis.

To this end, it extends the pointcut matching of the ANALYZE plug-in. The current implementation computes a specific call graph with qualified edges as described in Section 5.3. This call graph does not only represent additional and lost call paths it also shows modified execution conditions within a call path. The qualified edges indicate if a change affects the statically approximated execution likeliness of a call path. Every specified cflow property is evaluated to a set of matching call paths which are stored in

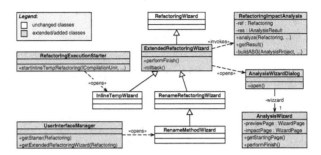

Figure 7.2: Integration of the SOOTHSAYER refactoring wizard.

an extended version of the pointcut selection.

SOOTHSAYER::VISUAL presents affected advice declarations, the individual effects on pointcut expressions and altered pointcut matches within the refactoring wizard. It provides a specific visualization of the change impact measures and the computed heuristics for the update decision making. VISUAL supports the developer in accepting, modifying or deferring the proposed updated decisions. Also the customization of computed pointcut adjustments is supported by the VISUAL plug-in. It allows for comparing the selection of the adjusted update with the original pointcut selection. In the current implementation we propose a tree-map [48] or seesoft [25] visualization for properties of static program representations and a graph-based visualization for cflow properties.

7.2 Extended Refactoring Workflow

The standard refactoring workflow of the Eclipse JDT was extended to support our aspect-aware refactoring process. The Eclipse JDT provides two kinds of refactorings: processor-based, e.g., *Rename Method*, and non-processor-based refactorings, e.g., *Inline Local Variable*. Both kinds are executed through user interactions in the UI. For non-processor-based refactorings the class `RefactoringExecutionStarter` is responsible for starting the corresponding refactoring wizard, which we have extended to start the adapted refactoring support. For processor-based refactorings the class `UserInterfaceManager` creates specific starter for each refactoring wizard.

Figure 7.2 illustrates which classes are extended for integrating our refactoring support. Since the refactoring wizards of Eclipse cannot be extended with additional wizard pages we need to integrate a new dialog `AnalysisWizardDialog` that is opened after the last parameter page of a refactoring wizard is closed. We insert a new superclass to all refactoring wizards `ExtendedRefactoringWizard` that shows our analysis wizard pages as additional refactoring steps[1]. The `AnalysisWizard` provides an extended preview

---

[1]Such an extension requires to copy the original refactoring plugin and to replace it with the modified version. Unfortunately, the UI implementation of the JDT refactoring support is so well encapsulated that no other extension was possible.

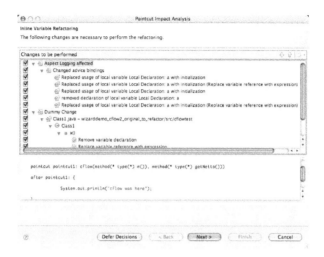

Figure 7.3: The extended *Refactoring Preview* illustrates which advice is affected by what change of the refactoring.

page, the pointcut impact page, and access to the pointcut edit dialog.

Our **Refactoring Preview** page additionally shows the change effects on advice declarations of existing aspects. For each aspect the effects on its advice declarations is presented, as illustrated by Figure 7.3. The tree view of planned changes also lists the affected program elements whose executions are selected by a pointcut. These additional entries state what will happen with the referenced elements if the refactoring is carried out. The tree gathers the entries and associates them to the affected advice code.

The advice code is displayed in the code view in the lower part. The presentation of affected advice code together with the program code it is assigned to, allows the developer to estimate whether the expected effects on the program behavior are crucial. In cases where only unimportant behavior is affected, e.g., some logging aspect, she could press the *Finish* button immediately and leave the remaining decisions to the refactoring tool.

The **Pointcut Impact Page** presents invalidated pointcuts and proposed update decisions. As shown in Figure 7.4 the page is divided into two parts. The upper part presents invalidated pointcuts, update decision, and describes the impact situation, whereas the lower part illustrates the impact for each selected pointcut. The left tree view depicts any pointcut expression and (if selected) shows the affecting changes. On the right side the impact is illustrated with different visualizations. The current implementation provides seesoft and tree-map visualizations for static properties and a graph-based visualization for cflow properties. The figure shows a partial call graph (with qualified edges) because the cflow expression is selected in the tree view on the left side. As one can see the *Inline Variable Refactoring* causes four new and one lost edge in the call graph.

The developer is asked to review all proposed updates. She can accept, decline, defer,

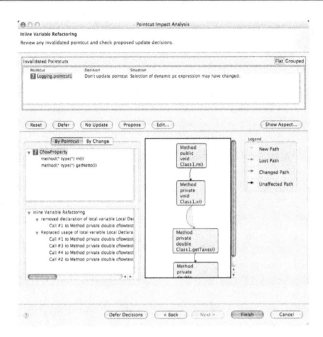

Figure 7.4: An additional *Pointcut Impact Dialog* shows invalidated pointcuts and the concrete change effects.

or edit a pointcut update using the buttons below the table in the upper part. Also the corresponding aspect can be displayed using the *Show Aspect...* button. The *Finish* button is disabled as long as some pointcuts are undecided. A click on this button would perform the refactoring and update all pointcuts as decided in this wizard page. The developer can also go back to the preview page using the *Back* button or defer all decisions (*Defer Decisions*). The *Cancel* button will rollback the complete refactoring.

The *Edit...* button displays the dialog shown in Figure 7.5. It allows for a customized update of a pointcut. If the developer edits the pointcut manually (check box *Manual Update*), she has to define the pointcut in our intermediate representation. In a future version, we will also allow developers to edit the pointcut in the syntax of the actual pointcut language. Every click on the button *Evaluate* re-evaluates the customized pointcut and compares its selection either with the selection of the original or refactored program. Also the selection delta can be displayed by the visualization in the lower part. The *Ok* button applies the customization and the *Cancel* button makes the edit undone.

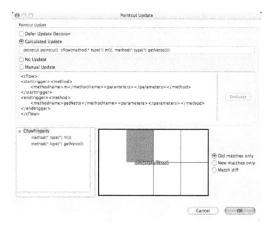

Figure 7.5: An additional *Pointcut Update Dialog* allows for customized pointcut update that can separately be evaluated.

7.3 Implementation of the Refactoring and Analysis Steps

In Figure 7.6 we illustrate the information flow in the implementation of our refactoring tool. It shows the program representations that are used and produced in every analysis step. In this section we describe each refactoring and analysis step in detail and present important classes that implement the particular steps.

7.3.1 Aspect-aware Refactoring

Our refactoring tool gets the original source code and the refactoring input to perform the selected refactoring. The refactoring is virtually performed, i.e., the tool executes each constituent program transformation on the code, but produces a working copy of modified program elements. The virtual modification is already implemented by Eclipse to preview what will happen when the refactoring is carried out. The program representations of Eclipse for the original and refactored program are used to compute our abstract syntax graph (ASG) in the next step.

In addition, the extended refactoring wizard invokes the impact analysis before our `AnalysisWizard` is opened to show the analysis results. The integration of our aspect-aware refactoring workflow into the JDT refactoring support is already described in Section 7.2.

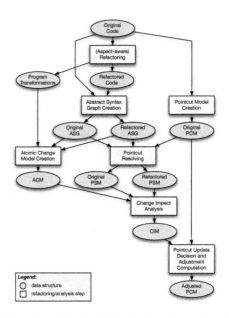

Figure 7.6: Overview of the individual refactoring and analysis steps.

7.3.2 Abstract Syntax Graph Creation

Our analysis uses a specific representation of the program, a so called abstract syntax graph (ASG). Such a graph represents containment and usage relationships of program elements. It is created for the original and the refactored program in order to reveal pointcut expressions that match different elements in both program versions. The ASG is implemented in package `org.soothsayer.asg.nodes` and consists of program elements ranging from project to statement, like `Package`, `Type`, `Method`, and `MethodCall`.

Figure 7.7 shows the classes that are involved in the ASG creation. The ASG is created by the class `ASGBuilder`, which uses the Java Model and the public AST of the Eclipse JDT. The Java Model is an AST that represents every declared program element, but no statement-level elements. It is used in the IDE for displaying syntactic elements in the UI, for user interactions with individual elements (e.g., selection) and target selection for code manipulations. The public AST is more complete. It additionally represents statement-level code and is used in the IDE for code manipulation and code generation. However, it is only created for a single compilation unit, i.e., it does not represent the structural dependencies of several collaborating classes that are implemented in different files. We use therefore the Java Model and the public AST for the creation of our representation.

Our ASG is more complete in two dimensions, even if it represents only some parts of the program. It contains all types and their enclosed elements that are possibly referenced

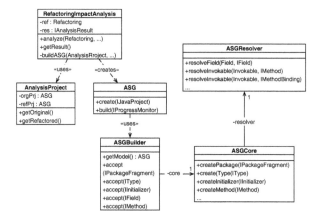

Figure 7.7: Implementation of the ASG creation.

by a pointcut, down to every statement that can be referenced by existing pointcut languages. Other statements and expression, such as local assignments, type casts, and literals, are ignored.

7.3.3 Pointcut Model Creation

The creation of a pointcut model is realized in two different subclasses of `IAnalysisProvider`. Figure 7.8 shows all classes and their relationships that are involved in this creation process.

The `PointcutModelProvider` triggers the pointcut parsing to create a `PointcutModel` (PCM). An implementation of an `IAspectParser` reads the pointcuts from the original program and builds the `PointcutModel`. The current implementation of this provider uses an XML parser that parses an XML representation of pointcuts. The `PointcutModelProvider` can be used with other parsers for supporting other pointcut languages. The class `PointcutFractionizationProvider` expands every pointcut that is represented by the PCM and defines in which sequence the individual pointcut expressions are evaluated. Both providers are implemented in package `org.soothsayer.internal.match.analysis`. The resulting PCM contains the decomposed pointcuts in which every expression is a subclass of `PointcutExpression` (PCE).

A PCE can have subexpressions (children) and a parent expression. A pointcut definition is represented by the class `Pointcut`.

7.3.4 Pointcut Resolving

Every decomposed pointcut is evaluated two times, in the original and the refactored program. The classes that implement the pointcut resolving are shown in Figure 7.9.

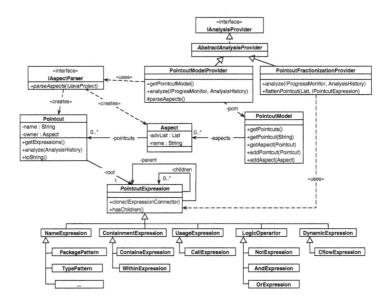

Figure 7.8: Overview of the pointcut model implementation and classes that are used to create it.

For each independent pointcut expression and partial aggregation of expressions (result of the `PointcutFractionizationProvider`) the `IProgramElement` objects are ascertained that match the specified properties. The class `PointcutExpressionResolver` has three subclasses that implement the evaluation of properties of a concrete program representation, i.e., `ASGPropertyResolver`, `TypeHierarchyPropertyResolver`, and `DynamicPropertyResolver`.

The pointcut resolving is triggered by an instance of `MatchAnalysisProvider` and results in a `PointcutSelection` object for each pointcut. Every pointcut selection contains the matching elements for each pointcut expression and the selection of a single pointcut expression is represented by objects of class `PropertySelection`. Since multiple pointcut expressions can refer to the same program element the individual matches need to be distinguished. A single reference to a program element is represented by an instance of class `PropertyMatch`. A property match connects a matching element with the pointcut expression and allows for an individual assessment of each match.

This relationship is presented in Figure 7.10. An instance of a `PointcutExpression` represents the specification of a joinpoint property. The `PropertySelection` objects represent the bunch of references to program elements for each expression. Objects of class `PropertyMatch` represent a single reference to an element which can be individually assessed.

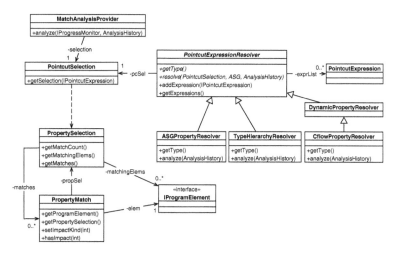

Figure 7.9: Collaborating classes that create a pointcut selection for a pointcut.

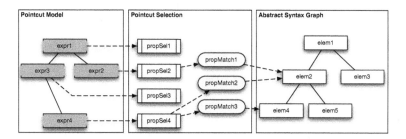

Figure 7.10: The relationships between pointcut model, pointcut selection, and program
elements.

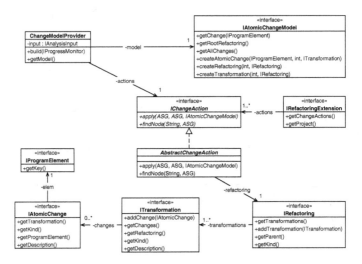

Figure 7.11: Classes that implement the atomic change model and their relationships.

7.3.5 Atomic Change Model Creation

Our impact analysis requires additional change information from a refactoring. For each extended refactoring the individual transformations are detected and represented in subclasses of `AbstractChangeAction`. These representations of elementary transformations are implemented in package `org.soothsayer.refactor.acm.actions`, such as extract, inline, move, and rename. The representation of a refactoring by these actions makes the reasons for detected change effects explicit. The relationship represent the interface between the refactoring tool and our impact analysis.

The atomic change model basically associates instances of three classes: `Refactoring`, `Transformation`, and `AtomicChange`. Figure 7.11 illustrates the relationships between these classes. The class `AtomicChangeModel` encapsulates a particular change model for a specific refactoring and target program. It is created by a `ChangeModelProvider`. The provider class uses an `IAnalysisInput` to receive the ASGs of the original and refactored program, and it gets the list of `IChangeAction` objects from the refactoring.

An instance of the `AtomicChangeModel` is created to associate any modification of a program element with the responsible `Transformation` of the `Refactoring`. The changes that are computed by the existing JDT refactorings cannot be assigned to program elements of our ASG. These changes are designed to be directly executed on the program code but not to represent reasons for change effects. We solve this problem by extending the refactorings to provide the performed program transformations as instances of `IChangeAction`. The `ChangeModelProvider` receives these change actions and assigns it as change reasons with affected elements of the ASG.

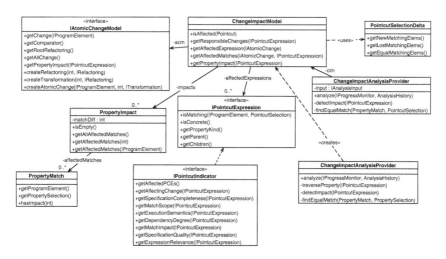

Figure 7.12: Classes that implement the change impact model and their relationships.

7.3.6 Change Impact Analysis

This analysis step computes a `PointcutSelectionDelta` object that contains instances of `IProgramElement` with altered matches. The analysis result is represented by the class `ChangeImpactModel` which contains only program elements with new or lost matches. Figure 7.12 presents the class diagram of the change impact model and collaborating classes that are used to represent the change impact.

The class `ChangeImpactModel` represents the complete impact for all existing pointcuts in the program. It associates every affected `IPointcutExpression` with a `PropertyImpact`. For each pointcut (root expression) the `PropertyImpact` object stores the new and lost matches. An instance of class `IPointcutIndicator` stores the values for the defined impact indicators.

A `ChangeImpactModel` is created by the class `ChangeImpactAnalysisProvider` (CIAP). The provider requires the `PointcutSelection` objects of the original and refactored program, and an `IAtomicChangeModel`. The CIAP triggers first the computation of the selection delta entries for every expression of a pointcut. To this end, it compares the `PropertyMatch` objects in both pointcut selections.

If the original selection contains a property match but the refactored selection does not, then the match is labeled as lost and added to the `PointcutSelectionDelta`. Newly matching elements are treated in the same way, except that matches are labeled as new matches. The `AtomicChangeModel` is used to differentiate moved and renamed elements that still match the pointcut but with a different ID from matches that are really lost or added.

Not every affected `IPointcutExpression` with altered matches is directly associated with an `IAtomicChange` object. For example, indirectly affected expressions that use

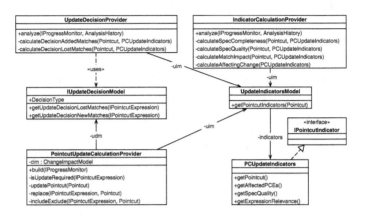

Figure 7.13: Implementation of the pointcut update decision making and update computation.

a directly affected expression. For such indirectly affected expressions the change reasons are ascertained separately. The algorithm for creating a pointcut update described in Section 6.3 uses a function that computes the smallest directly affected expression. The algorithm is implemented by the method detectImpact(IPointcutExpression) in CIAP. The function for finding the affecting changes for indirectly affected expressions is implemented in method calculateAffectingChange(PCUpdateIndicators). It invokes an individual search specific to the expression kind. For instance, a WithinExpression is either directly affected or indirectly through an change that modifies an element that encloses a matching element. Every parent node in the ASG is visited to find the affecting atomic change.

7.3.7 Pointcut Update Computation

In the final step, the impact indicators are calculated for every affected IPointcutExpression. The calculation of each measure is triggered by the class IndicatorCalculationProvider. The class provides a method for each measure, like calculateMatchImpact(), calculateSpecQuality(), as shown in Figure 7.13.

The values of the specification quality and the expression relevance are used for determining an update decision. For every affected PropertyMatch an update decision is computed such as described in Section 6.2. The actual update decision making is implemented in the UpdateDecisionProvider. It separately computes an update decision for new and lost matches and additionally distinguishes change and add from remove transformations. For every kind of decision a separate method is provided. The individual decisions are stored in an instance of the IUpdateDecisionModel. The class associates each altered PropertyMatch with an update decision.

If the algorithm decides to update a pointcut expression with altered matches, then the

`PointcutUpdateCalculationProvider` tries to compute the least intrusive replacement. If the provider successfully computes a replacement the adjusted `PointcutModel` is evaluated using the refactored ASG. If the comparison with the property matches of the original ASG results not in a similar pointcut selection (or no replacement could be computed), then the original PCM is extended with an explicit exclusion or inclusion. The updated `PointcutModel` is a cloned representation of the original pointcut. In this way, the original pointcut can anytime be recovered. This pointcut rewriting is implemented in the class `PointcutUpdateCalculationProvider` which returns an updated pointcut model that contains only updated pointcuts.

7.4 Summary

In this chapter, we have presented important implementation details of our refactoring tool SOOTHSAYER. We have introduced its constituent components ANALYZE, REFACTOR, DYNAMIC, and VISUAL in Section 7.1. Each of these components is an Eclipse plug-in, and DYNAMIC and VISUAL can be used optionally. ANALYZE implements the fundamental analyses and the creation of program representations. REFACTOR implements the actual refactoring extensions and additional UI elements. DYNAMIC realizes the approximation of cflow properties and VISUAL provides the visualizations to illustrate the change impact and resulting pointcut adjustments.

In Section 7.2 we have presented how existing JDT refactorings are extended and how our aspect-aware refactoring tool supports the developer. In particular, individual UI elements are presented and the displayed information discussed.

In the main part of this chapter, Section 7.3, we have described how the overall analysis process is implemented and which implementation details and design decisions were important for each analysis step. We have also depicted important classes and their relationships with UML diagrams and described how the functionalities of these classes can be used.

Chapter 8

Evaluation

The refactoring approach developed in this work was evaluated using our refactoring tool
SOOTHSAYER. In this chapter we describe the employed evaluation methodology, elucidate expected results, and present three case studies in which independently developed
aspect-oriented programs are refactored using our approach. For each experiment, we
describe the program, the refactoring scenarios and the source code changes. Furthermore, we present the detected effects on pointcuts, proposed update decisions as well as
the adjusted pointcuts. In the end, we discuss the evaluation results, expose the kinds
of pointcuts that cannot be properly handled by our refactoring tool and elucidate the
particular reasons.

8.1 Methodology

Our prototype refactoring tool SOOTHSAYER supports our approach for refactoring AspectJ programs. The tool was used in three different applications in order to evaluate
our approach. The applications were selected according to the characteristics of their
pointcuts, primarily because the major goal of this evaluation was to apply our approach
to very different pointcuts. The application size may affect the scalability of our analysis
approach, and the proportions between aspects and classes may result in more unsolvable
inter-aspect conflicts, but neither have been the focus of this evaluation. The applications
where chosen for whether a refactoring can affect:

- pointcuts that specify various properties of all possible program representations;
- pointcuts that specify these properties with a different level of completeness;
- pointcut expressions at different nesting levels of a pointcut.

For each of the chosen programs we have identified a set of refactorings that affect the
program representations that are referenced by the pointcuts in a certain way. Each
program was tested by a suite of unit tests, that reveal altered executions of existing
advice more easily. This way, unexpected side effects of a refactoring can be made
visible. The test suite is run before and after a refactoring. The comparison of test
failures demonstrates whether all expected effects are detected by our analysis and if the

proposed pointcut updates achieve the expected results.

The particular update decision is validated during a refactoring. Our impact analysis shows the effects on any pointcut and we have decided what is the most likely expected update decision. When our analysis proposed an adjustment the updated pointcut was used in the refactored program. In cases where no update was proposed we have run the test suite against the original pointcut in the (refactored) program.

8.2 Experiment 1: Telecom Application

For the first experiment we have chosen a small example program from the AspectJ distribution. The *Telecom* example, available from AspectJ's website [5], is a simple simulation of telephone connections to which timing and billing features are added using aspects. We augmented the program with unit tests to expose the effects on the adapted base code functionality. The tests are used to ensure advice invocation is altered unnoticeably.

The application has three core functionalities: a basic functionality that simulates customers, calls and connections, a timing feature and a billing feature. The timing and billing features are implemented by aspects. The timing aspect manages the total time per customer and is added as a timer to each connection. The billing aspect calculates a charge per connection and builds upon the timing aspect.

8.2.1 Involved Aspects

The application defines three aspects `Timing`, `TimerLog`, and `Billing`. The `TimerLog` aspect was not considered in the experiment, because it is a too simple aspect with pointcuts similar to those defined by the other aspects.

Timing. The Timing aspect records the duration of each connection and associates the total connection time with each customer. It extends the structure of the classes `Customer` and `Connection` and defines two pointcuts:

> (Connection c): **target**(c) && **call**(**void** Connection.complete())
> PM: *call(within(*
>   *type("Connection"),*
>   *method(<..>, type("void"), "complete", <>)))*

> endTiming(Connection c): **target**(c)&& **call**(**void** Connection.drop())
> PM: *call(within(*
>   *type("Connection"),*
>   *method(<..>, type("void"), "drop", <>)))*

The pointcuts intercept all executions of any call to the two methods `Connection.complete()` and `Connection.drop()`. Both pointcuts are quite simple, using signature patterns and containment-based scopes. They can be transformed directly into our intermediate representation. The dynamic types specified by *target* expressions would then be approximated by a static inheritance-based scope $within(subtypes(type("T")), ...)$. The specified containment-based scoped however is more restrictive, and so, the dynamic types are ignored in our pointcut representation.

TimerLog. The `TimerLog` aspect is used in the program to log when the timer is started or stopped. Any time the timer is started or stopped it prints some log information to standard output. The aspect contains two pointcuts:

> (Timer t): **target**(t) && **call**(∗ Timer.start())
> **PM:** $call(within(type("Timer"), method(<..>, type("*"), "start", <>)))$

> (Timer t): **target**(t) && **call**(∗ Timer.stop())
> **PM:** $call(within(type("Timer"), method(<..>, type("*"), "stop", <>)))$

Both pointcuts are quite similar to the pointcuts of aspect `Timing` regarding the referenced program representations and the way in which the joinpoint properties are specified.

Billing. The `Billing` aspect implements the billing functionality on top of the `Timing` aspect. It declares additional features in the classes `Connection` and `Customer` for storing the customer who pays for the call, and for charging local and long distance calls differently. In addition, the aspect defines the following pointcut:

> (Customer cust): **args**(cust, ..) && **call**(Connection+.**new**(..))
> **PM:** $call(within($
> $\qquad subtypes(type("Connection")),$
> $\qquad constructor(<..>, <subtypes(type("Customer")), ..>)))$

The pointcut is used to receive the caller who pays for the call. It intercepts any invocation of a constructor in `Connection` (or its subclasses) and receives the constructor's first argument in a parameter. The pointcut refers to more program representations than the pointcuts of previous aspects. It uses signature patterns, an inheritance-based scope, and dynamic typing information. The pointcut can be directly transformed into our pointcut model, which represents the dynamic type of the *args* expression as a static subtypes relationship.

8.2.2 Refactoring Scenarios

In this experiment, three different refactorings were performed within the class `Connection`: Rename Method, Rename Type and Inline method. The measured indicators and proposed updated decisions are shown in Table 8.1.

In the table as well as in the descriptions we use the following abbreviations:

- Specification Completeness (SC),
- Match Scope (MS),
- Specification Quality (SQ),

- Execution Semantics (ES),

- Degree of Dependency (DD),

- Expression Relevance (ER), and

- Match Impact (MI).

(S1) Rename Method: "Connection.complete()". The *Rename Method* refactoring changes the name of method `complete()` to `completeConnectionCall()`. It obviously affects any pointcut that matches the method's name.

Our impact analysis computes the pointcut selection for the original and the refactored program. The comparison of both selections indicates the loss of all selected joinpoints for the first `Timing` pointcut:

```
1 (Connection c): target(c) && call(void Connection.complete())
```

The tool analyzes its pointcut selection and reveals a lost match of expression *within*(*type* ("*Connection*"), *method*(< .. >, *type*("*void*"), "*complete*", <>)) as the cause for the effects on the pointcut. For this expression a Match Scope (MS) of 100% is computed, which indicates that the pointcut selects the lost match explicitly.

The further analysis recognizes the pointcut expression *method*(< .. >, *type*("*void*"), "*complete*", <>) as the smallest expression that is directly affected by the refactoring's *RENAME* transformation. This expression is completely defined (SC 100%), which, in combination with MS 100%, results in a specification quality (SQ) of 100%. A complete specification quality is an indicator that the pointcut has explicitly selected the lost match in the original program. Two additional indicators are used to ascertain the relevance of the affected expression for the pointcut. The expression specifies no execution related properties (ES 0%) and is located on nesting level 2 (DD 100%) of our pointcut representation. The SQ 100% in combination with a high relevance (ER) of 100% of the effect for the pointcut leads the decision: "update the pointcut".

The update computation algorithm is executed with a Match Impact (MI) 100% for the affected expression and results in a REPLACE proposal. The evaluation of the updated pointcut:

> *call*(*within*(*type*("*Connection*"),
> **method**(<..>, **type**("void"), "**completeConnectionCall**", <>)))

in the refactored program shows that all lost pointcut matches are recovered.

(S2) Rename Type: "Connection". *Rename Type* refactoring changes the name of class `Connection` to `TelConnection`. This obviously affects any pointcut that matches the original class name. The tool compares the pointcut selections in the original and the refactored program and reveals three affected pointcuts of the aspects `Timing` and `Billing`:

```
1 (Customer cust): args(cust, ..) && call(Connection+.new(..))
2 (Connection c): target(c) && call(void Connection.complete())
3 endTiming(Connection c): target(c) && call(void Connection.drop())
```

The refactoring's *RENAME* transformation has caused the loss of all matches for these pointcuts. Each affected pointcut refers to the complete name of class `Connection`. The impact analysis reveals the lost matches of the expression *type("Connection")* in each pointcut as the cause of this effect. The type name is scoped (MS 100% through import statements) and completely defined (SC 100%). The affected pointcut expressions specify a type as the location for the behavior, which we rate with ES 5%, and they are located on the second or third nesting level (DD 100%). As result, a precisely defined match is lost (SQ 100%), which is specified by a highly relevant expression (ER 95%), thus our tool proposes to "update the pointcut".

The update computation starts with a Match Impact (MI) of 100% for the expression *type("Connection")* and is able to replace the expression directly in each pointcut:

> *call*(*within*(
>   *subtypes*(**type("TelConnection")**),
>   *constructor*($< .. >$, $< subtypes$(*type*("*Customer*")), $.. >$)))
> *call*(*within*(
>   **type("TelConnection")**,
>   *method*($< .. >$, *type*("*void*"), "*complete*", $<>$)))
> *call*(*within*(
>   **type("TelConnection")**,
>   *method*($< .. >$, *type*("*void*"), "*drop*", $<>$)))

(S3) Inline Method: "Connection.complete()". *Inline Method* targets the method `complete()`, replacing any call to this method with its body, and removing the original method declaration. Our impact analysis detects lost matches of pointcut:

```
1 (Connection c): target(c) && call(void Connection.complete())
```

The analysis detects the lost match of expression *within*(*type*("*Connection*"), *method*($<$ $.. >$, *type*("*void*"), "*complete*", $<>$)) (MS 100%) and reveals the expression *method*($<$ $.. >$, *type*("*void*"), "*complete*", $<>$) as directly affected by the refactoring's *REMOVE* transformation. Since the affected expression is precisely specified (SQ 100%) and highly relevant for the evaluation of the pointcut (ER 100%) the tool proposes to "update the pointcut".

The update computation tries to determine the property value in the refactored program version, but deals with a *REMOVE* transformation. Since matches of removed elements cannot be recovered, it proposes to CANCEL the refactoring.

8.2.3 Discussion

All pointcuts in the *Telecom* application are fairly simple. They specify only a few properties, each with 100% specification quality. Due to the high specification quality the refactorings cause only lost matches of precisely specified elements. Our tool has detected all lost matches and was able to propose the correct update decision in all tested cases.

In this experiment our analysis approach identified the lost matches correctly and associated them with the responsible program transformations. Also the update decisions based on this association and on our (quite primitive) heuristics lead to the expected results. For the Inline Method refactoring, which tries to remove a precisely specified element, the cancel decision was the only possibility for the tool to preserve the affected pointcut. In the other cases, a suitable pointcut update was proposed that resulted in replacements of the smallest affected anchor expressions. These updates preserved the pointcut's appearance; even multiple of these updates would keep it recognizable to the developer who originally defined the pointcut.

In addition, the proposed updates did not only preserve the pointcut they also restored the original program behavior. This was possible because of completely specified static properties. In this experiment the prototype worked well for simple but commonly used pointcuts.

8.3 Experiment 2: Spacewar Application

In the second experiment, we use an AspectJ implementation of the video game "Spacewar". The program is slightly bigger than the Telecom application and uses significantly more aspects for various functionalities in the application. It is also available from the AspectJ's website [5].
The basic functionality for synchronizing and coordinating different threads upon entering and exiting methods is implemented by the `Coordination` aspect. Also the game synchronization is an aspect that ensures synchronized access to methods of the game in the presence of several threads. In addition, the `Registry` and `RegistrySynchronization` for managing any space object that is floating around are implemented as aspects.
Most of these aspects use very simple pointcuts similar to the pointcuts in the *Telecom* application. In this experiment we have focussed on the pointcuts of the aspects `Debug`, `DisplayAspect` and `Ship`, which leaded to new situations when refactoring the program.

8.3.1 Involved Aspects

We consider the pointcuts of the following three aspects as interesting targets for an evaluation of our approach. They either match incompletely specified elements or use irregular nesting of pointcut expressions.

Table 8.1: Change impact measures and updates for pointcuts in the Telecom Application.

Refactorings		Billing	Timing
	AspectJ pointcut	(Connection conn): args(cust, ..) && call(Connection+.new(..))	(Connection c): target(c) && call(void Connection.complete()) endTiming(Connection c): target(c) && call(void Connection.drop())
	Decomposed pointcut	call(within(subtypes(type("Connection")), constructor(<..>, <subtypes(type("Customer")), ..>)))	call(within(type("Connection")), method(<..>,type("void"),"complete",<>))) call(within(type("Connection")), method(<..>,type("void"),"drop",<>)))
(S1) Rename Method "complete" to "completeConnectionCall"	Affected PCE	-	method(<..>,type("void"),"complete",<>)
	Measures	-	-Match RENAME SQ: 100 (SC:100, MS:100) ER: 100 (ES:0, DD:100)
	Decision	-	UPDATE MI: 100 Loss REPLACE
	Proposal	-	call(within(type("Connection")), **method(<..>,type("void"),"completeConnectionCall",<>)))**
(S2) Rename Type "Connection" to "TelConnection"	Affected PCE	type("Connection")	type("Connection")
	Measures	-Match RENAME SQ: 100 (SC:100, MS:100) ER: 95 (ES:5, DD:100)	-Match RENAME SQ: 100 (SC:100, MS:100) ER: 95 (ES:5, DD:100)
	Decision	UPDATE MI: 100 Loss REPLACE	UPDATE MI: 100 Loss REPLACE
	Proposal	call(within(subtypes(**type("TelConnection")**)), constructor(<..>, <subtypes(type("Customer")), ..>)))	call(within(**type("TelConnection")**), method(<..>,type("void"),"complete",<>)))
(S3) Inline Method "complete()"	Affected PCE	-	method(<..>,type("void"),"complete",<>)
	Measures	-	-Match REMOVE SQ: 100 (SC:100, MS:100) ER: 100 (ES:0, DD:100)
	Decision	-	UPDATE MI: 100 Loss CANCEL
	Proposal	-	-

Debug. The Debug aspect specifies debugging information that is displayed in the information window. It basically allows to set the amount of tracing information that is to be displayed, at runtime. Optionally, the aspect can be included in a build to provide additional debugging information. It defines a more complex pointcut:

allMethodsCut(): **execution**(∗ (spacewar.∗ && !(Debug+ || InfoWin+)).∗(..))
PM: *and(*
  execution(within(
   package("spacewar"),
   method(<..>, type(" ∗ "), " ∗ ", <..>))),
  not(execution(within(
   subtypes(type("Debug")),
   method(<..>, type(" ∗ "), " ∗ ", <..>)))),
  not(execution(within(
   subtypes(type("InfoWin")),
   method(<..>, type(" ∗ "), " ∗ ", <..>)))))

The pointcut selects all executions of any method in the package spacewar with the exception of methods that are defined in classes Debug or InfoWin. In the AspectJ pointcut these scopes are enumerated in a nested expression. Our pointcut model expands this pointcut to three distinct specifications in order to compute their matching elements separately.

DisplayAspect. The class Display defines the look and feel of the application, and is sub-classed by concrete display implementations. A game can have multiple displays which all accept keyboard input. The aspect DisplayAspect within class Display defines two particularly interesting pointcuts:

(Display display): **call**(**void** setSize (..)) && **target**(display)
PM: *call(within(*
  subtypes(type("Display")),
  method(<..>, type("void"), "setSize", <..>)))

(): **call**(Display+.**new**(..))
PM: *call(within(*
  subtypes(type("Display")),
  constructor(<..>, <..>)))

The first pointcut selects all executions of setSize() method calls with an incompletely specified signature pattern within classes of class Display. Our pointcut model approximates the dynamic type with an inheritance-based scope. The second pointcut intercepts all executions of any constructor call of class Display (or its subclasses). It specifies an incomplete signature pattern for the constructors and restricts its selection with an inheritance-based scope.

Ship. A ship is the vehicle that is moved through space by the user (direction, acceleration etc.). Other relevant properties are: amount of fuel and sustained damage. A ship is implemented as an aspect with the following pointcut:

```
1 helmCommandsCut(Ship ship): target(ship)
2     && (call(void rotate(int))
3         || call(void thrust(boolean))
4         || call(void fire()))
```

> **PM:** *or(*
> *call(within(*
> *subtypes(type("Ship")),*
> *method(<..>, type("void"), "rotate", <type("int")>))),*
> *call(within(*
> *subtypes(type("Ship")),*
> *method(<..>, type("void"), "thrust", <type("boolean")>))),*
> *call(within(*
> *subtypes(type("Ship")),*
> *method(<..>, type("void"), "fire", <>))))*

The pointcut enumerates three different methods for intercepting their invocations. It restricts the scope in which methods with the specified signatures are selected through a dynamic type. Our pointcut model approximates the dynamic type with the corresponding static type hierarchy and represents the pointcut in its disjunctive normal form (DNF). This normalization of pointcuts is important for locating the least affected part of the pointcut.

8.3.2 Refactoring Scenarios

In this experiment four different refactorings were performed. The measured indicators and proposed updated decisions are shown in Table 8.2. In the table as well as in the descriptions we use the same abbreviations as for the previous experiment.

(S4) Extract Method from "Game.run()". The *Extract Method* refactoring is performed within method Game.run() to extract lines 84-90 into a new method (cf. [83]). It creates a new method named createRobots(), moves the selected statements into this method and creates at their original location a method call that invokes the newly created method. The creation of the new method affects the following pointcut of aspect Debug:

```
1 allMethodsCut():
2     execution(* (spacewar.* && !(Debug+ || InfoWin+)).*(..))
```

The refactoring's *CREATE* transformation causes additional pointcut matches which are detected by our change impact analysis. The analysis reveals additional matches of *within(package("spacewar"), method(<..>, type("*"), "*", <..>))* which are not fully scoped (MS: 50%). In combination with the specification completeness (SC 0%) of the directly affected expression $method(<..>, type("*"), "*", <..>)$ our analysis computes a precision SQ 0%. Even with a relevance of ER 100% the affected expression selects no explicit element. Our tool proposes not to update the pointcut, i.e., it proposes to accept the new pointcut match.

(S5) Extract Method from "Display.initializeOffImage()". The *Extract Method* refactoring is performed within method `Display.initializeOffImage()` to extract the image size setup (lines 73-76) into a new method. It creates a new method `setSize(double, double)`, moves the selected statements into this method and creates at their original location a method call that invokes the newly created method. The creation of the new method affects the following pointcut of aspect `DisplayAspect`:

```
1 (Display  display):  call(void  setSize(..))  && target(display)
```

This pointcut specifies its anchors more precisely than the pointcut of the preview refactoring scenario. The newly created call causes an additional match of the unscoped expression $call(within(subtypes(type("Display"))), method(<..>, type("void"), "setSize", <..>)))$ (MS 0%). The same expression is directly affected by the refactoring's *CREATE* transformation (SC 68%) which results in a measured precision (SQ) of 34%. The additional match is not scoped by its corresponding expression, but its anchors are restricted with an inheritance-based scope (ES 100%). The affected expression is located on nesting level 0 (DD 33%) which indicates that the effect on the pointcut is of low relevance (ER 0%).

The update decision computation proposes not to update the pointcut. This decision is comprehensible if we consider the impact measures, but it may be unexpected for the developer. The newly matching method call belongs to a method that neither overrides a "setSize" method from a superclass, nor implements it the same behavior. Even if this call corresponds to all specified properties, it simply represents a different behavior as represented by the other methods.

(S6) Move Type "Display". The refactoring moves the type `Display` from package `spacewar` to package `spacewar.core`. This change indirectly affects the following two pointcuts for aspect `DisplayAspect`:

```
1 ():  call(Display+.new(..))
2 (Display  display):  call(void  setSize(..))  && target(display)
```

Both pointcuts refer to the fully qualified type name of class `Display`. However, package declarations are not part of pointcuts. They are defined in the import statements of the aspect. Import statements are generally adjusted by the standard Java refactorings. Our impact analysis does not recognize any change effect, because it is performed after the standard refactoring was executed.

(S7) PullUp Method "Ship.rotate(int)". The *Pull Up Method* refactoring moves the method `rotate(int)` from class `Ship` to its superclass `SpaceObject`. The following pointcut is affected:

```
1 pointcut helmCommandsCut(Ship ship):
2     target(ship) && ( call(void rotate(int))
3         || call(void thrust(boolean))
4         || call(void fire()) )
```

The pointcut selects (among others) all methods named `rotate(int)` within class `Ship` and its subclasses. The refactoring's *MOVE* transformation affects the expression *within(subtypes(type("Ship")), method(< .. >, type("void"), "rotate", < type("int") >))* but does not cause any altered anchor match. Since the method is moved to a super class it is still available in the class `Ship`. Our static impact analysis does not recognize the change and thus does not propose an update for the pointcut.

8.3.3 Discussion

This experiment mainly deals with change effects on incomplete specifications. The first two refactoring scenarios cause additional matches of incomplete specified properties which represent a special challenge for refactoring tools. The third refactoring was done to see what happens if we modify program elements on which pointcuts depend on but which are not explicitly treated by our approach. The last refactoring was expected to affect a fully specified property, but surprisingly did not cause any impact.

In the first scenario, the refactoring caused a new match of an unspecified but partially scoped expression. It shows that our approach can deal with intentionally under-specified properties, and accepts corresponding matches. Our impact measures indicate that the effect on the pointcut is relevant for its evaluation, but also that the pointcut does not specify any particular expectation. Hence, our heuristics seem to work well for these imprecise specifications.

The second refactoring creates a newly matching method call to a method that almost overrides a method from the superclass. The nearly correct match can only be distinguished from correct matches by locating the overridden methods, which do not exists for this match. It fulfills all other specified properties. These situations are among of the most challenging for aspect-oriented refactoring tools, because the recognized similarities are completely unintended.

The last refactoring moves a feature to a super class, i.e., out of a specified hierarchy-based scope. However, a pull up method refactoring cannot remove a feature from a subtype hierarchy, because any subtype inherits it from any possible refactoring target class. Thus, it is not surprising that this refactoring did not affect the pointcut.

8.4 Experiment 3: Simple Insurance Application

The third experiment underlines the usability of our tool for projects that have properties more comparable to real projects in size, proportion between aspects and classes and the usage of libraries[1]. We refactor the extended version of the *Simple Insurance Application* that we have described in Chapter 2 (cf. Section 2.3). The program is a scaled down version of an insurance application that keeps track of customers and policies of a fictitious insurance company.

The extended version additionally implements a treatment of statistical data for contracted life policies. It defines a new aspect `LifePolicyStatistics` that uses an *cflow* pointcut and adapts the class `CustomerEditor.AddPolicyListener`. In addition, we have changed the pointcut `findPolicies` of aspect `TrackFinders` to have another pointcut that differs in its characteristics from the other pointcut[2]. Again unit tests are used to reveal altered invocations of the aspects.

8.4.1 Involved Aspects

The application defines three aspects `TrackFinders`, `PolicyChangeNotification` and `LifePolicyStatistics`. In this experiment every performed refactoring affects one of these aspects.

TrackFinders. The `TrackFinders` aspect tracks the executions of queries for policies. It intercepts any "findPolicy" method and captures how many results they return. It defines the following pointcut:

```
1 findPolicies(String criteria):
2     (execution(Set SimpleInsurance.findPoliciesById(String)
         )
3         || execution(Set SimpleInsurance.
              findPoliciesByCustomerId(String))
4         || execution(Set SimpleInsurance.
              findPoliciesByCustomerLastName(String)))
5     && args(criteria)
```

---

[1]The project contains 3752 lines of code, defines 59 types and 3 aspects, and makes use of several libraries.

[2]For a more detailed description of the application see [80]

Table 8.2: Change impact measures and updates for pointcuts in the Spacewar Application.

Refactorings		Debug	Display	Ship
	Aspect) pointcut	allMethodsCut(): execution(* (spacewar.* && !(Debug+ || InfoWin+)).*(..))	(Display display): call(void setSize(..)) && target(display)	pointcut helmCommandsCut(Ship ship): target(ship) && (call(void rotate(int)) || call(void thrust(boolean)) || call(void fire()));
	Decomposed pointcut	and(execution(within(package("spacewar"), method(<..>, type("**"), * , <..>))), not(execution(within(subtypes(type("Debug")), method(<..>, type("**"), * , <..>)))), not(execution(within(subtypes(type("InfoWin")), method(<..>, type("**"), * , <..>)))))	call(within(subtypes(type("Display")), method(<..>,type("void"),"setSize",<..>)))	or(call(within(subtypes(type("Ship")), method(<..>,type("void"),"rotate", <type("int")>))), call(within(subtypes(type("Ship")), method(<..>,type("void"),"thrust", <type("boolean")>))), call(within(subtypes(type("Ship")), method(<..>,type("void"),"fire",<>))))
(S4) Extract Method: line 84–90 of "Game.run()" to "createRobots()"	Affected PCE	method(<..>, type("**"), "**", <..>)	–	–
	Measures	+Match CREATE SQ: 0 (SC:0, MS:50) ER: 100 (ES:0, DD:100)	–	–
	Decision	NO UPDATE	–	–
	Proposal	–	–	–
(S5) Extract Method: line 73–76 of "initializeOfImage()" to "setSize(double, double)"	Affected PCE	–	call(within(subtypes(type("Display")), method(<..>,type("void"),"setSize",<..>)))	–
	Measures	–	+Match CREATE SQ: 34 (SC:68, MS:0) ER: 0 (ES:100, DD:33)	–
	Decision	–	NO UPDATE	–
	Proposal	–	–	–
(S6) Move Type "spacewar.Display" to "spacewar.core"	Affected PCE	–	–	–
	Decision	–	In AspectJ package declaration are not part of the pointcut. The affected import statements are updated by the standard Java refactoring.	In AspectJ package declaration are not part of the pointcut. The affected import statements are updated by the standard Java refactoring.
	Proposal	–	–	–
(S7) Pullup Method "Ship.rotate()" to "SpaceObject"	Affected PCE	–	–	within(subtypes(type("Ship")), method(<..>, type("void"), "rotate", <type("int")>))
	Measures	–	–	MOVE SQ:100 (SC:100, MS:100) ER: 0 (ES:100, DD:67)
	Decision	–	–	NO UPDATE
	Proposal	–	–	–

PM: *or(*
      execution(within(
        type("SimpleInsurance"),
        method(<..>, type("Set"), "findPoliciesById",
          <type("String")>))),
      execution(within(
        type("SimpleInsurance"),
        method(<..>, type("Set"), "findPoliciesByCustomerId",
          <type("String")>))),
      execution(within(
        type("SimpleInsurance"),
        method(<..>, type("Set"), "findPoliciesByCustomerLastName",
          <type("String")>))))

The pointcut enumerates the three methods (pointcut anchors) explicitly by specifying their complete signatures and their enclosing type. It is a typical enumeration-based pointcut with a low abstraction level. It explicitly states which program elements implement the selected behavior (joinpoints), rather than specifying the behavior itself. The pointcut can be translated directly into our pointcut representation.

PolicyChangeNotification.   The `PolicyChangeNotification` aspect implements a notification mechanism to observe updates of policies. It defines the following pointcut to select all executions of *setter* methods of type `PolicyImpl`:

policyStateUpdate(PolicyImpl policy): **execution**($*$ **set**$*$(..)) && **this**(policy)
PM: *execution(within(*
      subtypes(type("PolicyImpl")),
      method(<..>, type(""), "set*", <..>)))*

The pointcut identifies *setter* methods by the first three characters "set" of their names. This is a typical example for an incomplete pointcut that uses a signature pattern, even if it would additionally restrict its selection to a specific containment-based scope, it belongs to the most challenging pointcuts. The intention what should be selected by the pointcut is not completely expressed it, but remains to a large extent in the developer's mind.

LifePolicyStatistics.   The last aspect `LifePolicyStatistics` implements a treatment of statistical data for contracted life policies. It defines a *cflow* pointcut to intercept any creation of a `LifePolicyImpl` object "after" the Add-Button was pressed in the user interface:

```
5  policyContracted():
6      cflow(execution(public void *.widgetSelected(
           SelectionEvent)))
7      && execution(LifePolicyImpl.new(Customer));
```

PM: *cflow(*
 execution(
  method(<"public" >, type("void"), "widgetSelected",
   <type("SelectionEvent")>)),
 execution(within(
  type("LifePolicyImpl"),
  constructor(<..>, <type("Customer")>))))

The point in time "after pressing the Add-Button" is specified as "being in the control flow of a method" that is invoked when the Add-Button is pressed. Thus, the pointcut only selects executions of the LifePolicyImpl constructor that are inside the control flow of the method `widgetSelected(SelectionEvent)`. Both anchors are selected by completely specified signature patterns. Such a pointcut describes a particular behavior, even if it refers to elements of the program source. Our pointcut model directly represents such pointcuts and makes any referenced program representation explicit.

8.4.2 Refactoring Scenarios

In this experiment we performed two Rename Method refactorings and one Inline Local Variable refactoring in different classes. Every refactoring has caused different effects on the pointcuts which are shown in Table 8.3. In the table as well as in the descriptions we use the same abbreviations as in the previous experiments.

(S8) Rename Method: "SimpleInsurance.findPoliciesByCustomerLastName(String)".
The *Rename Method* changes the name of `findPoliciesByCustomerLastName(String)` in class `SimpleInsurance` to `findPoliciesByCustomerName`. It affects the pointcut `findPolicies(String)` in `TrackFinders`:

```
1 pointcut findPolicies(String criteria):
2    ( execution(Set SimpleInsurance.findPoliciesById(String))
3       || execution(Set SimpleInsurance.findPoliciesByCustomerId(
          String))
4       || execution(Set SimpleInsurance.
          findPoliciesByCustomerLastName(String)))
5    && args(criteria)
```

The pointcut specifies three orthogonal sets of joinpoints. Only the third specification is affected by the refactoring. The lost anchor match is exactly specified (SQ 100%), and completely relevant for the evaluation of the pointcut (ER 100%). Our impact analysis proposes to update the pointcut.
Since the affected expression loses all matches (MI 100%), the tool proposes to replace

the affected expression and generates the following pointcut:

or(
    execution(within(
        type("SimpleInsurance"),
        method(<..>, type("Set"), "findPoliciesById", <type("String")>))),
    execution(within(
        type("SimpleInsurance"),
        method(<..>, type("Set"), "findPoliciesByCustomerId",
            <type("String")>))),
    execution(within(
        type("SimpleInsurance"),
        method(<..>, type("Set"), "findPoliciesByCustomerName",
            <type("String")>))))

(S9) Rename Method: "PolicyImpl.createPolicyID()"   The *Rename Method* changes the name of method `createPolicyID()` in class `PolicyImpl` to `setupPolicyID`. The renaming causes a newly matching pointcut anchor in pointcut `policyStateUpdate(Policy-Impl)` of aspect `PolicyChangeNotification`:

```
1 pointcut policyStateUpdate(PolicyImpl policy):
2     execution(* set *(..)) && this(policy)
```

The additional match of the expression *within(subtypes(type("PolicyImpl")), method(<..>, type("*"), "set*", <..>))* is completely scoped (MS 100%), but the directly affected expression *method(<..>, type("*"), "set*", <..>)* is only partially defined (SC 17%). Since the precision of the specification of the additional match is not sufficiently precise (SQ 17%), and the affected expression is quite relevant for the pointcut (ER 75%), the tool proposes to update the pointcut.

The update computation is performed with a Match Impact of 7%, i.e., it tries to exclude the additional match explicitly. The proposed update extends the original pointcut with the most precise exclusion of the unwanted match:

and(
    execution(within(
        subtypes(type("PolicyImpl")),
        method(<..>, type(""), "set*", <..>))),*
    not(execution(method(<private>, type("void"), "setupPolicyID", <>)))

(S10) Inline Local Variable "lp".   The *Inline Local Variable* refactoring is performed on the variable `lp` in method `widgetSelected` of class `CustomerEditor.AddPolicyListener`. This refactoring replaces all variable usages with its initialization and affects the pointcut `policyContracted` of aspect `LifePolicyStatistics`:

```
1 pointcut policyContracted():
```

```
2    cflow(execution(public void *.widgetSelected(SelectionEvent)))
3    && execution(LifePolicyImpl.new(Customer))
```

The pointcut captures any instantiation of type `LifePolicyImpl` that occurs in the control flow of any method `widgetSelected(SelectionEvent)`. The cflow property is used to filter instantiations that occur in other contexts. The refactoring duplicates the variable initialization and causes (unintentionally) an alteration of the base program behavior. Our impact analysis detects a new match path in the call graph between an already existing pair of start- and end-triggers. The additional match path is a new pointcut match with MS 60%. The directly affected expression $execution(within(type("Life-PolicyImpl"), constructor(< .. >, < type("Customer") >)))$ is completely specified which leads to SQ 80%. Our analysis proposes no update, because the definition of the expression is sufficiently precise and contains an inheritance-based scope (ES 100%). Nonetheless, an altered behavioral property, like cflow, always indicates a changed behavior of the base program, thus, the developer should cancel the refactoring if this alteration is not explicitly intended.

8.4.3 Discussion

The affected pointcuts in this experiment differ from each other in multiple characteristics. The first refactoring affects a pointcut that specifies three orthogonal sets of joinpoints. It enumerates three method declarations that are specified similar to a symbolic reference. Unexpected matches of the expressions are merely possible. Our analysis detects a lost match of one of these expressions and proposes to replace it with an updated signature pattern. The proposed update not only restores the pointcut, but also the (composed) program behavior.

The second refactoring affects an incompletely specified signature pattern that additionally contains a partial name pattern. The matching anchors are captured based on the "Java Beans Naming Standards" for properties, where names of *setter* methods start with `set`. However, it is impossible to decide whether an additionally matching method is a "setter" method simply by looking at its name. Our tool recognizes the additional match and decides that a partial method (even if scoped) is not sufficient to accept additional matches. Improved versions of this pointcut would, e.g., additionally specify the return type `void` and a single but arbitrary parameter type which would describe the intention "setter" method more precisely. Such pointcuts would select the same set of joinpoints in the program and their additional matches could be accepted.

The third refactoring affects the (base) program behavior in such a way that the dynamic property cflow is affected. Our tool detects this effect, which is an indicator that the (composed) program behavior is altered. Our approach works well from two points of view. First, the tool notifies the developer that the refactoring is going to change the behavior, which otherwise the developer might not have noticed because such side effects are usually not checked by standard refactoring tools. Second, our tool recognized an additional cflow match (path), which does not invalidate the specification. It is just an indicator of potentially more occurrences of the specified behavior. Accordingly, our tools has proposed the correct decision (no update), even if the developer probably wants to cancel the refactoring because of the base program behavior changes.

8.5 Summary

The primary goal of this evaluation was to show that our impact analysis approach can represent the change effects on pointcuts sufficiently concrete so that a minimal-invasive update proposal can be inferred automatically. More concretely, we wanted to show that our analysis can ascertain the smallest pointcut expression for any refactoring, propose the correct update decision, and generate a minimal replacement. In particular, we are interested in understanding why a minimal-invasive update cannot be proposed for some pointcuts.

To this end, we selected those three programs which differ most in their pointcuts from the AspectJ programs that are known to us. Unfortunately, it was not easy to find proper AspectJ example programs for our experiments. Most programs were toy programs with suitable pointcuts but not much room for reasonable refactorings. We have selected the refactorings and their targets in the source code, that would have at least some effect on one of the pointcuts in the programs.

As the primary result, our prototype refactoring tool provided the correct update decision (and adjustment if proposed) in 9 of 10 refactoring scenarios. In three scenarios, the affected expressions could be directly replaced, whereas in one scenario the pointcut was extended with an explicit exclusion. Also, in two situations new matches of intentionally fuzzy specifications were correctly recognized. In Table 8.4 we present an overview of the experiment, enumerating every refactoring scenario in these experiments.

Regarding our two heuristics (specification quality, expression relevance) the refactoring scenarios have dealt with four kinds of pointcuts:

Precise and relevant expressions — For these pointcuts, all lost matches were detected and affected expressions were directly replaced (cf. S1, S2, S3, S8) Hence, as long as a refactoring does not try to remove a matching element, those pointcuts are the most suitable for a reliable refactoring. Since these expressions do not specify dynamic anchors (i.e., ER = high) neither new nor lost matches can be accepted. In particular because of their precise specification any adjustment keeps the pointcut recognizable even after multiple updates. Due to the high match impact of precisely specified elements, the updates of such pointcuts not only preserve the pointcut, but also preserve the original program behavior.

Imprecise but relevant expressions — Imprecisely specified properties often cause new matches which represent a special challenge for refactoring tools (cf. S4, S9). For newly matching elements, the refactoring tool has to determine whether they are specified sufficiently complete, or if they just match accidently. Our approach measures the name-based completeness (SC) and the specified scope of any match for this decision. The heuristics based on these measures have been shown to be able to deal with intentionally under-specified matches. Since this kind of expressions is

Table 8.3: Change impact measures and updates for pointcuts in the Simple Insurance Application.

Refactorings		TrackFinders	PolicyChangeNotification	LifePolicyStatistics
	Aspect/ pointcut	findPolicies(String criteria): (execution(Set SimpleInsurance.findPoliciesById(String)) || execution(Set SimpleInsurance.findPoliciesByCustomerId(String)) || execution(Set SimpleInsurance.findPoliciesByCustomerLastName(String))) && args(criteria)	policyStateUpdate(PolicyImpl policy): execution(* set*(..)) && this(policy)	policyContracted(): cflow(execution(public void * .widgetSelected(SelectionEvent)) && execution(LifePolicyImpl.new(Customer))
	Decomposed pointcut	or(execution(within(type("SimpleInsurance"), method(<...>,type("Set"), "findPoliciesById", <type("String")>)), execution(within(type("SimpleInsurance"), method(<...>,type("Set"), "findPoliciesByCustomerId", <type("String")>))), execution(within(type("SimpleInsurance"), method(<...>,type("Set"),"findPoliciesByCustomerLastName", <type("String")>))))	execution(within(subtypes(type("PolicyImpl")), method(<...>, type("*"), "set*", <...>)))	cflow(execution(method(<"public">, type("void"), "widgetSelected", <type("SelectionEvent")>)), execution(within(type("LifePolicyImpl"), constructor(<...>, <type("Customer")>))))
(S8) **Rename Method** **"findPoliciesByCustomer** **LastName(String)"**	Affected PCE	method(<...>,type("Set"),"findPoliciesByCustomerLastName", <type("String")>)	-	-
	Measures	-Match RENAME SQ: 100 (SC:100, MS:100) ER: 100 (ES:0, DD:100)		
	Decision	UPDATE MI: 100 REPLACE		
	Proposal	or(execution(within(type("SimpleInsurance"), method(<...>,type("Set"), "findPoliciesById", <type("String")>)), execution(within(type("SimpleInsurance"), method(<...>,type("Set"), "findPoliciesByCustomerId", <type("String")>))), execution(within(type("SimpleInsurance"), method(<...>,type("Set"),"findPoliciesByCustomerName", <type("String")>))))		
(S9) **Rename Method** **"createPolicyID" to** **"setupPolicyID"**	Affected PCE	-	method(<...>, type("*"), "set*", <...>)	-
	Measures		+Match RENAME SQ: 17 (SC:17, MS:100) ER: 75 (ES:25, DD:100)	
	Decision		UPDATE MI: 7 EXCLUDE	
	Proposal		and(execution(within(subtypes(type("PolicyImpl")), method(<...>, type("*"), "set*", <...>))), not(execution(method(<private>, type("void"), "setupPolicyID", <>))))	
(S10) **Inline Local Variable "ip"**	Affected PCE	-	-	execution(within(type("LifePolicyImpl"), constructor(<...>, <type("Customer")>)))
	Measures			+Match CREATE SQ: 80 (SC:100, MS:60) ER: 0 (ES:100, DD:67)
	Decision			**NO UPDATE**
	Proposal			

Table 8.4: Overview of all refactoring scenarios in the evaluation.

Scenario	SC	MS	SQ	DD	ES	ER	Matches	Transform.	Decision	Update
S1	100	100	100	100	0	100	lost	rename	update	replace
S2	100	100	100	100	5	95	lost	rename	update	replace
S3	100	100	100	100	0	100	lost	remove	update	cancel
S4	0	50	0	100	0	100	new	create	noupdate	-
S5	68	0	34	33	100	0	new	create	noupdate	-
S6	-	-	-	-	-	-	-	-	-	-
S7	100	100	100	67	100	0	-	move	-	-
S8	100	100	100	100	0	100	lost	rename	update	replace
S9	17	100	17	100	25	75	new	rename	update	exclude
S10	100	60	80	67	100	0	new	create	noupdate	-

relevant for the evaluation of other parts of the pointcut, we only accept matches of unspecified properties.

Imprecise and irrelevant expressions — Such expressions should only refer to elements which are closely connected to the targeted behavior (i.e., a joinpoint), because any change can cause new and lost matches, and no analysis of the pointcut can determine whether such matches are acceptable. And even if such an expression directly addresses a joinpoint shadow, it can lead to ambiguous update decisions. For example, in scenario S5, the refactoring created an element with similar properties but the affected pointcut specified the properties incompletely. The result, a nearly correct match, cannot be recognized as different match because its similarity to the correct matches was not intended (and is without any effect in the base program). Hence, such expressions are most challenging for aspect-oriented refactoring tools, because the intention whether their matches are wanted remains in the developer's mind.

Precise but irrelevant expressions — Our refactoring tool was able to accept the most impact of such expressions. The moved method in scenario S7 has even no effect on the selected joinpoint set. The almost completely specified cflow property in scenario S10 also belongs to this category. The only downside is that it is more expensive to differentiate additional occurrences of already specified behavior from alterations of the specified behavior introduced by the refactoring. Accordingly, our tool has proposed the correct decisions, even though the developer probably wants to cancel the refactoring because the base program behavior changes.

Aside from the result, that the pointcut updates have been successful in all experiments, we also have learned several lessons from these experiments. Specifications of meta-level properties for selecting program elements are much more difficult to maintain them as symbolic references. There are two reasons for this: (i) a pointcut does not necessarily state that a certain element is referenced, and (ii) any adjustment of a pointcut can lead to a different selection of elements (which does not necessarily recover the originally matching elements).

Moreover, incomplete specifications represent the biggest challenge in refactoring aspect-oriented programs. More precisely, our approach had to deal with two kinds of incompleteness: pointcuts with incompletely specified matches (i.e., matching program elements), and pointcuts with incompletely specified properties. The former kind specifies too few properties for restricting its selection to a single element, similar as symbolic references refer to a single element. A refactoring may split the set of matching elements into different sets, which causes a explicit extension of the pointcut and is thus the main reason for pointcut bloating. The latter specify a single property only partially, which may thus already match multiple times. Such incomplete specifications complicate the generation of a suitable adjustments of the specified parts the need to be updated. A refactoring tool could incrementally propose new adjustments of such expressions, making the specification more and more complete. Such incremental proposition of update would require an evaluation of every proposal before it could be compared. In addition, incomplete and nested expressions can interfere with the required update decision for aggregated specifications, such as in scenario S5. Here an almost overridden method is created, but the wrong match is caused by the creation of one of its calls.

Finally, the refactoring tool SOOTHSAYER worked as expected. All pointcuts could be represented by our intermediate representation, and any altered match was detected by our impact analysis. Also, the responsible program transformations and directly affected expressions were ascertained in every scenario. This means that our proposed impact analysis was able to detect all effects, and provided a suitable representation for the impact classification.

Furthermore, the analysis for cflow pointcuts worked successfully in a nontrivial case, where new occurrences of already matching behavior had to be distinguished from the selection of altered behavior.

Our analysis approach worked well in determining which transformation causes what kind of effect on which expression of a pointcut. Also, we have observed a significantly higher computation effort for our impact analysis. However, none of the algorithms were optimized, so much higher response times for larger programs are actually not unexpected.

Chapter 9

Concluding Remarks

This last chapter is dedicated to summarize the work presented in the proceeding chapters. In particular, we summarize the contributions of this dissertation, give an overview of the limitations of the approach and its implementation, present "lessons learned" particularly with regards to refactoring compliant AOP, and outline directions for future work.

9.1 Summary of Contributions

This research has explored how tool-supported refactoring for object-oriented programs can be made aware of behavioral composition defined in aspect-oriented programs, and which particular attributes of existing AOP approaches are suitable for refactoring tool support. The principal artifact of this research is a change impact analysis framework, that is integrated in a refactoring tool for aspect-oriented programs, called SOOTHSAYER. In particular, the following contributions have been made:

SOOTHSAYER provides a specific **change impact analysis framework** for pointcuts. This static program analysis detects alterations of matching program elements, and provides concrete information about affected pointcut expressions and responsible changes so that pointcut updates can be proposed automatically. The analysis considers any program element that is referenced by a pointcut, and reveals altered matches regardless of the quality of their specifications.

In addition, the analysis provides a specific call graph that allows for a **precise evaluation of statically represented cflow properties**. The call graph is optimized for representing partial control flows statically, including the execution likeliness of potential call paths at runtime. Our static matching algorithm for evaluating cflow properties of this graph not only detects cycles, but also computes cflow matches as qualified call paths (i.e., using the execution likeliness information). This static representation enables SOOTHSAYER to detect changes of the execution likeliness in addition to alterations of complete call paths.

A *second contribution* of this work is a **change impact classification** for pointcuts. For this classification, we developed a **model for the decomposition of pointcuts** that represents every property specified by a pointcut in a single pointcut expression and reflects the dependencies of (extrinsic) properties directly. This intermediate representation of pointcuts allows for an explicit assessment of change effects on every single pointcut expression. The resolving of this pointcut model associates every matching program element with the corresponding expression (pointcut selection model). Because of this direct association, the change impact on every matching element can be assessed in terms of the corresponding pointcut expression.

We have developed a set of five *change impact measures* for the impact classification, which classify the change effects in terms of the affected pointcut expression, i.e., how complete an affected expression is defined, how precise an altered match is specified, how much the affected property is related to a particular program behavior, and how many other expressions depend on an affected pointcut expression.

The *third contribution* is the **prototype refactoring tool**. It extends object-oriented refactorings with the detection of pointcut-affecting changes and an update computation for invalidated pointcuts. The implementation is based on the Eclipse JDT and enhances the JDT refactoring workflow as well as its individual refactorings. The enhanced workflow provides an extended change preview (showing also change effects on aspects) a pointcut impact analysis review, and a pointcut update customization dialog. The enhanced refactorings additionally determine the kind of every performed transformation (e.g., rename, move, create) and associate its atomic changes with any lost or new match of program elements.

The refactoring tool runs on this explicit change information a set of qualitative heuristics to decide whether affected pointcuts have to be adjusted.

The *fourth contribution* is the **heuristic-based pointcut update computation**. Two qualitative heuristics were developed based on the change impact measures. They determine whether altered matches are intended or accidental by assessing quality and relevance of the affected pointcut expressions. Predefined ranges for both heuristics recommend to accept new matches of precisely specified and less relevant expressions, and lost matches of almost unspecified and less relevant expressions. For all other values the expressions are labeled as invalidated (i.e., to be updated).

Our update computation algorithm uses **pointcut update patterns** to propose the least intrusive replacement, i.e., a complete replacement on invalidated expressions whose matches are completely lost or new, or a direct exclusion or inclusion of altered matches. Any update recovers the originally matching elements which were selected before the refactoring, and hence restores the original program behavior. Complete replacements of pointcut expressions preserve the pointcut's appearance and keep the pointcut recognizable even after multiple updates. If original matches should be recovered but the cannot, e.g., because they were removed from the program, the algorithm proposes to cancel the refactoring.

The *fifth and last contribution* is a **taxonomy for the attributes of joinpoint models and pointcut languages** used by existing AOP approaches. The influences of each attribute on the predictability of change effects are presented in the context of tool-supported refactoring. The analyzability of joinpoint properties, the completeness of their specification, and their dependency of other properties were identified as the primary reasons for problems when refactoring programs of existing AOP approaches. From the resulting challenges *criteria for refactoring compliant AOP* were developed.

9.2 Lessons Learned

The ways in which pointcuts can be expressed by existing pointcut languages lead to various challenges for tool-supporting the refactoring of aspect-oriented programs. Our approach integrates a change impact analysis for pointcuts into a refactoring tool for assessing the effects of source code changes in terms of existing pointcuts. Based on the computed impact measures an update decisions is proposed and for invalidated pointcuts an update is computed.

The evaluation of our work has shown that our approach can deal with a variety of pointcuts. In terms of the thesis' statement we have shown that an explicit representation of the change impact on pointcuts, stating which part of a pointcut is affected by which program transformation, allows for the computation of minimal-invasive adjustments.

The following more specific issues could be observed if we consider our taxonomy for attributes of existing joinpoint models and pointcut languages. The following attributes have been identified as *unrelated attributes* to aspect-aware refactoring:

Visibility — The visibility does not influence our approach, but (if restricted) it can lead to additional refactoring constraints.

Granularity — As long as the pointcuts refer to elements of program representations that are statically computed, the granularity does not influence the result of our refactoring approach.

The issues for the following attributes could be solved by our approach and thus are considered as *unproblematic attributes*:

Dependency — The specification of particularly extrinsic properties can depend on specifications of anchor properties. These dependencies cannot always be recognized from the pointcut's structure, our intermediate representation of pointcuts makes them explicit, and enables our impact analysis to detect changes of the pointcut semantics.

Aggregation — A pointcut can specify a joinpoint property by aggregating several (nested) expressions. The properties specified by the nested expressions can interfere with the required adjustment of the aggregated expression. Adjustments for specifications of such more complex properties can require to replace multiple dependent pointcut expressions with a single expression, which has been shown by our approach for computing pointcut updates.

Meaning — Pointcuts can restrict a selection of matching elements by properties that are more or less related to a particular program behavior. Properties with a strong behavioral meaning, like cflow properties, are rarely affected by refactorings and their specifications cannot automatically be adjusted. Properties with a pure structural meaning are more easily affected by refactoring but their specifications can often directly replaced. Effects on both kinds can be handled by our approach properly.

The issues for the following attributes could only partially be solved by our approach. These attributes are the primary reasons for unpredictable effects on the program behavior which cannot be solved with existing program analysis approaches. Even if our analysis is able to detect interferences with such pointcuts, it can be impossible to determine the pointcut update, because of an imprecise or statically not determinable specification. These attributes are considered as **problematic attributes**:

Analyzability — Pointcuts can specify properties of dynamic program representations that cannot be sufficiently precise approximated (with reasonable effort). Dynamic properties that are not restricted to runtime information which occur only in specific executions of the program (like, specific execution sequences, values of unscoped variables), are particularly problematic. Those properties often require a static representation of all possible program executions and an analysis of the entire representation. Such dynamic information cannot be supported with reasonable computation effort.

Since refactoring tools use static program analysis some of these conditions cannot be statically represented and, thus, not checked by a refactoring tool.

Completeness — Pointcuts can under specify joinpoint properties, e.g., if a similar behavior is added in a future program version, a pointcut may intentionally bind advice to it. However, such pointcuts do not necessarily state such an intention. They specify a set of elements incompletely, i.e., a matching element is specified with too vague properties or the matching property is just partially specified. In both cases important information, for deciding whether a matching element is intentional or accidental, is not expressed in the pointcut.

Imprecisely specified properties can be handled with our heuristics-based approach, however adjustments of such expressions can require additional analysis steps. Updates may need to be incrementally proposed, which require multiple evaluation steps of gradually broadened or narrowed updates, so that the adjustment is minimal-invasive and does not bloat the pointcut.

Symmetry — Joinpoint models that also provide access to joinpoints in the execution of aspect code can merely be found in existing AOP approaches. Hence, properties provided by such models were not investigated by the research of this dissertation.

To summarize, not only pointcut expressions that precisely specify an affected property are properly handled by our approach. A heuristics-based refactoring approach can also determine whether matches of imprecisely specified properties are sufficiently complete specified, so that the pointcut has to be updated. For our approach, particularly path-based specifications which reflect the dependencies in the program seem to simplify the update computation.

9.3 Limitations

SOOTHSAYER is the first implementation of an aspect-aware refactoring approach, and, being a research prototype, it does not provide the final commercial-grade refactoring support for AOP. One the one hand, there are limitations that result from features of existing pointcut language approaches, which generally cannot be solved by program analysis. On the other hand, there are some technical limitations of the current implementation of SOOTHSAYER.

During the work on SOOTHSAYER we have explored several possibilities for approximating dynamic joinpoint properties. We have developed a model for statically representing properties of the execution history and discussed limitations of this model in particular for cflow and execution sequence properties. In particular, we have highlighted the differences in computation effort and accuracy for static representations of these properties. We concluded that static program analysis approaches are not suitable for an efficient and precise **approximation of the execution sequence property**. Potential alternatives for such highly dynamic properties are, for example, model checking approaches, which we have not investigated in this work.

The current **implementation of the pointcut model** does not support unification (as introduced by LMP approaches, like [36]). We therefore could not investigate the effects of unification on our impact analysis and the generation of updated pointcuts. Since some very powerful pointcut language approaches support unification, we are planning to investigate the influences of unification on the evolvability of pointcuts in future work. In addition, abstract pointcuts are not supported by our pointcut model. Such pointcuts are important for specifying some already known properties but defer more precise definitions to other aspect modules. Abstract pointcuts can refer to other pointcuts and state some arbitrary properties which cannot be resolved to a set of matching program elements.

The implementation is also limited to AspectJ-like pointcut languages. Although our pointcut model can be used as intermediate representation for other pointcut languages, we have not evaluated if an implementation, e.g., of path-based or LMP-based pointcut languages, causes new problems when generating pointcuts.

Various pointcut languages allow for **nested OR expressions**. Our implementation of the pointcut resolver has to consider aggregations with OR expression as individual pointcuts. We therefore normalize pointcuts with nested OR expressions, by pulling every OR expression to the most top nesting level (i.e., its DNF form). This is crucial for the current change impact classification approach. However, updates of such a normalized pointcut can significantly differ in its appearance from the original pointcut. It is also not clear if every normalized and updated version of a pointcut can be retranslated into its original (but updated) form.

The current implementation of SOOTHSAYER cannot deal with pointcuts that use other pointcuts. Such **dependencies between pointcuts** are used to refine a specification of joinpoint properties in different aspect modules. Also pointcuts that share the same joinpoint are not considered in the current implementation. A proper treatment of such dependencies between pointcuts would integrate our approach closer into AOP languages.

Finally, most AOP languages provide *mechanisms for composing the structure* of different implementation modules. The current version of SOOTHSAYER only focusses on the preservation of the behavioral composition in aspect-oriented programs. Defined structural compositions are not considered.

9.4 Future Work

A long-term goal of this research is the development of a practical refactoring extension for aspect-oriented programs. To support this goal, several of the issues raised by the current work deserve further attention.

Perhaps most importantly, a mechanisms that can incrementally compute *gradually narrowed or broadened scopes of a pointcut update*. The current update decision algorithm can propose complete replacements of the smallest affected expression, but if this is not possible it explicitly enumerates matches to exclude or include them. In case such an extension is computed for a pointcut that was already extended, an incremental update computation could try to combine both extensions to a more general specification. Such a composition of explicit exclusions or inclusions would allow for recognizable pointcuts even if affected expressions could not be replaced.

The current update computation allows for additionally matching elements if they are sufficiently concrete specified. However, we do not consider yet almost matching elements in our update computation algorithm. A presentation of almost matching elements could be particularly helpful when a user decides to define a customized update.
To this end, we are planning to integrate a *computation of boundary matches*, as proposed by Anabalagan and Xie [4]. Similar to this approach a predefined threshold can be established, which is used to additionally present program elements that nearly correspond to all specified properties. In contrast to Anabalagan and Xie, we are planning to extend the distance measure to all properties that can be represented by our pointcut model, rather than considering only signature patterns.

As one result of this dissertation, we have identified path-based pointcut languages, like the XQuery approach of Eichberg et al. [24], as most suitable for our refactoring support. We are planning an *integration of path-based pointcut specifications* with our pointcut model into a future version of SOOTHSAYER.

The impact measures on which both heuristics where defined are configured very conservatively, i.e., they propose to recover the original pointcut selection in some cases where an altered selection could be accepted. A further evaluation, with less conservative configurations of both heuristics and systematically defined pointcut examples that lead to extreme decision scenarios, can result in a configuration that allows for an automated computation of valid updates in more cases.

The current implementation of our intermediate representation for pointcut does not support unification (as introduced by LMP approaches, like [36]). We want to investigate whether **unification** can be integrated into our pointcut model in such a way that the dependencies between joinpoint properties are still explicitly reflected.

Also, **abstract pointcuts** are not supported by the current pointcut model. Such pointcuts are an important means for specifying some already known properties but leave more precise definitions to pointcut definitions. Abstract pointcuts can refer to other pointcuts or just state some arbitrary properties which cannot be evaluated to set of matching program elements.

In future work, we want to investigate whether our update computation can deal with such dependencies between different pointcuts and if the pointcut model can support incomplete pointcut definitions like:

```
1 pointcut interestingPage ( ) :
2     within ( AspectJProjectPropertiesPage )  ||
3     within ( AJCompilerPreferencePage ) ;
```

Finally, we are planning to **complete the current implementation** of SOOTHSAYER. A closer integration into the IDE, for example, can provide specific error messages when a refactored program with deferred updated decisions is going to be executed. We also plan the integration with other language features of a particular AOP language, like AspectJ, or OT/J.

Moreover, an optimized approximation of dynamic joinpoint properties could speed up the refactoring process and allows for refactorings in larger programs. We plan to optimize the algorithms for constructing the approximated program representations and for evaluating the properties.

Appendix A

Examples for Dynamic Program Representations

A.1 An Object Graph Example

This example demonstrates the general structure and its changeability of an object graph during the execution of a program. Any point in execution has a specific execution context that defines the entry points for accessing an object graph. In this example, we use the program shown in Figure A.1 and discuss three points during the execution of this program depicted by Figure A.2, A.3, and A.4.

The current execution context at the considered point in execution is shown on the left side of each figure. The current point in execution is indicated by the black arrow.
Starting from method `main(String[])` in class `ObjectGraphExample`, several new objects are instantiated and connected to each other through corresponding method calls. First, a list is instantiated in line 6, then objects a, b, and c are instantiated (till line 10).

In Figure A.2, the object graph after these instantiations is illustrated. The figure shows that the instantiation of type `MyLinkedList` has also caused an instantiation of type `Entry`, as well as the creation of an edge connecting the both objects.
Figure A.3 shows the point in execution directly before the return from method `add-(Object)` in method `main(String[])`. It illustrates that occurrences of new nodes in the graph cause always changes to existing edges or at least an additional edge connecting the new node. The current execution context is still the context of method `add(Object)`. The assignments in `add(Object)` caused an addition of a new node for object *elem2* as well as new and changed edges, making the object *a* part of the list.
After three additional invocations of method `add(Object)` the execution returns to the method `main(String[])` (line 13). In Figure A.4 is illustrated, which changes lead to a disappearance of edges and nodes in the graph. The invocation of method `remove(Object)` removes the object *elem4* from the list, which causes a disappearance of the edge connecting both objects. The object *elem4* can now only be accessed from the execution context of method `remove(Object)`. After the execution is returned to

```
1  public class ObjectGraphExample
2  {
3    public static void
4      main(String[] args)
5    {
6      MyLinkedList list =
7        new MyLinkedList();
8      Object a = new Object();
9      Object b = new Object();
10     Object c = new Object();
11     list.add(a);
12     list.add(b);
13     list.add(c);
14     list.remove(c);
15   }
16 }
```

(a)

```
1  public class Entry{
2    Object element;
3    Entry next;
4    Entry previous;
5
6    Entry(Object element,
7          Entry next,
8          Entry previous)
9    {
10       this.element = element;
11       this.next = next;
12       this.previous = previous;
13   }
14 }
```

(b)

```
1  public class MyLinkedList{
2    private Entry header =
3      new Entry(null, null, null);
4
5    public MyLinkedList(){
6      header.next = header;
7      header.previous = header;
8    }
9
10   public void add(Object o){
11     Entry newEntry =
12       new Entry(o,
13       header,
14       header.previous);
15     newEntry.previous.next =
16       newEntry;
17     newEntry.next.previous =
18       newEntry;
19   }
20
21   public boolean remove(Object o){
22     for (Entry e = header.next;
23       e != header;
24       e = e.next)
25     {
26       if (o.equals(e.element)){
27         remove(e);
28         return true;
29       }
30     }
31     return false;
32   }
33   private void remove(Entry e) {
34     e.previous.next = e.next;
35     e.next.previous = e.previous;
36   }
37 }
```

(c)

Figure A.1: Source code of object graph example.

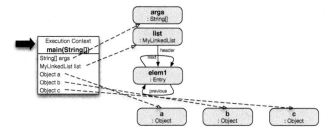

Figure A.2: Object graph after execution of all instantiations in `main(String[])`

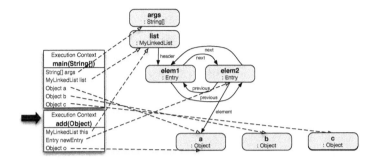

Figure A.3: Object graph before return from first call of method add(Object)

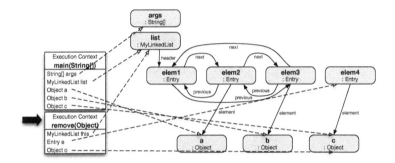

Figure A.4: Object graph before return from call of method remove(Object)

method main(String[]), the last reference to *elem4* (the execution context of method remove(Object)) is removed and the node *elem4* disappears from the graph.

A.2 An Execution Sequence Example

The following example uses the *tracematches* approach to illustrate how execution sequences can be specified. It is based on the program presented in Figure 5.4 (a) and refers to Figure A.5 which depicts its execution. The specification of an execution sequence can require the occurrence of a specific pattern of joinpoint entries and exits. The example pointcut requires an entry of method m5() (indirectly) followed by an entry of method m3(), before an entry of method m9() is considered as selected joinpoint. The corresponding pointcut in the *tracematches* syntax is shown in Listing A.1.

```
1 tracematch () {
2     sym entM5 before : call(void Example.m5());
3     sym entM3 before : call(void Example.m3());
4     sym entM9 before : call(void Example.m9());
5
6     entM5 entM3 entM9
7
8     { /* Advicebody A */}
9 }
```

Listing A.1: Tracematches   Example
specification of an execution sequence using the
tracematches approach.

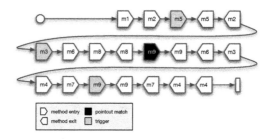

Figure A.5: A visualized execution of the program shown in Figure 5.4 (a)

In Figure A.5 several occurrences of method m9() entries are shown, but only occurrences after the specified execution pattern are considered as selected joinpoints. The specified sequence of the example is a strict specification, i.e., if the second occurrence of the entry of method m9() should be a selected joinpoint, the sequence could be specified as: **entM5 entM3 entM9 entM9**.

Following the *tracematches* approach, an execution sequence is specified in two different parts (cf. Listing A.1). A first part defines so-called *symbols*, and a second defines a *regular expression* using these symbols. This expression is then compared with actually occurred events in the program execution. An selected joinpoint occurs, i.e., the bound advice is invoked, if the last symbol of the regular expression occurs in the execution. The symbols comprise a **before** or **after** construct and can be combined with other pointcut designators. A specification of **before** or **after** for a symbol is necessary, otherwise a symbol would not denote an atomic point in the execution[1].

The example above shows a strict specification of an execution sequence. In addition, more "fuzzy" execution patterns can be defined, e.g., with optional symbols or symbol repetitions. Such a specification could lead to a selected joinpoint for every execution of method m9() in the example.

---

[1] The last symbol can also be augmented with an **around**, **after returning**, or **after throwing**.

Appendix B

Additional Properties of Dynamic Program Representation

B.1 Object Graph Properties

Several dynamic properties of a joinpoint can be provided using an object graph or the execution context. Pointcut languages, such as *Alpha* [72], provide access to the complete graph, others make use of the execution context only. Moreover, not all variables of the execution context are accessible. Often access is provided to the current object (under execution), arguments of called methods, the target object at which a method or field is accessed, the return value of a method, and globally accessible fields[1]. Pointcuts can specify these properties using the syntax defined by the pointcut language. In the following four paragraphs, we give typical examples for such properties and illustrate how they can be specified.

B.1.1 Dynamic Type

Many pointcut languages provide a means to specify the type of a node within an execution context. This allows a pointcut to consider only joinpoints whose dynamic type is conform to a specific type. Mainly, this is allowed for directly accessible nodes from the execution context, e.g., the current object under execution and actual parameters. For example, consider the following AspectJ pointcut:

```
1 pointcut stringMethods(): execution(* *.*(..)) && this(String);
```

The pointcut selects any execution of a method that is executed for objects of type String (or its sub-types). The designator this refers to the object currently under execution and specifies the required dynamic type.

---

[1]In Java such field are defined by the modifiers public static.

B.1.2 Identity of Objects

Another property, for which the object graph is used, is the identity of objects. It allows a pointcut to specify the identity of two objects, even at different points in execution. The object graph is constructed at the potential joinpoint and allows for a comparison of different nodes. For example, the following pointcut specifies the identity of two method arguments:

```
1 ?jp matching
2     reception(?jp, ?selector, <?arg, ?arg>)
```

The example uses a logic programming syntax provided by a pointcut language proposed by Gybels et al. [36]. The pointcut specifies the identity of two successive arguments of an arbitrary method invocation of arbitrary objects. The identity is specified using a specific mechanism, called *unification*, i.e., for elements with the same identifier the same value is required.

B.1.3 Reachability of Objects

Also the directed edges of a call graph between different nodes can be used for the specification of properties. The pointcut language *Alpha* introduces the reachability between two graph nodes as specifiable property. A joinpoint can be required to be reachable from another joinpoint, i.e., a specific node in the object graph has to be connected to another node through graph edges. For example, consider the following pointcut in the Alpha syntax:

```
1 class Exmpl extends Object{
2     after set(P, F, _), reachable(Q, P), instanceof(Q, 'String')
3     {
4         /* advicebody: do something */
5     }
6 }
```

It selects any field assignment to a field whose type P is reachable from the type String (or its subtypes) in the object graph. The property "reachable" is specified between nodes in the object graph, representing a type of a field and a node of type String. The pointcut language uses unification over the variables Q and P for specifying the reachable property.

B.1.4 Dynamic Value-based Conditionals.

Some pointcut languages allow for the use of conditionals for specifying a particular value of a variable. For example, the following pointcut illustrates how a value-based conditional can be specified in AspectJ:

```
1 aspect AnAspect {
2     before(Withdrawal amount) : if(amount.value > 1000.0)
3         && execution(void *.withdraw(Withdrawal)) && args(amount)
4     {
5         /* advicebody: since this is much money make a more intense check */
6     }
7 }
```

The pointcut selects every execution of method `withdraw(Withdrawal)` if its argument has a value bigger than 1000. It refers to the argument node in the object graph and accesses a dynamic value of the underlying object. The specification combines an `execution`-designator with an `args`-designator, i.e., the object graph node is required to be a method and its argument has to be of type `Withdrawal`. The condition is specified using the `if`-designator, i.e., the field `value` of the graph node `amount` is expected to be bigger than 1000. Every invocation of a method `withdraw` with an withdrawal of a higher value than 1000 is considered as desired joinpoint.

B.2 Combined Properties of Object Graph and Execution History

```
1 tracematch (Subject s, Observer o) {
2
3   sym create_observer after returning(o):
4
5       call(Observer.new(..))
6
7   && args(s);
8
9   sym update_subject after:
10
11      call(* Subject.update(..))
12
13  && target(s);
14
15
16
17  create_observer update_subject*
18
19  {
20
21    o.update_view();
22
23  }
24
25 }
```

Listing B.1: Implementation   of
            the Observer Pattern's update mechanism using
            variable bindings in *tracematches*.

In addition to a specific sequence of executions, the identity of objects at a particular execution step (trigger) can be specified. The pointcut can access the object graphs at different triggers and specify the identity of a certain node. At every point in execution different object graphs are available, providing access to different execution contexts and associated nodes. A pointcut that specifies a specific execution sequence can additionally define a so-called *variable binding*. In Listing B.1, an example implementation of the observer pattern is shown[2].

The listing shows a pointcut expressed in the *tracematches* syntax. It selects every subject update, after the observer was created, if it is the same subject for which the observer was created. To this end, the pointcut specifies the identity of `Subject`'s object in the observer pattern and the object in the update process. For the specification of the identity the *tracematches* approach uses unification, a language feature introduced by logic programming approaches, but also *Stateful Aspects* and *tracematches* make use of it.

---

[2]Example is taken from [3], the term *observer pattern* is defined in [29] p. 239

Bibliography

[1] Homepage of the AspectJ Development Tools (AJDT) for Eclipse. http://www.eclipse.org/ajdt/.

[2] A. V. Aho, R. Sethi, and J. D. Ullman. *Compilers: Principles, Techniques, and Tools*. Addison-Wesley Longman Publishing Co., Inc., Boston, MA, USA, 1987.

[3] C. Allan, P. Avgustinov, A. S. Christensen, L. Hendren, S. Kuzins, O. Lhotak, O. de Moor, D. Sereni, G. Sittampalam, and J. Tibble. Adding trace matching to AspectJ. Technical Report abc-2005-1, Programming Tools Group, University of Oxford University, UK; BRICS, Group of Aarhus, Denmark; Sable Research, McGill University, Montreal, Canada, 2005.

[4] P. Anbalagan and T. Xie. APTE: Automated pointcut testing for AspectJ programs. In *Proceedings of the 2nd Workshop on Testing Aspect-Oriented Programs (WTAOP 2006)*, pages 27–32, July 2006.

[5] Homepage of the AspectJ Programming Language. http://www.eclipse.org/aspectj.

[6] L. Bergmans and M. Akşit. Principles and Design Rationale of Composition Filters. In Robert E. Filman, Tzilla Elrad, Siobhán Clarke, and Mehmet Akşit, editors, *Aspect-Oriented Software Development*, pages 63–95. Addison-Wesley, Boston, 2004.

[7] Lodewijk Bergmans, Johan Brichau, Peri Tarr, and Erik Ernst, editors. *SPLAT: Software engineering Properties of Languages for Aspect Technologies*, March 2003.

[8] D. Binkley, M. Ceccato, M. Harman, F. Ricca, and P. Tonella. Automated Refactoring of Object Oriented Code into Aspects. In *ICSM* [45], pages 27–36.

[9] Andrew P. Black, editor. *ECOOP 2005 - Object-Oriented Programming, 19th European Conference, Glasgow, UK, July 25-29, 2005, Proceedings*, volume 3586 of *Lecture Notes in Computer Science*. Springer, 2005.

[10] M. Braem, K. Gybels, A. Kellens, and W. Vanderperren. Automated Pattern-Based Pointcut Generation. In Welf Löwe and Mario Südholt, editors, *Software Composition*, volume 4089 of *Lecture Notes in Computer Science*, pages 66–81. Springer, 2006.

[11] M. Braem, K. Gybels, A. Kellens, and W. Vanderperren. Inducing Evolution-robust Pointcuts. In *Proceedings of the International ERCIM Workshop on Software Evolution*, Lille, France, april 2006.

[12] G. Brcan. Extension of object-oriented Refactoring for the aspect-oriented Programming Language ObjectTeams/Java. Diploma thesis (in german), Technical University Berlin, Berlin, Germany, October 2005.

[13] S. Breu and J. Krinke. Aspect Mmining using Event Traces. In *19th International Conference on Automated Software Engineering*, pages 310–315, Los Alamitos, California, September 2004. IEEE Computer Society.

[14] H. Chen and D. Wagner. MOPS: An Infrastructure for Examining Security Properties of Software. In *CCS '02: Proceedings of the 9th ACM Conference on Computer and Communications Security*, pages 235–244, New York, NY, USA, 2002. ACM Press.

[15] C. Clifton. *A Design Discipline and Language Features for Modular Reasoning in Aspect-oriented Programs*. Ph.d. thesis, Iowa State University, Ames, IA, USA, 2005. Major Professor-Gary T. Leavens.

[16] A. Colyer, A. Clement, G. Harley, and M. Webster. *Eclipse AspectJ*. The Eclipse Series. Addison-Wesley, Upper Saddle River, NJ, 2005.

[17] T. Cormen, C. Leiserson, R. Rivest, and C. Stein. *Introduction to Algorithms, Second Edition*. The MIT Press, Cambridge, MA, USA, September 2001.

[18] J. Dean, D. Grove, and C. Chambers. Optimization of Object-Oriented Programs Using Class Hierarchy Analysis. In W. Olthoff, editor, *ECOOP '95 - Object-Oriented Programming: 9th European Conference*, volume 952 of *Lecture Notes in Computer Science*, pages 77–101, London, UK, August 1995. Springer-Verlag.

[19] R. Douence, O. Motelet, and M. Südholt. A Formal Definition of Crosscuts. In A. Yonezawa and S. Matsuoka, editors, *Metalevel Architectures and Separation of Crosscutting Concerns 3rd International Conference (Reflection 2001), LNCS 2192*, pages 170–186. Springer-Verlag, September 2001.

[20] M. Eaddy and A. Aho. Statement Annotations for Fine-Grained Advising. In Y. Coady W. Cazzola, S. Chiba and Gunter Saake, editors, *3rd ECOOP Workshop on Reflection, AOP and Meta-Data for Software Evolution (RAMSE)*, pages 89–99, July 2006.

[21] Homepage of the Eclipse Project. http://www.eclipse.org.

[22] Homepage of the Eclipse Java Development Tools (JDT) Subproject. http://www.eclipse.org/jdt/.

[23] Homepage of the Eclipse Test and Performance Platform (TPTP) Project. http://www.eclipse.org/tptp/.

[24] M. Eichberg, M. Mezini, and K. Ostermann. Pointcuts as Functional Queries. In Wei-Ngan Chin, editor, *Programming Languages and Systems: Second Asian Symposium, APLAS 2004*, Lecture Notes in Computer Science, pages 366–382, Taipei, Taiwan, November 2004. Springer-Verlag Heidelberg.

[25] S. G. Eick, J. L. Steffen, and E. E. Summer. SeeSoft – A Tool for Visualizing Line Oriented Software Statistics. In *IEEE Trans. on Software Engineering, 18(11)*, pages 957–968, 1992.

[26] Erik Ernst, Johan Brichau, and Lodewijk Bergmans, editors. *SPLAT: Software engineering Properties of Languages for Aspect Technologies*, March 2006.

[27] R. E. Filman, T. Elrad, S. Clarke, and M. Akşit, editors. *Aspect-Oriented Software Development*. Addison-Wesley, Boston, 2005.

[28] M. Fowler, K. Beck, J. Brant, W. Opdyke, and D. Roberts. *Refactoring: Improving the Design of Existing Code*. Addison-Wesley, 1999.

[29] E. Gamma, R. Helm, R. Johnson, and J. Vlissides. *Design Patterns: Elements of Reusable Object-Oriented Software*. Addison-Wesley Longman Publishing Co., Inc., Boston, MA, USA, January 1995.

[30] A. Garcia, C. Sant'Anna, E. Figueiredo, C. Lucena, K. Uira, and A. von Staa. Modularizing Design Patterns with Aspects: A Quantitative Study. *LNCS Transactions on Aspect-Oriented Software Development, Springer*, 2006.

[31] A. Garrido and R. Johnson. Challenges of refactoring C programs. In *IWPSE '02: Proceedings of the International Workshop on Principles of Software Evolution*, pages 6–14, New York, NY, USA, 2002. ACM Press.

[32] A. Garrido and R. Johnson. Refactoring C with Conditional Compilation. In *ASE*, pages 323–326. IEEE Computer Society, 2003.

[33] James Gosling, Bill Joy, Guy Steele, and Gilad Bracha. *Java(TM) Language Specification, Third Edition*. Addison-Wesley Professional, June 2005.

[34] P. Greenwood, T. Bartolomei, E. Figueiredo, M. Dosea, A. Garcia, N. Cacho, C. Sant'Anna, S. Soares, P. Borba, U. Kulesza, and A. Rashid. On the Impact of Aspectual Decompositions on Design Stability: An Empirical Study. In *21st European Conference on Object-Oriented Programming (ECOOP'07)*, Germany, July 2007.

[35] W. G. Griswold, K. Sullivan, Y. Song, M. Shonle, N. Tewari, Y. Cai, and H. Rajan. Modular Software Design with Crosscutting Interfaces. *IEEE Softw.*, 23(1):51–60, 2006.

[36] K. Gybel and J. Brichau. Arranging Language Features for Pattern-based Crosscuts. In Mehmet Akşit, editor, *Proc. 2nd Int' Conf. on Aspect-Oriented Software Development (AOSD-2003)*, pages 60–69. ACM Press, March 2003.

[37] K. Gybels, S. Hanenberg, S. Herrmann, and J. Wloka, editors. *European Interactive Workshop on Aspects in Software (EIWAS)*, September 2004.

[38] K. Gybels and A. Kellens. An Experiment in Using Inductive Logic Programming to Uncover Pointcuts. In Gybels et al. [37].

[39] S. Hanenberg, C. Oberschulte, and R. Unland. Refactoring of Aspect-Oriented Software. In R. Unland, editor, *NetObjectDays*, volume 2591 of *Lecture Notes in Computer Science*. Springer, 2003.

[40] J. Hannemann, T. Fritz, and G. C. Murphy. Refactoring to Aspects: An Interactive Approach. In *eclipse '03: Proceedings of the 2003 OOPSLA workshop on eclipse technology eXchange*, pages 74–78. ACM Press, 2003.

[41] J. Hannemann, G. Murphy, and G. Kiczales. Role-Based Refactoring of Crosscutting Concerns. In Tarr [92], pages 135–146.

[42] W. Harrison, H. Ossher, and P. Tarr. Asymmetrically vs. Symmetrically Organized Paradigms for Software Composition. In Bergmans et al. [7].

[43] S. Herrmann. Object Teams: Improving modularity for crosscutting collaborations. In *Proc. Net Object Days 2002*, 2002.

[44] Homepage of the IntelliJ IDEA Java IDE. http://www.jetbrains.com/idea/.

[45] IEEE Computer Society. *21st IEEE International Conference on Software Maintenance (ICSM 2005), 25-30 September 2005, Budapest, Hungary*, 2005.

[46] M. Iwamoto and J. Zhao. Refactoring Aspect-Oriented Programs. In O. Aldawud, M. Kandé, G. Booch, B. Harrison, D. Stein, J. Gray, S. Clarke, A. Z. Santeon, P. Tarr, and F. Akkawi, editors, *The 4th AOSD Modeling With UML Workshop*, October 2003.

[47] Homepage of the JHotDraw Open-Source Project. http://www.jhotdraw.org/.

[48] B. Johnson and B. Shneiderman. Tree-Maps: A Space-Filling Approach to the Visualization of Hirarchical Information Structures. In *In Proceedings of IEEE Visualization Conference*, pages pages 284–291., 1991.

[49] A. Kellens, K. Mens, J. Brichau, and K. Gybels. A Model-Driven Pointcut Language for More Robust Pointcuts. In Ernst et al. [26].

[50] A. Kellens, K. Mens, J. Brichau, and K. Gybels. Managing the Evolution of Aspect-Oriented Software with Model-based Pointcuts. In Dave Thomas, editor, *ECOOP*, volume 4067 of *Lecture Notes in Computer Science*. Springer, July 2006.

[51] J. Kerievsky. *Refactoring to Patterns*. Addison-Wesley Professional, August 2004.

[52] G. Kiczales, E. Hilsdale, J. Hugunin, M. Kersten, J. Palm, and W. G. Griswold. An Overview of AspectJ. In J. L. Knudsen, editor, *Proc. ECOOP 2001, LNCS 2072*, pages 327–353, Berlin, June 2001. Springer-Verlag.

[53] G. Kiczales, J. Lamping, A. Mendhekar, C. Maeda, C. Lopes, J.-M. Loingtier, and J. Irwin. Aspect-Oriented Programming. Technical Report SPL97-008 P9710042, Xerox PARC, February 1997.

[54] G. Kiczales and M. Mezini. Aspect-oriented Programming and Modular Reasoning. In Roman et al. [76], pages 49–58.

[55] G. Kiczales and M. Mezini. Separation of Concerns with Procedures, Annotations, Advice and Pointcuts. In Black [9], pages 195–213.

[56] C. Koppen and M. Störzer. PCDiff: Attacking the Fragile Pointcut Problem. In Gybels et al. [37].

[57] U. Kulesza, V. Alves, A. Garcia, J. P. Carlos de Lucena, and P. Borba. Improving Extensibility of Object-Oriented Frameworks with Aspect-Oriented Programming. In *9th International Conference on Software Reuse (ICSR'06)*, Turin, Italy, 2006.

[58] R. Laddad. Aspect-Oriented Refactoring Parts 1: Overview and Process. Technical report, TheServerSide.com, 2003.

[59] R. Laddad. Aspect-Oriented Refactoring Parts 2: The Techniques of the Trade. Technical report, TheServerSide.com, 2003.

[60] R. Laddad. *AspectJ in Action: Practical Aspect-Oriented Programming.* Manning, 2003.

[61] M. Lehman, J. Ramil, P. Wernick, D. Perry, and W. Turski. Metrics and Laws of Software Evolution - The Nineties View. *Software Metrics Symposium, 1997. Proceedings., Fourth International*, pages 20–32, 1997.

[62] M. M. Lehman. The Programming Process. Res. Rep. RC 2722, IBM, 1969.

[63] M. Marin, A. van Deursen, and L. Moonen. Identifying Aspects Using Fan-In Analysis. In Stroulia and Lucia [87], pages 132–141.

[64] H. Masuhara, G. Kiczales, and C. Dutchyn. Compilation Semantics of Aspect-Oriented Programs. In Ron Cytron and Gary T. Leavens, editors, *FOAL 2002: Foundations of Aspect-Oriented Languages (AOSD-2002)*, pages 17–26, March 2002.

[65] T. Mens, K. Mens, and T. Tourw'e. Aspect-Oriented Software Evolution. *ERCIM News*, 58:36–37, July 2004.

[66] M. Monteiro and J. Fernandes. Towards a Catalog of Aspect-Oriented Refactorings. In Tarr [92], pages 111–122.

[67] M. P. Monteiro. Catalogue of Refactorings for AspectJ. Technical Report UM-DI-GECSD-200401, Universidade Do Minho, 2004.

[68] M. P. Monteiro and J. M. Fernandes. Towards a Catalogue of Refactorings and Code Smells for AspectJ. *T. Aspect-Oriented Software Development I*, 3880:214–258, 2006.

[69] Homepage of Object Teams. `http://www.ObjectTeams.org`.

[70] W. F. Opdyke. *Refactoring Object-Oriented Frameworks.* Ph.d. thesis, University of Illinois at Urbana-Champaign, Urbana-Champaign, IL, 1992.

[71] H. Ossher and P. Tarr. Operation-Level Composition: A Case in (Join) Point. In Serge Demeyer and Jan Bosch, editors, *ECOOP Workshops*, volume 1543 of *Lecture Notes in Computer Science*, pages 406–409. Springer, 1998.

[72] K. Ostermann, M. Mezini, and C. Bockisch. Expressive Pointcuts for Increased Modularity. In Black [9], pages 214–240.

[73] X. Ren, B. G. Ryder, M. Stoerzer, and F. Tip. Chianti: A Change Impact Analysis Tool for Java Programs. In Roman et al. [76], pages 664–665.

[74] Research on Object-Oriented Technologies and Systems Department at University of Bonn. *Homepage of the LogicAJ Project.* Available from http://roots.iai.uni-bonn.de/research/logicaj/.

[75] D. B. Roberts. Practical Analysis for Refactoring. Ph.d. thesis, University of Illinois at Urbana-Champaign, Champaign, IL, USA, 1999.

[76] Gruia-Catalin Roman, William G. Griswold, and Bashar Nuseibeh, editors. *27th International Conference on Software Engineering (ICSE 2005)*, St. Louis, Missouri, USA, May 2005. ACM Press.

[77] S. Rura. Refactoring Aspect-Oriented Software. Bachelor thesis, Williams College, May 2003.

[78] S. Rura and B. Lerner. A Basis for AspectJ Refactoring. http://www.mtholyoke.edu/~blerner/papers/gpce04.pdf, 2004.

[79] B. G. Ryder and F. Tip. Change Impact Analysis for Object-oriented Programs. In *PASTE '01: Proceedings of the 2001 ACM SIGPLAN-SIGSOFT workshop on Program analysis for software tools and engineering*, pages 46–53, New York, NY, USA, 2001. ACM Press.

[80] Source Code of the Simple Insurance Example. http://www.awprofessional.com/content/images/0321245873/sourcecode/org.cchw.ajdt.examples_1.0.0_archive.zip.

[81] Software Technology Group at Technical University of Darmstadt. *CaesarJ Programming Guide.* Available from http://caesarj.org/index.php/ProgrammingGuide/Contents.

[82] D. Sokenou, K. Mehner, S. Herrmann, and H. Sudhof. Patterns for Re-usable Aspects in Object Teams. In *Proc. Net.Object Days 2006 (NODe'06)*, Erfurt, 2006.

[83] Source Code of the Spacewar Example Program. http://dev.eclipse.org/viewcvs/index.cgi/org.eclipse.ajdt/AJDT_src/org.eclipse.ajdt.examples/examples/spacewar/?root=Tools_Project.

[84] M. Stoerzer, B. G. Ryder, X. Ren, and F. Tip. Finding Failure-inducing Changes in Java Programs Using Change Classification. In *Proceedings of the ACM SIGSOFT 14th Symposium on the Foundations of Software Engineering (FSE 2006)*, pages 57–68, Portland, OR, USA, November 7–9, 2006.

[85] M. Störzer and J. Graf. Using Pointcut Delta Analysis to Support Evolution of Aspect-Oriented Software. In *ICSM* [45], pages 653–656.

[86] M. Störzer and J. Krinke. Interference Analysis for AspectJ. In Gary T. Leavens and Curtis Clifton, editors, *FOAL: Foundations of Aspect-Oriented Languages*, March 2003.

[87] Eleni Stroulia and Andrea De Lucia, editors. *11th Working Conference on Reverse Engineering (WCRE 2004), 8-12 November 2004, Delft, The Netherlands*, Los Alamitos, 2004. IEEE, IEEE Computer Society.

[88] Homepage of the Standard Widget Toolkit (SWT). http://www.eclipse.org/swt/.

[89] System and Software Engineering lab (SSEL) at the Department of (Applied) Computer Science (Faculty of Sciences) at Vrije Universiteit Brussel (VUB). *JAsCo Language Reference*. Available from `http://ssel.vub.ac.be/jasco/documentation:main`.

[90] R. E. Tarjan. Depth-First Search and Linear Graph Algorithms. *Siam Journal on Computing*, 1(2):146–160, June 1972.

[91] P. Tarr and H. Ossher. *Hyper/J User and Installation Manual*. IBM Corporation, 2000.

[92] Peri Tarr, editor. *Proc. 4rd Int' Conf. on Aspect-Oriented Software Development (AOSD-2005)*. ACM Press, March 2005.

[93] P. Tonella and M. Ceccato. Aspect Mining through the Formal Concept Analysis of Execution Traces. In Stroulia and Lucia [87], pages 112–121.

[94] T. Tourwé, J. Brichau, and K. Gybels. On the Existence of the AOSD-Evolution Paradox. In Bergmans et al. [7].

[95] T. Tourwé, A. Kellens, W. Vanderperren, and F. Vannieuwenhuyse. Inductively Generated Pointcuts to Support Refactoring to Aspects. In Ernst et al. [26].

[96] T. Tourwé and K. Mens. Mining Aspectual Views using Formal Concept Analysis. In *SCAM*, pages 97–106. IEEE Computer Society, 2004.

[97] Tom Tourwé, Andy Kellens, Mariano Ceccato, and David Shepherd, editors. *Linking Aspect Technology and Evolution*, March 2005.

[98] K. van den Berg, J. Conejero, and R. Chitchyan. AOSD Ontology 1.0 - Public Ontology of Aspect-Orientation. Technical report, AOSD-Europe-UT-01, D9, AOSD-Europe, May 2005.

[99] W. Vanderperren, D. Suvée, M. Agustina Cibrán, and B. De Fraine. Stateful Aspects in JAsCo. In F. Gschwind, U. Aßmann and O. Nierstrasz, editors, *Proc. SC 2005, LNCS 3628*, pages 167–181, Edinburgh, April 2005. Springer-Verlag.

[100] B. Verheecke and M. A. Cibrán. Dynamic Aspects in Large Scale Distributed Applications – An Experience Report. In Lodewijk Bergmans, Kris Gybels, Peri Tarr, and Erik Ernst, editors, *Software Engineering Properties of Languages and Aspect Technologies*, March 2005.

[101] J. Wloka. Aspect-aware Refactoring Tool Support. In Tourwé et al. [97].

[102] J. Wloka. Towards Tool-supported Update of Pointcuts in AO Refactoring. In T. Tourwé, A. Kellens, M. Ceccato, and D. Shepherd, editors, *Linking Aspect Technology and Evolution*, March 2006.

[103] Xerox Corporation. *AspectJ Programming Guide*. Available from `http://eclipse.org/aspectj`.

[104] C. Zhang, H.-A. Jacobsen, J. Waterhouse, and A. Colyer. Aspect Refactoring Verifier. In Tourwé et al. [97].